mycool~~sixties~~

Lennon, Jagger
&
The Rest

Tony Norman

www.mycoolsixties.co.uk

Steampacket Publishing
Ennis House
59-65 Enys Road
Eastbourne BN21 2DN
East Sussex

www.mycoolsixties.co.uk

First published in Great Britain in 2012

A catalogue record for this book is available from the British Library

Printed in Eastbourne by Plan Ahead
Bound in Hove by Kensetts Limited
Layout and design: David Pringle
Cover design: Michael Baldry

Front page photographs of John & Yoko Lennon and Mick Jagger
reproduced by kind permission of Chris Walter
www.chriswalterphotography.com

ISBN 978-0-9570298-0-4

The Rest (photo opposite)
(l to r) : Tony Norman, bass guitar; Shay McKeown, drums; Colin Green, lead vocals;
Graham Lynch, 12-string rhythm guitar (seated); Fred Giulianotti, lead guitar (insert)

For Colin, Gray, Shay
and Fred of The Rest

and the friends and lovers
who shared that special time...

London in the Sixties... the weekend starts here!

It's called *my**cool**sixties.*

I'm not saying I was *cool* in the Sixties. In fact the working title of this book was *Sex, Drugs and Rock 'n Roll... I Got Them All Wrong.* I was like a million other kids, exploring the twists and turns of a decade we'd never forget, making mistakes, getting into scrapes, acting crazy and, just once in a while, reaching for the stars and feeling their silver light dancing in our hands. We weren't *cool,* but the times were *cool,* being young was *cool,* the music was *cool,* feeling the world move every day and knowing in your heart anything was possible was *cool...* a special time, like no other.

So, how to write about it?

I wanted to ride the excitement I felt first time around, with the reader as a friend who shares the journey. Dates give a time frame but this is not a dusty old diary from *waybackwhen*. It's a book of memories, fresh and clear, starting in the heady rush of '69 then backtracking to '63 when I was 16 and chasing two dreams...

Dream # 1 to be a journalist. At school sour-faced men told me I had no chance, but with a naive mix of stubborn belief and rose-tinted optimism I set out to prove them wrong.

Dream # 2 to have a hit with Colin, Gray and Shay... The Rest. The four of us were in a teenage group playing American R&B. By '65 we were Mods with Fred on lead guitar, playing Motown at all-night gigs in Soho, longing to meet Cathy McGowan on *Ready Steady Go!* and tour the USA.

Truth is, we never got close to the Beatles or the Stones, but we're sharing the billing with them now... *Lennon, Jagger & The Rest*. It's got a certain ring, don't you think? And there is a true life connection: I interviewed John Lennon, Mick Jagger and many more. Rapping with rock stars often felt surreal, but playing in The Rest with mates I loved like brothers, that was reality. Young and free in London: no better place to be.

Most of this story is true. Some names and scenes have been amended to protect the privacy of those I knew at the time. Poetic licence apart, we'll travel those years the way I remember them. Was it hard to get back to the Sixties? No, I loved stepping out on the streets I knew so well and finding them still full of wonder.

Welcome to the magic carpet ride...

Tony Norman,
Eastbourne 2011

April 1969

Lennon

Once upon a time, or maybe twice,
this is the story of how I first met John...

Apple Corps, 3 Savile Row, London.

Beatles buddy Derek Taylor sits on his throne-like chair smiling benignly as a track called *Music Now* fills his press office. It's an enthusiastic mix of acoustic guitars, flutes and hippy harmonies. Okay, it's a fly-me-to-the-moon longshot, but would the Fabs like to put my song out on Apple?

George Harrison walks in and listens. One of my favourite musicians on the planet is standing right beside me and I fight to avert my eyes. George likes his space: everyone knows that. The record ends.

'Was that you singing?'

He's talking to me! George Harrison is talking to *me*. I nod and give a nervous smile.

'He wrote it too,' adds Derek warmly.

'Needs sitar,' says George, his voice matter-of-fact. 'See you at Abbey Road, Thursday night, okay?'

It feels like a dream... and, of course, that's exactly what it is.

But only the last part.

I *do* know Derek Taylor. I *was* in the press office at Apple. George Harrison *did* walk in, but that's where fantasy separates from fact. Truth is George had a quick listen, before giving Derek Taylor a *what the hell is this?* look and making a hasty exit. George was right. Derek knew it and so did I, this song was no classic. Check out the opening lines: *If music be the food of love, give us Music Now.* Not good, right? We're planning a name change at the music paper I work for, swapping *Top Pops* (corny) for *Music Now* (cool). Having our jingle on Apple would've been a thrill, but it's not going to happen.

Ah well, can't win 'em all...

Derek passed on the record in the kindest possible way and I appreciated that. He's a really nice guy. I guess I've known him for about a year now and I liked him the first time we met. As trusted publicist and advisor to the Beatles he gets calls from newspapers and magazines worldwide. He could easily give our little paper the big-time cold shoulder but, along with his excellent assistant Mavis Smith, Derek always treats us with respect. Why? Well, I think he sees us as underdogs taking on the giants of the UK rock press, like *Melody Maker* and *NME*. He can see we love the music... even if our theme song isn't up to much.

Walking into Apple is a buzz. The Beatles are forever top of my interview wish list. I met Paul, George and Ringo last summer at the press launch of their *Yellow Submarine* movie. It was all a bit crazy, journalists shouting, cameras flashing, and three of the Fabs answering questions with a string of neat one-liners, like a scene out of *Hard Day's Night*. John didn't make it - he sent a cardboard cut-out instead. My quest to meet him went on hold until this morning, then everything changed in a hurry...

*

It's April and I'm a fool in love. Alison and I have been together a long time, but now our future is a question mark. I couldn't sleep last night, in work before nine, an hour to myself before the rush of the day. I like our basement office in central London, right now it feels like a hideaway, I can lose myself here. Three years ago I was still in school dreaming of making it as a writer. Now I'm reviewing rock concerts and albums, interviewing some of the best musicians on the planet. This is where life makes sense.

Today I'm typing up an interview with Bill Wyman about the next Stones album. Wyman doesn't play the rock star game, what you see is what you get. He told me he never sees the rest of the group when he's not working. He probably gets on best with Charlie Watts, but they're not close friends. The Stones have a good working relationship, and Bill's happy with that.

My editor, John Halsall, has heard the interview tape and he loves it. In fact, we're giving the Stones a four page spread next week, so the pressure is on to write a good piece. I make a coffee, light a cigarette and attack my typewriter with two fingers. The machine's so old I have to punch the keys with psycho stabs to get the words down on paper, as the office comes to life around me. I'm so caught up in my writing I jump when my phone rings.

'Tony, it's Chris Walter. Are you free?'

'When?'

'Now.'

'What's happening?'

'John and Yoko are giving a press conference at Heathrow, want to come?'

'Yeah... sure... thanks.'

'Pick you up in ten.' Chris sounds focused, business-like, but my heart skips a beat.

Thirty minutes later we are speeding out of London on the M4. Chris and I work well together. He's like David Hemmings in *Blow-Up*, a freelance photographer with a cool image and an open-top sports car. If something's happening in London, Chris knows about it. He does a great job for us, never misses a beat.

The motorway traffic is light. It's chilly but sunny and Chris hugs the outside lane with the speedo kissing ninety. John and Yoko are on their way home from their *Bed-In for Peace* in Amsterdam and we'll be there to meet them. Chris does all the talking when we get to the airport and we're ushered into a small VIP lounge already packed with journalists. I take one of the last free seats and Chris spirits himself into prime position in front of the two chairs waiting for the Lennons.

Looking round, I can't see many music journalists. This is the Fleet Street crowd. They can be very cold and cynical and they've been having piss-take fun recently at John and Yoko's expense. What will happen today? There's a definite air of anticipation.

The door bursts open and in they walk, looking cool in white. John peers out belligerently through his granny glasses.

'Where's Zec?' he snaps.

The Lennons are here to talk peace, but John is gunning for Donald Zec, an outspoken columnist for the *Daily Mirror*. Zec mocked John and Yoko in a vitriolic piece on their offbeat campaign. He said they looked like *two gurus in drag*. John did not appreciate that description of his wife of just a few days. Right now he's ready to take on Zec and cut his pomposity to the bone. A tongue lashing from Lennon is something to fear, but Zec is a wily old fox. He knew better than to show up here today.

No Zec, but John still looks edgy. He's expecting trouble from the national press. He knows talk of love and peace, acorns, bagism and bed-ins is way over their heads. Before Amsterdam, the word on the (Fleet) street was that John and Yoko were going to celebrate their honeymoon by making love in front of the world. In room 902 of the

Amsterdam Hilton to be exact. Of course, that was never going to happen. John and Yoko put on their pyjamas and talked about peace for a week.

Were they mad? No, they knew exactly what they were doing. Their antics were sure to stir up controversy and if that meant people were talking about peace, then that was their aim.

Now, back in the UK, John and Yoko are ready to face their fiercest critics. I look at John, try to read what he's thinking. He looks confident, but his eyes are wary. Yoko is more mysterious, her face half-hidden beneath a floppy hat and huge dark shades. The stage is set, but the big fight never comes.

Fleet Street's finest congratulate John and Yoko on their wedding in Gibraltar and ask polite questions about Amsterdam. *What did the Bed-In achieve?* John says people are thinking about peace now and that's a good thing. *What about the acorns?* Plant them for peace and see a tree grow. *Is world peace really possible?* If people are positive, it can happen. *Yesterday you gave a press conference in Vienna in a bag. What was that all about?* Bagism is a tag for what we are doing. All we're saying is give peace a chance. *Will there be more Bed-Ins?* Yes. John and Yoko are determined to continue their work for peace. That's their main focus now.

Then John comes up with a quote that's sure to hit the headlines tomorrow. He says his bank balance is running dry. 'I could put my hands on £50,000 cash, but that's scratching the deck for me.' He doesn't want to go into details, but everyone here instantly knows the trip out to the airport has been worthwhile. The papers have their front page story and so do I. Will the Beatles go back on the road? They recently turned down an offer of four million dollars to play four shows in the States. With money getting tight, will their attitude change? Beatles live onstage after a three year break... it might just happen.

The mood in the stuffy little room mellows. Someone asks John what he thinks of the critics who mock him and Yoko. He says they are happy to be seen as clowns, if that's what it takes to get their message across. Nods of approval all round from the assembled journalists.

The press conference is over. As John gets up to leave, a lady writer steps forward and asks for his autograph. He looks surprised, but signs, then guides Yoko from the room. I stare at the writer in amazement. Asking for Lennon's autograph, how uncool is that?

That's how I felt this morning, but now I'm back in the office, part of me wishes I'd asked for one too. I'd never do that, of course, not in front of the Fleet Street Pack, but if I meet John one-on-one, who knows. Will it ever happen? Question mark, but I'm working on it. Come on Apple, give me a call...

So, what did John and Yoko *really* think of what happened at Heathrow? John was ready for a scrap, but there were no snide remarks about *gurus in drag* today. Nobody wanted to dish out that kind of bullshit to his face. In fact, the press were on their best behaviour, very polite, very respectful, all *very* strange.

A penny for your thoughts John... bet you hated it.

TOP POPS

Week Ending April 12, 1969 Issue 67 1s Weekly

BEATLES TO TOUR SHORTLY?

Foundations rush album

THE FOUNDATIONS are currently crash-recording their new L.P. which must be completed by April 16, before they leave for America. They are working from 11 a.m. to midnight, daily. They had to cancel the S.O.S. show at Wembley, much to their disappointment, in order to fulfil their recording demands. The album will contain their singles. "Build me up Buttercup" and the "Bad, bad old days", plus 12 others. Six of the numbers have been written by the group, whilst the other six are Tony McCauley/John McLeod compositions. The record is being produced by John McLeod, and is being rush-released on both sides of the Atlantic. It's entitled "Digging the Foundations", and is a double-sleeved album, depicting the boys as convicts, complete with picks and shovels. Inside, there are portraits of the seven with life lines.

Hobby

Two members of the group, Tony and Alan, have a new hobby. They are firm members of the Top Ten Football Eleven.

The Foundations leave on the 16th to record a new single in Detroit. They are, at present, the first British group since the Beatles to have two records in the U.S. Top 50. The single will be their first ballad, written by McLeod and McCauley, called "No place on earth could find you."

On the 18th and 19th April, they open in New York, and on May 24th and 25th, in Los Angeles.

AT LAST it seems that the Beatles are likely to tour again. They have not played a live concert for over three years, and at one time it seemed that they would never play to a live audience again.

However, John Lennon made it clear that he was keen to "go back on the road", when he arrived back in Britain with his wife, Yoko Lennon, last week.

"My bank balance is scratching the deck," he told surprised journalists. "I could put my hands on £50,000 cash, but that's scratching the deck for me."

Although Lennon has a great deal of money tied in shares, he is not keen to sell-out. He knows that the Beatles could earn a phenomenal amount if they decided to tour again. In March they were offered four million dollars to play four major venues in the States.

The live show never materialised, but now fans of the group have more reason for optimism. Even if they concentrate on the lucrative American market, it seems likely that they would play at least one big concert in Britain.

The Beatles' new single has been rush-released this Friday, April 11. It is "Get Back".

June 1969

Crossroads

Her bedroom was small and welcoming.
A raga from Ravi Shankar traced circles in the joss stick air.
The stranger with Afro hair walked towards me with a gentle smile.
Her face was free of make-up. She slipped the thin cotton dress over
her head and stood naked in the candlelight. The hippy culture of
free love was everywhere and now it was my time to drink from the
perfumed cup. Funny really, because sex was
the last thing on my mind tonight...

I'm at the crossroads, literally, figuratively, every which way. I was right about Alison. It's over, she's gone, and for the last few weeks my life has been a mess. So many songs about broken hearts, but when it happens to you for the first time it feels like the pain will never end. I keep imagining Ali in the arms of her new lover. I run the movie over and over in my head. I know I could have done more to keep her, treasure what we had, but it's too late now. Sadness and regret twist inside me like twin vipers. Can't talk to anyone about it: don't even care to try.

Now I'm sitting here on a bench by Whitestone Pond at the top of Hampstead Heath. It's late and orange street lights glimmer on the shallow waters. Busy roads from Hampstead, Highgate and Golders

Green run along the shores of this concrete island, but there's not much traffic now. It's quiet and I'm happy to sit back, light another cigarette and relive the last couple of hours. Suddenly I'm laughing, really laughing. What a night, great night, bizarre to say the least.

It happened this way...

Since Alison and I broke up, I've got into the habit of staying late at work, delaying the trip home. Tonight the tube to Golders Green was almost empty. I sat slumped in a corner, lost in gloom. I was so down, I was sick of *myself*. On impulse, I got out at Hampstead and walked down to the Freemasons Arms. I bought a pint and found an empty table in the garden. I wanted to be alone, but dark thoughts of Alison soon crowded in all around me.

'Hi.'

The stranger's voice was spacy. I knew straight away she was on something.

'Hi,' I said.

She smiled, I filled the silence.

'Drink?'

'I don't,' she said softly, sitting down close beside me.

Okay, so she wasn't drunk. What then? Hash? A couple of joints? Alice B. Toklas cookies? No, she was more out of it than that. A trip?

Yes, that was my best guess. We sat in silence for a while. It was all a bit weird, but she was oblivious. I finished my beer and put the empty glass on the table.

'Shall we go?' she asked, as if it was the most natural thing in the world. She took my hand and led me back to her flat in the Vale of Health on Hampstead Heath. We didn't talk on the way. No words were necessary. She was tripping and I was happy to play along with her game. It beat brooding on my own.

Minutes later, she stood naked in the candlelight. She was older than me and I was being seduced. She was leading the dance and I liked it that way. We lay down on her big bed and I was soon naked too. Her kisses were warm and unhurried, first on my lips, then my nipples. Her mouth moved slowly down over my stomach and I felt the thrill of a new sensual delight. I was a stranger to the joys of oral sex, but she was an expert. Giving head really turned her on. She gave little moans of pleasure as her mouth and lips took me on my own trip through the looking glass. Her tongue teased me in the naughtiest ways, fast then slow, until I felt my excitement rising and knew I wouldn't be able to hold back much longer.

I tried to gently move her head away as I started to come, but she wanted to enjoy the moment with me. It was beautiful and afterwards she lay quietly in my arms, smiling, saying nothing. It was a long time since I'd had sex and soon my passion started to rise again. I lifted her face to mine and kissed her deeply. She held me close for a moment, kissed me softly, then got up and walked from the room. Seconds later I heard a shower running.

At first, I thought she'd soon slip back into bed, refreshed and ready to take me on a new trip of discovery. I wanted that to happen, to continue the sensual game and repay the pleasure she'd given me, but time passed... five minutes, ten. Time to go, definitely.

I dressed quickly and went into the hall. The bathroom door was open and the shower was still running. I started to call goodbye, but realised I didn't know her name. I felt a sudden stab of guilt about leaving, but then she peered out through the steam and her glazed eyes told me she had no idea who I was. Her trip had moved on.

'I've got to go now.'

'Groovy,' she said.

She smiled at me like a child on a sunny day.

It was good to get out into the night air. The Vale of Health was quiet and deserted. High above me, I could see the orange glow of the streets lights at the top of a steep grassy slope. I started to climb, stumbling in the shadows, then an already strange evening twisted into horror.

I tripped and fell on a dead body. It was a man, lying face down.

'Oh God, no!'

The shock in my voice told its own story, then the corpse's head moved.

'Piss off will you mate?'

I looked closer and realised that beneath the dead man lay the body of a dead woman. Or maybe it was just a loving couple who had been happily making out, until some long-haired weirdo crashed uninvited into their world.

'Sorry man,' I stammered. 'I thought ... sorry.'

I clambered to my feet and hurried up to the street. If the lights momentarily glowed red instead of orange, you'll know the reason why. I walked across the road to Whitestone Pond, sat on a bench and lit a cigarette...

That's how it happened and I'm still here, feeling the best I have for weeks.

'Piss off will you mate?'

Every time I think of that guy's voice it cracks me up.

And that gentle, trippy sister of mercy definitely shone the light for free love. Will we meet again? Probably not, but I won't forget her. I was at the crossroads and suddenly I see it's time to move on. Alison is gone, face it, she's never coming back. The last summer of the Sixties is coming alive and I want to be part of it.

The future's all ahead...

and tomorrow

I'm interviewing

Mick Jagger.

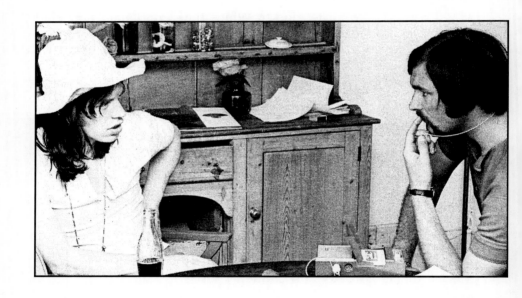

'What does it do for me?'

Mick Jagger echoes my question.

London 1969

June/July 1969

Jagger

June '69

What does marijuana do?'

I hear my voice ask the question and wait for Mick Jagger's reply. He's been relaxed so far, but now his eyes narrow with suspicion and disdain.

'Different things for different people,' he says cagily.

'What does it do for you?'

'What does it do for me?'

Jagger echoes my question, his voice thick with sarcasm. Friendly Mick has left the building and I'm left facing a sneering Stone who looks absolutely and non-ambiguously pissed off.

'Mick can't answer that Tony,' says publicist David Sanderson, with a look that says I've betrayed his trust. 'That subject is way off limits...'

Silence fills the room and suddenly I feel like a fool. I'm known as a journalist who always sides with the musicians I interview. I tend to avoid the rapier thrust, preferring to give my articles a gentle spin that accentuates the positive. But lately I've been reading *Rolling Stone,* a really cool magazine from the States. Last month they ran features on Hendrix and Joni Mitchell and I loved their direct style. No bullshit. Just good intelligent writing. With the arrival of *Rolling Stone,* rock journalism has grown up and come of age. I'm 21 now, it's time I did the same.

I've done okay with *Top Pops*, but now I want to follow what's happening in the States, where underground writers are getting to the heart of things. I came here today wanting something special from the man who launched a thousand headlines, to get him talking in depth about a secret chamber of his private world. Now, as I sit here melting under the laser stares of Jagger and Sanderson, I realise I am way out of my depth. When it comes to sharp, incisive assignments, I'm as cutting edge as Hiram Holliday.

I mumble my apologies and wind things up in a hurry. Chris Walter has to stop taking photos too. He's a cool guy, man of few words, but I know exactly what he's thinking. I don't blame Chris for being angry. I'm still determined to learn from *Rolling Stone*, I will change and grow as a writer, but today I rushed in and found myself up to my neck in thorns. Naive, that's the word, or maybe it's just plain *stupid.*

I should have known Jagger wouldn't talk about drugs, no way, why would he after that drug bust with Keith Richards two years ago? All charges against Mick were eventually quashed and he was given a conditional discharge, but not before a lonely night in Brixton jail. So why start asking him about drugs now? Honest answer, I was on an ego trip, trying for a major exclusive. I blew it and now I've got to go and tell my editor, John Halsall. Getting Jagger was big news for *Top Pops* and I've fucked things up.

Time to face the music back at the office... wish me luck.

*

The good news is, I've still got a job.

John's pretty cool about the whole thing.

'Play me the tape,' he says, as I sit cringing.

'What does marijuana do?'

'Different things for different people.'

'What does it do for you?'

'What does it do for me?'

The irritation in Jagger's voice hangs heavy in the air.

'Well, you walked straight into that one, didn't you?' says John, quietly.

'Yeah, sorry.'

'Why did you even go there? I mean *drugs*, you must have known...'

'I just... *Rolling Stone*... wanted to be like *Rolling Stone*.'

'I'd stick to being Tony Norman if I were you.'

'Right.'

'Is that the start or end of the tape?'

'Last question.'

'Good. Write up everything else you got... *and don't mention drugs!!*'

'Sure, thanks.'

'I'll ring the Stones' office and sort things out. Don't worry.'

I hang my head and feel like a naughty kid in the schoolyard. On the way back to the office I'd convinced myself I was heading for the sack. I wouldn't have blamed John if he'd kicked me out the door. I know a few editors who would have done just that, but mine is backing me and I can't tell you how relieved I feel. I owe you one John, big time.

Okay, time to wipe the drugs *faux pas* from my brain and get to work on the Jagger interview we're running next week. So please ignore everything I've told you so far, and let's cut back to the start of an afternoon that promised so much...

I arrive at the Rolling Stones' Maddox Street office in London's West End. It's just a few minutes walk from Apple. In January, the Beatles filmed a live show on the roof there for their next movie. No such extravagance for the Stones. The band who built their legend on outrage and controversy prefer to protect their privacy. The entrance to their inner sanctum is all low-key elegance.

Inside, the atmosphere is laid-back and focused. Major tours, new singles and albums, all the planning starts here. The manic management days of Andrew Loog Oldham and getting arrested for pissing against a petrol station wall are a lifetime away. Allen Klein has seen to that. The Stones are big business now and the man I'm here to interview is at the heart of it all.

Jagger is running late and that's fine by me. The office is full of pretty girls and one of them tells me she has known the Stones since *Come On*. Beatles or the Stones? That question teased a million teenagers back in the day, but for this lady there was only ever one choice. She started the first Rolling Stones fan club and as she talks about them now, it's clear the magic has never faded, she's still a fan.

Would I like a Coke? She gives me a tall glass, tinkling with ice, and I sit back and think what a strong character Mick Jagger must be. He's the front man for everything that's happening here but he rides it all like a surfer, never seems nervous or uptight.

'Sorry.'

The voice is unmistakable. I look up to see the man himself beckoning me into a quiet room where we can rap. He wears a floppy canvas hat and a short-sleeved cotton shirt. His long dark hair brushes his shoulders: instant charisma, effortless cool.

David Sanderson from the Les Perrin PR office explains time is tight, so I switch on my tape and launch into the question everyone is asking. Why did Brian Jones leave the Stones two weeks ago? Mick doesn't want to go into details. The official line is *musical differences*. Brian wanted to go one way and the rest of the Stones are headed in another. I get the feeling there's definitely more to the story, but Mick's wearing his poker face.

Chris Walter arrives to take photographs and the interview moves on. The Stones have been recording tracks for a new album for release later this year. Working title is *Let It Bleed*, but that might change. The new single is their first record in 14 months, a double A-side featuring two Jagger-Richards songs. *You Can't Always Get What You Want* is a bluesy ballad that builds to a crescendo with a 60-piece choir. *Honky Tonk Women* is a raunchy rocker introducing the band's new guitarist Mick Taylor. Jagger's happy with the way the new tracks have turned out and if the rest of the album sounds this good, I'm already standing in line.

The Stones can't wait to play live again. The first show will be a free concert in Hyde Park at the start of July. Jagger can hold an audience in the palm of his hand and squeeze the last ecstatic cries of pleasure from them. After six years at the top, he still gets a kick out of being onstage.

He's spreading his wings as an actor too. He recently completed work on *Performance* with James Fox and will be spending this summer in Australia filming *Ned Kelly*. He enjoys acting, but it will never take the place of singing. He wants to do one film a year maximum. If he's going to play gigs for free, he smiles, he needs to make films that pay.

Talk of free shows brings us back to Hyde Park. Mick Taylor's debut will mark the start of a whole new era for the Rolling Stones. How much longer can they keep going? Mick Jagger doesn't want to waste time thinking about that, he lives in the present and the immediate future. The band's philosophy has never changed. Their aim is simple: to make music that turns on the fans and themselves in equal measure.

Stones in The Park... be there.

I pull the last sheet of paper from of my typewriter and think about the drugs question I've cut from the Jagger feature. Have I copped out by doing that? No, I don't think so, that went nowhere. If you want to step into controversial areas, you need to follow Dylan's advice and know your song well before you start singing. Careful preparation, deep research, considered thought - I had none of these things in my locker and I paid the price. But I'm no fool, I will learn from this.

Okay, enough soul-searching, my brain hurts. I'm going to buy John a beer in the pub across the street. I'm ready for a drink – it's been one hell of a day!

I am forgiven!

The Stones office – I'm guessing that includes the man himself – have seen my interview with Jagger and they're happy with what I've written. And what I left out. So, I'm getting a press pass for the Hyde Park show. They said I can pick it up this afternoon, when I go to interview Mick Taylor.

Think I'll start by asking him to list his favourite Top Five Drugs.

Joking, just joking.

Taylor's at a fascinating moment in his life and I'm looking forward to meeting him. Following in the footsteps of Eric Clapton and Peter Green as lead guitarist with John Mayall's Bluesbreakers was a big breakthrough, but replacing Brian Jones in the Stones, that's on a whole other level.

See you there...

*

Mick Taylor is used to being a nobody.

The harsh glare of recent publicity has left him with the startled expression of a rabbit in the headlights. As the new Rolling Stone, he will have to get used to the circus that goes with the gig. His world changed the day he took a call from Jagger, asking him down to a recording session. Since then things have happened in a hurry.

Taylor played on a few tracks, including *Honky Tonk Women*, and the Stones obviously liked what they heard because they asked him to join full-time.

With his boyish good looks and baby blue eyes Taylor looks vulnerable, but after two years on the road with Mayall, he's paid his dues. His debut with the Stones will be a very big deal indeed. Thousands of fans will be there and a film crew will record the concert for TV. Taylor says the pressure won't faze him, he's looking forward to it. So far there's been a lot of talking (publicity) and not enough action (music). Once he's onstage with Jagger, Richards, Wyman and Watts, he will start to feel he really belongs.

Have the Stones told him how they want him to play? No, they picked him because they like his guitar style and he'll be free to express his own musical ideas. Cynics might share a sly grin when Taylor says he joined the Stones for their music, not the money and fame, but he seems a genuine guy and I believe him.

Truth is the trappings of success will come, whether he wants them or not. When an unknown musician joins a top band, they are often put on a weekly wage. Good money, but not life-changing. The day

Taylor joined the Stones, Mick Jagger told him he'd be on an equal split with the rest of the band for live gigs and records. Taylor wasn't pushing for a dream deal, the Stones handed it to him on a plate.

When it comes to the fame game, Taylor knows back-slappers will want to know him just because he's a Rolling Stone, but he's confident he'll spot that type a mile away. And if he needs any advice on his new lifestyle, the rest of the group will be happy to help. He gets on well with them and is looking forward to riffing with Keith Richards in the greatest rock 'n roll band in the world.

Mick Taylor is living a dream. It's life in the fast lane from now on. Our interview is over, but a line of other people are waiting to speak to him. The new Rolling Stone... right place, right time.

July '69

Brian Jones is dead.

He was found at the bottom of his swimming pool in the early hours of this morning. Everyone was talking about it when I arrived at the *Top Pops* office. I started making calls, trying to get more details, but the circumstances surrounding his death were clouded in mystery. Was it an accident, suicide, or something darker? You know what people are like, rumours have already started to fly, but the truth is nobody really knows what happened at Brian's farm in Sussex last night.

Brian Jones... at his best he shone brightly

The news is shocking, but not surprising. London's rock world is like a tiny village and the gossip machine has been buzzing for months. Everyone knew Brian was on his way out of the group, and in many ways he only had himself to blame. Recently he has often looked bloated and glazed when seen in public. He was arrested again last month for the possession of cannabis, and that proved to be another step on his sad and lonely downward path. The jury found him guilty, but the judge showed sympathy for the fading Stone, and let him off with a fine. The irony is, of course, if Brian had gone to prison he would still be alive today, but for how long?

When I met Mick Jagger a couple of weeks ago, he looked fit and full of life. He was keen to talk about his plans for worldwide tours and a new Stones album. How could Brian's failing health possibly cope with Jagger's vibrant vision? He had to go. Thinking about it now – and this is just my opinion – I think the Stones agreed to protect Brian from the indignity of being sacked. They let him announce the split, to give the impression he was in control of the situation. I guess Mick, Keith, Charlie and Bill figured they owed him that much. Did his departure from the Stones play any part in his death? Who can say: only Brian knew how he felt inside.

So we are left with the cold facts. Brian Jones is dead at the age of 27. At his best he shone brightly with brilliant bottle neck guitar on *Little Red Rooster,* silken sitar on *Paint It Black*, lyrical dulcimer on *Lady Jane,* wailing harmonica on *Not Fade Away*, hook line marimba on *Under My Thumb*, the list goes on and on, but now it's over. There will be tears and a funeral, rock star dies, the stuff of legends. And a single thought keeps running through my mind: what a waste.

The Stones are due to play in the park two days from now. Will they cancel? I call David Sanderson to find out. It takes ages to get through, engaged, engaged, then I hear the latest news. The Stones have made a decision. Saturday's concert goes ahead... as a tribute to Brian.

*

Saturday July 5th and midday traffic flows easily down Abbey Road. I pass the studio where the Beatles have made history, but today is all about the Rolling Stones. I park my Mini near Marble Arch and walk into Hyde Park. It's a humid day, the sun peeping through scattered clouds. Luckily, it didn't rain last night. Hundreds of fans slept here, in sleeping bags, on deckchairs, all eager to claim a prime spot to see the Rolling Stones.

I walk past the Serpentine. Young kids fish in the lake, as family groups drift past in rowing boats they've hired by the hour. It's lunchtime in the park and life goes on as normal, apart from the rising rumble of live music. Then rock show reality kicks in, mini skirts, cotton shirts, kaftans, shades, and long hair everywhere.

I flash my backstage pass and immediately see my friend Jennie Halsall (sister of *Top Pops* editor John) who's looking good in her blue and white dress and hippy hat. She tells me she first saw the Stones in Watford a few years ago and only about 20 people turned up. It's a bit different today: the press enclosure at the foot of the stage is packed but we squeeze into a space on the grass and enjoy the support bands. My favourites are Family, with Roger Chapman's gravelly vocals punching out songs from their excellent album, *Music in A Doll's House*.

As the crowd rises to them, I realise I need to take a pee and curse the tin of Coke I bought out in the park for the rip-off price of two shillings. Ice creams at the same stall were 1/6d, so the spirit of love and peace obviously hasn't filtered through to London's small-time hustlers. As I stumble through the crowd - trying to preserve my cool and avoid stepping on someone's toes – I regret breaking my golden rule. At big gigs like this I try not to drink, which is a drag but a lot better than coming face-to-face with the backstage toilets. They're better than the ones outside shared by thousands, I know that, but it's still a horror trip.

I hold my breath while I pee and reel out into the fresh air just as the Stones arrive in what looks like an army truck. Concerts like this need security, but was importing gangs of Hells Angels to do the job really wise? With their leather jackets, metal helmets and swastika badges, they ooze menace. Now, as the Stones make their way to their backstage caravan, the Angels shove people aside with needless force. For me they don't fit with a day like this, nuff said.

The Stones look focused as they disappear from sight to prepare for the show. They haven't played live for over a year and the death of Brian Jones has added an extra dimension. How will they deal with the tragedy? We'll soon find out. I say a quick hello to Chris Walter on my way back to sit with Jennie, then check out the crowd which stretches back as far as the eye can see. I'm hearing there are upwards of 300,000 people here today and so far not one arrest.

Tall oaks are dotted around the grassy slope above the stage, offering shade but blocking views. Most people are cool with that, but a few kids climb the trees to score a prime seat. Some branches are broken in the process and when the man on the mike gives the culprits a hard time for being selfish, the rest of the fans applaud. Nobody wants bad vibes, just great music. Dark clouds roll in as the big moment approaches: please don't rain on us, not today.

A huge roar greets the Stones as they walk out onstage.

Jagger looks instantly at ease, waving and blowing kisses to the crowd, as the rest of the band take their places. Mick Taylor stands to the left beneath palm trees imported to decorate the stage. Next it's Charlie Watts behind his drums, then Keith Richards and Bill Wyman in front of a huge wall of speakers. Jagger, in what looks like a white cotton dress, has the front of the stage in which to weave his magic.

But first... a tribute Brian Jones.

'Okay, will you cool it just for a minute?' Mick asks the crowd. 'I really would like to say something for Brian, and I'd really dig it if you would be with us, with what I'm gonna say... about what I feel about Brian... and I'm sure you do too... about him just going when we didn't expect him to.'

Jagger is emotional, stumbling over his words.

'I really don't know how to do this sort of thing, but I'm gonna try,' he explains. Some idiots in the crowd are still shouting. Amazing how insensitive some people can be, even at a time like this. 'Are you gonna be quiet or not?' Mick snaps, and peace finally settles as he reads some lines from Shelley and the Stones stand in silence, their heads bowed. The hassles that split the band are forgotten. At this moment they are thinking of a lost friend.

> *'Peace, peace, he is not dead, he doth not sleep,*
> *he hath awakened from the dream of life...'*

Jagger's voice echoes with a raw brand of emotion rarely seen at a rock show. Harsh reality is difficult to deal with in the warmth of a summer's day. The poem ends and I sense relief in the polite applause that follows. Time for the Stones to do what they do best. Thousands of white butterflies fill the air as the band kick into one of Brian's favourite tracks, *I'm Yours And I'm Hers.* The raw power of the Johnny Winter song lifts the mood and Marianne Faithfull smiles for the first time from the side of the stage.

Mick is dancing, strutting, pouting, and singing with the ease and grace of a master showman. He has to be the best front man in the world. I always enjoy seeing Daltrey with The Who, but he has one main move, whirling the mike high above his head. Jagger has a thousand moves, gestures, expressions, all flowing from the self-belief that underlines every performance. He is the ringmaster who leads the show.

I'd love to tell you we are being treated to a classic concert, but sadly that's not true. The sound is ragged. Watts and Wyman are rock solid, but the two guitars often sound out of tune. Mick Taylor plays some nice bluesy slide, but as he said when we met, it will take time for him to feel part of the Stones. It's too early for any real rapport between him and Keith, they're still finding their way.

The songs are great, of course. Hits like *Jumpin' Jack Flash* and *Satisfaction*, plus *Midnight Rambler* and *Love in Vain* from their next album, and the new single *Honky Tonk Women,* all have their moments but there's something missing. Maybe the band are rusty after that long layoff, maybe recent events have caught up with them. Whatever the reason, from where I'm sitting it all feels a bit flat. It's Jagger who keeps the show alive. He knows the band are playing way short of their best but he shows no weakness, holding it all together with his unique brand of ego and wizardry.

The show finally kicks into gear with the last two songs, both from *Beggar's Banquet*. *Street Fighting Man* is powerhouse rock. Question: how does Charlie Watts do it? He's not like Keith Moon, pounding the kit like a madman. Charlie looks cool and relaxed, almost like a sleepy commuter on a morning train, but he delivers killer rhythms that could stop traffic. Wyman's pounding bass drives the song forward and, at last, Keith Richards comes alive. Taylor's guitar senses the lift in mood and weaves its own tasty patterns.

Jagger's prancing, having fun. His vocals have been strong all afternoon and now the band have finally shown up he's on the high wire, living the moment. It's time for the last song, *Sympathy For The Devil*. African drummers join the Stones onstage, at one with the menacing beat. The lyrics are dark, but the mood is light, as Mick dances with a tribal warrior complete with spear. It's all a bit cheesy, but he carries it off with a smile, before kneeling down at the front of the stage and teasing the young girls who reach up to touch him.

Excitement grows, shades of early tours, teenage fans with tear-stained faces, longing for Jagger, the shaman who makes their hearts race. The girls claw their way up onto the stage, things are getting a little out of hand, Mick knows the signs, it's time to go. One last message for the crowd, *really had a good time, really had a good time*, he repeats the words over and over like a mantra, as the band build to a crescendo, African drums pounding, stoned crowd rising, voodoo song shining for the one who has fallen, no need to explain, no sugar and spice, this is how it should be, rock 'n roll gypsies at one with their music... the music of the Rolling Stones.

Jennie and I are up on our feet as the final chords crash and tumble. This wasn't just a rock show, it was a worldwide event. Paul McCartney is leaving at the same time as us, no security men, no big fuss. I'd love to talk to him but I chicken out. He looks happy, like he's *really had a good time*. Jennie and I feel the same way.

The Stones came through... thanks to Jagger.

THOUSANDS PAY HOMAGE TO BRIAN

By Tony Norman
PICS: CHRIS WALTER

"PEACE, PEACE. HE IS NOT DEAD, HE DOES NOT SLEEP. HE HATH AWAKENED FROM THE DREAM OF LIFE."

Mick Jagger, his face pale and drawn, read these lines from Shelley to the thousands who squatted uncomfortably, but silently together on a warm Summer afternoon in Hyde Park. This was his tribute to the memory of a friend. But the greatest tribute to Brian was that soon the tragedy of his death was forgotten as the music started and people relaxed and enjoyed the group that he had been such a vital member of during the last years of his life.

The Stones were back. With Jagger leaping and strutting, Richard twirling, Wyman attentive and Watts mildly curious, something came back to pop music which has been missing for 13 months. Mick Taylor looked far too young to be faced with the emotional strain of the part he had to play. The sea of people which stretched as far as the eye could see remained seated for some time, but the familiar beat of "Satisfaction" brought them to their feet in a spontaneous wave of enthusiasm. It is still easy to see, still, while the Stones are at work!

EXTORTION

Some of the audience had slept in the park overnight to win the right to a place near the start. They were rewarded with some fine music and the superb generosity of the small businessmen who saw this as a funny item to sell small ice creams for 1/6d and cans of coke for 2/-. A few crophaired youths jeckled this would be a good time to play "Cowboys and Indians" rumours found in small packs clapping their hands and beginning their automatic muscularity and mischief. But the real majority were content to sit back in the sun and enjoy the music.

STANDING OVATION

King Crimson were one of the outstanding successes of the afternoon. A progressive band, they refused to go too far beyond the field of our comprehension and won a standing ovation. Alexis Korner, one of the few true British Blues artists gave us the true, raw stuff and we thanked him for it. Family were disappointing only in that they were not on stage for long enough. Yells for more were frustrated because of problems with the amplification. Screw, and The Battered Ornaments seemed overawed by the occasion, but this was understandable.

As the afternoon drifted past dark clouds jumbled over each other to smother the sun. Various people persuaded and argued their way into the cramped press enclosure at the foot of the stage where a black leather line of Hell's Angels stood between the mikes and the masses. The official stewards, they enjoyed their role, strutting around steely-eyed like so many extras from an early Marlon Brando movie. Pretty girls in see-through dresses and girls in jumpy jumpers and laddered stockings, long haired Hippies all beads and sandals, short-haired lads in shirts and suits, the occasional mum with the estranged dad and a little toddler imitating Mick Jagger. They were all there and many many more besides, listening to the Stones as white butterflies flew into the air in a confused white cloud.

TREMBLING HAND

Songs of the past, songs of the future, excitement building, hands clapping, tambourines beating, Taylor succeeding, a spot of trouble, Jagger glares, Watts, Angels moving, strength in numbers, pushing and pushing — and for nothing. O.K. now it's starting to happen, young girls screaming, Jagger squatting, mascara running, fingers stretching, wanting to touch him, feel him, hold him, have him — but they can't. Jagger holds a small trembling hand . . . . memories of one-nighters . . . . memories of Chicago, of African drummers with their fingers beating out the rhythm, of excitement, of the peak of the evening. The park is full of happy people, but time is passing, it's nearly over.

● Jagger smiles and announces, "WE'VE HAD A GOOD TIME, WE'VE HAD A GOOD TIME." And then they are gone. This was joy, this was excitement, this was The Stones, this was the music, this was away from the scandal and the court cases, this was a happy release of so much tension. This was a tribute to Brian Jones a thousand times more meaningful than all the words that have been written by those who hounded him and invaded his privacy while he was alive. I am one of those people as I cannot write about him now as if I have lost a dearly-loved brother.

But on Saturday the people who really cared about Brian Jones, his true friends, forgot their grief for a short time and shamelessly enjoyed the music that was so much a part of the man . . . the music of the Rolling Stones.

There have been good times . . .

Midnight on Tuesday and I'm lying on my hotel bed thinking over the past few whirlwind days. I wrote my Stones in the Park review in the office yesterday then caught the train to Middlesbrough. This is where we print *Top Pops* and it's my job to make sure there are no major goofs with layouts, photos and stories. It's always a thrill to see the presses roll as our paper zips out at the end of the line. I like the guys I work with up here, plenty of banter about my long hair and Zapata moustache, but it's cool, no problem.

This morning we did a full page layout on the Hyde Park show headlined *Thousands Pay Homage To Brian* using my words and some great live shots from Chris Walter. The eyes of the world were on London that day and I was lucky enough to be there at the heart of it all. I love being a writer, love this life, and can't quite believe how much has happened since I was a schoolboy in Cricklewood, dreaming of being a journalist and hitting the charts with my mates in The Rest.

We didn't know it then, but a golden age was dawning...

September – November '63

The Inferno

September '63

Wednesday 25th

I'm getting old.

I was 16 last week and a few things need to change in a hurry. I'm still a virgin. Well, let's face it, I've never even had a proper girlfriend. Mind you, most of my friends are the same. Mr Pastry the prime minister is famous for saying *you've never had it so good*. He should try being a teenager in Cricklewood. It's alright for politicians and spies chasing Christine Keeler around Big Ben. Maybe that's why most of them look so shagged out these days. Nobody's feeling shagged out round here. Nobody's feeling anything... or anyone.

The Sixties are coming alive, but it feels like we're stuck down an empty street. I want to meet the Beatles, see them play. I bought their *Please Please Me* LP with my birthday money and I love that weird twangy sound they get on their voices. It's new and exciting like *Ready Steady Go!* Did you see the one with the Rolling Stones?

Brilliant. Best TV I've ever seen. *RSG!* feels like a cool club that's happening... right now. I want to be there, dancing to the music and kissing the girls. And if you think I sound desperate, just take a look at my love life. No need to call the *News of the World* for this bit. No sexy scandals, no nights of passion with Mandy Rice-Davies, except in my dreams.

Here's the story so far...

Cindy

The first girl I kissed was a dancer from the USA.

Cindy's mum dressed her in style. Cute little coats and dresses from the US Air Force base at Ruislip, where her dad worked as an officer. She was beautiful and I was... well... *Just William.* One winter afternoon we climbed into the garden of bushes and trees across from our homes and my world changed forever. We were nine years old.

Back home in the States Cindy was a tap dancer but she had a rock 'n roll heart and that first kiss led to many. We were like babes in the wood, safe in our frosted hiding place, but all too soon our cozy little world fell apart. She cried when we said our last goodbye and I waved until her dad's car drove out of sight. My first romance was over, but my love affair with the States still burns bright. I'd love to go there someday, but how many people do you know who've been to America, or *anywhere*? Jumping on a plane to the sun: that's a rich man's game.

Pauline

Two years later, Clitterhouse Juniors took us on a trip to the Lake District. We went by train with steam blowing everywhere. It was the first time most of us kids had ever left London, a long long way from home, but I knew I'd be okay because I was with my best friend Graham Lynch. I was tubby and he was the fearless centre-forward of our school team. In some ways we were like chalk and cheese, but we hit it off from the start, talking, laughing, doing crazy kids stuff. Our holiday home was a scruffy old hut on a farm, but we loved it.

As the week went by, I spent more and more time with Pauline. She had pink National Health glasses and blonde hair cut like one of the *Famous Five*. On our last night, I asked if I could kiss her. She held my hand tight as we slipped into the shadows where our lips met with eyes shut tight. We enjoyed it but when we got home we both knew it had just been one of those holiday things!

Judy

Gray and I were like twins when we arrived at Whitefield Secondary Modern. We went under one name, *lynchandnorman,* and we got to be quite well known. I stood out because I grew tall and slim in a hurry, but nobody saw us the night we shared a three-on-a-bed passion session with the lovely Judy. Like so many great surprises, it happened on Christmas Eve. My parents were out and Gray came round with a bottle of cider he'd got from his brother. We were soon knocking it back in the sitting room, which was also my bedroom, the TV room, the dining room, and an indoor training pitch for Hendon football club to use on frosty nights. (The last bit's crazytalk, but you get the idea: this room was and is *crowded.)*

Christmas was in the air. Small tree with coloured lights, coal fire flickering in the grate, and Radio Luxembourg's yuletide hit parade fading in and out on the radiogram. We were ready for action, only trouble was no girls and we were used to that, believe me. But we'd just been thrown a lifeline, a glimmer of hope in a cold, cold world. We were walking out of school at the end of term when some girls from our class pushed a piece of paper into Gray's hand.

'What's that all about?'

'They've had a vote,' said Gray.

'What about?'

'Best looking boy.'

'Who won?'

'You.'

'Really?'

'Yeah, I was runner up.'

'Always said I was better looking than you, Lynchy!'

'But ... hang on ... best personality ... winner ... me!'

'Runner up?'

'You.'

'We did alright then.'

'Great,' said Gray, 'so how come we never get near any of them?'

Good question.

We liked Whitefield, still do. It's a good school but the teachers have a golden rule that drives us crazy. Boys and girls must be kept apart *at all times*. Boys to the right of the class, girls to the left. Girls' playground one side of the school, boys' yard on the other. Cross those zones and you're in trouble, a few whacks of the cane, so we toe the line like good little zombies. But, after a couple of ciders on the night before Christmas, *lynchandnorman* were in the mood.

'Let's ring some of those girls, Tone. Have a party.'

'Party, right. Got any numbers?'

'No... phone books?'

'In my mum and dad's bedroom.'

It was freezing in there. No heat, just frost drawing patterns on the window panes. Yellow light from a single bulb. Not very romantic, but we got busy with the search.

'Christine Adams, she lives in The Vale, right?'

'No, Pennine Drive. I've seen her down the shops loads of times.'

'Right, Pennine Drive, I've got it. Speedwell 587. Give her a call.'

'Why me?'

'It's your phone.'

'Okay, what do I say?'

'We're having a party, does she want to come?'

We called quite a few girls and most of them were up for it, but then came the dull echo of an adult voice down the line. *Go out at 7.30 on Christmas Eve? Certainly not!*

We were struggling, then we called Judy and she said yes.

'What happens when she sees the party's just you and me.'

'She might like it that way,' said Gray.

And he was right!

Judy arrived with a smile and we gave her our last glass of cider. Then the three of us started dancing and in no time Graham was kissing her and taking her to the bed in the corner behind the couch.

I couldn't see what was going on so I carried on dancing, feeling like a prune.

'Aren't you lonely?' Judy's voice was full of promise.

'Yeah, come on Tone,' said Gray.

They didn't need to ask me twice. Judy lay in the middle of my single bed, with Gray and me either side. We took it in turns to kiss her soft pouting lips. She loved being there with the two of us and when she taught us how to French kiss, we couldn't wait for our turn to show what we could do. Every now and then we'd come up to sip our drinks, then it was back to our sexy little orgy. Well, it wasn't really an orgy, Judy was happy to kiss, but nothing more, and we were happy with that. Happy? We were *grateful.*

Judy stayed later than she should, but before she went she said she wanted to give us both a special Christmas present. She made us lie on the bed together, then lay across us like a luscious vampire, and gave us both a big love bite on the neck to remember her by. We offered to walk her home, but Judy did things her way. Warm kisses on the frosty doorstep, then with a final wave and sexy smile she melted into the night.

In the words of John Lennon... *Merry Crimble!*

*

What a night!

We tried to get Judy to come round again, of course, but I think it was one of those spur-of-the-moment-we-called-at-just-the-right-time type things. We all had fun and that was it, onto the next adventure. Well, we were 13 then and three years later I'm still waiting. I've had my moments, of course, but when it comes to sex and getting naked - you know, the real thing - I'm still strictly Mickey Mouse. Like I said, something's got to change. Having my own bedroom would be a start. Bit difficult to ask a girl round when your mum and dad are sitting there watching *Z-Cars*. Maybe baby that will change when we go to court to get our house back. My dad's really stressed, so we don't talk about it much. It's like a big drama waiting to happen.

October '63

Friday 4th

The Beatles were on *Ready Steady Go!* tonight and I've seen the light.

I know how to meet girls. Simple... start a group with my mates, like John, Paul, George and Ringo did in Liverpool. When Lennon sang *Twist and Shout* on *RSG!* I wanted to be like him, like all of them, singing and strumming their guitars, the eyes of every girl in the place glued to their every move. It must feel absolutely stunningly brilliant to be a Beatle. Good luck to them. They've worked hard in dodgy clubs in Germany and places like that to get where they are today. I'd love to go to the Cavern, but a kid at our school's got an aunty up there and she says it stinks of disinfectant. Well, if the Beatles are playing, who cares what the place smells like?

The Fabs did both sides of their chart topper, *She Loves You* and *I'll Get You,* but *Twist and Shout* was the one that really got me going. John screaming the song, Paul and George doing back-up vocals, Ringo pounding the drums. What a sound! Playing their records is great, but seeing them on TV was a whole new thing. Now I've *just got to* see them live, maybe pick up a few tips...

Monday 7th

Good news. Gray wants to be in the group. We talked about it walking home from school tonight. We're always the last to leave. We do extra football training with our-cool-mate-Johnny-who-we-call-Johnny-Cool. It's a good way to relax after sitting in class all day. Our O-levels are next Summer, so it's pressure on time if I want to make it as a journalist. I've always loved writing, playing with words, making them up, running them together to see how they look. Getting paid to write would be sheer honey heaven, so I won't be clowning when the exams roll around.

My plan is this:

1. Do well in O-levels
2. Get transfer to grammar school
3. Do well in A-levels
4. Get job as journalist on Fleet Street

People always want to trample on your dreams, tell you to forget it. I don't want to hear I've got no chance. I haven't even started yet!

Okay, where was I? Oh yeah... the group, right, Gray wants to be in the group, which is headline happy happy. He's got an old acoustic guitar and knows a few chords. I've never played a guitar, don't know the first thing about it, but Gray said he'll give me a few lessons so we're up and running. Watch out Beatles here we come...

Monday 14th

Gray's found a drummer.

His name is Shay McKeown and they play in the same football team, Kiwi United. I've only met Shay a couple of times, but he's a good laugh. He lives in a prefab in Cricklewood. His mum and dad sound dead Irish, but Shay's London all the way. He hasn't got any drums, but he's happy to get a kit as long as he can do it on tick.

He started joking about the Beatles making Liverpool famous and how we could do the same for Cricklewood. It's not very glamorous round here, but Shay reckons we can change all that. He even came up with a new catch phrase: *North-West 2 mate!* You have to say it like you're cheering on a team, but it's a bit tongue-in-cheek really. Shay on the drums, sounds good to me. All we need now is a singer and a bass guitarist.

But the search will have to wait... I'm in court tomorrow.

Tuesday 15th

I'm sitting in this stuffy room feeling really sorry for my dad. As he gets up to say his bit to the court, he drops his glasses and they spin away across the hard wooden floor. When he stands in front of the judge, I see his hands are shaking. Not for the first time, I feel really angry about the family who live upstairs from us. I call them the Piles because they are a pain in the... well, you get the picture.

We've shared a house with them for years. They've got two rooms and a kitchen upstairs; my mum, dad and me have the same downstairs. We all share the bathroom and toilet. It was even more crowded when my sister Mavis lived at home, but she's married now. Both flats are rented and bad feeling has built up between *us* and *them* like feudin' hillbillies. Truth is they've never really done anything bad to us, nor us to them, but we've been squeezed in together for too long. There's no love lost, that's for sure.

For years we were all sitting tenants. The landlord knew he couldn't get rid of us, so in the end he offered to sell the house to the highest bidder. My dad thought we'd have to fight the Piles every inch of the way, but his offer of £2000 won easily. Okay, it's a lot of money, but not bad for a semi in London. Why didn't the Piles put up more of a scrap? It was a mystery.

Then by a sheer fluke my dad was working by the Thames one day and saw Mr Pile in the garden of a very nice place on the banks of the river. Things went into Sherlock Holmes mode and the truth came out. The Piles had a home they used at weekends, only sleeping at our place a few nights a week, but leaving us squashed into the ground floor of the house we now owned.

And that's where we stand today. My dad wants the Piles to move out. It's not like we're throwing them onto the streets. I've seen photos of their place and it looks great. Why can't they enjoy their home and leave us to enjoy ours? You could cut the tension in this court with a knife. I try to keep my mind on all the legal talk, I know there's a lot at stake, but the voices drone on and I find myself slipping away into my own world and wondering who we can get as lead singer.

Then my dad's solicitor asks me to stand up to show the court what a big lad I am (six foot two) and how sad it is that I have to sleep in the sittingroom/TVroom/diningroom and do my homework in our little kitchen. I feel like telling them the main reason I need a bedroom is so I can ask girls round, but I keep my mouth shut. The judge stares at me and gives a sympathetic smile. I get the feeling a few people in here feel the same way, but Mr Pile never looks at me once.

I sit down and my big moment is over, nothing more I can do to help. The droning voices close in again and my mind drifts back to our new group. Who'd like to play bass guitar? Podge? Tommy? Stewart? Then I spin back to reality and hear the judge saying that the Piles can stay, but he feels they are hiding behind *the skirts of the law*. In other words, he doesn't think what they're doing is right, but he can't do a thing to stop them. The whole thing has been a complete waste of time and my dad's spent a lot of money he can't afford. Worse than that, the Piles have won and it looks like we're stuck with them forever. I feel sorry for my dad, sorry for my mum, sorry for myself.

What a shitty day...

Wednesday 16th

Had a chat with my dad last night. We don't find it easy to talk, but I wanted him to know I was sorry about the court thing. I thought he was taking it well, then I noticed his hands were still shaking. I get on much better with my mum than my dad, but I hate seeing him upset. He's a strong man, but this has really got to him.

What's the point of following the law when it turns round and kicks you in the teeth? Maybe I should go for a life of crime. Rob a few banks and buy a big house where I can live with mum and dad without having to share a toilet with people we can't stand. That's the worst thing about living the way we do. Hanging around at the foot of the stairs, listening to hear if the landing is clear above, then running up to the bathroom and shutting the door tight behind you. There's no privacy here: none at all

Sunday 27th

Needed to get out of the house so I went to the pictures to see the new James Bond film with my friend Podge. He's a really nice guy, mad on Peter Sellers, the Goons, all that crazy stuff. He's got a Sellers LP he plays all the time, knows the sketches off by heart. I asked him to do *Bal-ham: Gateway to the South* while we were waiting for 007. He went into this big Las Vegas accent and did the whole thing. I was rolling up.

We were really looking forward to the film. We saw *Dr. No* last year and that was great. When Ursula Andress walked out of the sea in that skin-tight white bikini I swear I nearly passed out on the spot, she is absolutely sexily gorgeous. *From Russia With Love* didn't even come close. There's quite a good bit where an old lady spy tries to kick Bond with a flick-knife hidden in her shoe, but Ursula's white bikini is still top of the Bond thrill zone.

When we came out the bright lights of Hendon were shining. Red, amber, green, and back to red. We fancied a coffee but everywhere was shut, so Podge did another Peter Sellers sketch down by the bus stop. It's about mad *Auntie Rotter* who does a radio show for kids that's a long long way from *Ding-de-dong*. I've been on the crest of a slump since the court thing, so it was good to be out with Podge and his Peter Sellers voices.

Enjoyed it.

Ursula Andress... absolutely sexily gorgeous

November '63

Tuesday 5th

Fireworks party at Jem's house. He lives four doors away and I've known him all his life. When I was a toddler, his mum used to take me for walks in the park, with Jem in the pram. Since then, he's felt like my kid brother, I watch out for him. Our parents get on well so mum and dad could relax for once. Mr Thomas started joking about the time Jem and I tried to dig to Australia. *The Beano* had this comic strip where Dennis the Menace dug a hole and came out in Oz. Seeing kangeroos sounded good to us, so we got busy in Jem's back garden. Only trouble was, when Jem's dad went out that night to get some coal... agghh!

It was good to see everyone laughing, like a big fat cloud was starting to lift at last.

Monday 11th

Ever heard of the Inferno?

It's the hottest new club in *North-West 2 mate!* I can get you in anytime you like, because I know the manager. Me. That's right, Dad came home from work on Friday with loads of wood. He told me he was going to put floorboards down in the loft to make a room for me and my mates. I felt quite choked. Dad's a quiet man, hardly ever speaks to me, then he does something like this out of the blue. My own room, how great is that?

Jem and I helped him with the boards on Saturday morning. Skip to tonight and the loft is ready. We've called it the Inferno coz we're hoping things will be a bit hot and spicy up there. I've bought a red bulb for that super sexy feeling when our girl fans come round. Of course, we'll have to get the group going first.

Friday 15th

Had a fab time in the Inferno tonight.

We took it in turns to swig from a bottle of cider I'd smuggled in and Shay soon had us cracking up. His brother Sean is a sailor, travels all over the world, and he brought a book back from Hong Kong last week. It's meant to be sexy, but the translation's all wrong. Shay read his favourite bit out loud:

> *Fugg me, fugg me, she crid,*
> *as the spug run down her thigs.*
> *Fugg me she crid,*
> *I'm in Exeter!*

Fugg me it's great to have my own place at last.

The Inferno is happy happy... he crid.

Blue

Christmas

November '63

Sunday 17th

Listened to *Pick of The Pops* this afternoon, the best show on the radio by about seven galaxies. It's the only place you can hear all the latest hits once a week, unless you tune to Radio Luxembourg which always fades out on the best songs. There's another new group from Liverpool in the charts, the Searchers with *Sweets For My Sweet.* They're not as good as the Fabs, but I still love that Mersey sound.

The deejay today was Don Moss. He's not as much fun as Alan Freeman, but he did play a great record called *Be My Baby* by the Ronettes. It's a real shiver-up-the-back job. You know Phil Spector, right? He's that crazy American who puts about 16 pianos,

25 guitars and six drummers on every song. He does some wild stuff but he makes great records, like *Da Doo Ron Ron* by the Crystals. I can't get enough of that *wall of sound*. I've seen photos of the Ronettes and they look very thrilling-steamy-exotic. *Be My Baby* will cost me 6/8d on Saturday, one third of my paper round money, but it's worth it. The Ronettes will be mine!

Unknown one minute, famous the next. That's the way it's running with with pop groups right now, they get famous in a hurry. It could happen to us, but we still need a singer and bass guitarist. We've asked all our mates but it's no go. Guitars and music gear cost a mint, so you've got to *really* want to do it. Shay and Gray both agree, *we must get going*, so the search goes on.

Wednesday 20th

I think he's too young.

Colin Green is in the same class as Jem, which makes him three years younger than us. Who needs a 13-year-old lead singer, right? But Shay lives across the street from him and he reckons Colin's quite grown up for his age. Then today Gray told me we should give the kid a chance, because George Harrison is three years younger than John Lennon and he's done alright. That made me feel like I'm the mean Troll saying Colin can't cross the bridge. So we're giving him a go on Friday, I've invited them all round to the Inferno. Gray's bringing his acoustic, Shay's got some drum sticks so he can bang on the beams and I'll do some backing vocals. Can Colin sing? Fugg me, I hope so. This could be the start of something big...

Friday 22nd

Silence.

A week ago the Inferno rocked with laughter. Tonight we sat together trying to make sense of a nightmare, no records spinning, no chords from Graham's guitar. President Kennedy is dead, gunned down on the streets of Dallas by a cruel coward, leaving the world to grieve for a man who gave us hope. Now that hope is gone and the future looks cold and bleak.

It had been just another Friday night. I watched the Stones, Gerry and the Pacemakers and Freddie and the Dreamers on *Ready Steady Go!* then came up to the loft to play my brand new LP, *With The Beatles.* It came out today and I ordered my copy three weeks ago. With the Piles away for the weekend, my Dansette was blasting out the new songs from the Fabs at top volume. I didn't hear mum calling me from the landing, then dad climbed up the ladder and stuck his head through the hatch. I thought I was in trouble for making too much noise, but it was far worse than that.

'President Kennedy has been shot.'

'Is he okay?'

'I'm afraid he's dead,' said dad quietly.

President John F. Kennedy... a man you could believe in

I just stared at him.

'Better turn your music off.'

'Yeah... right... sorry.'

I don't know why I apologised. I don't know anything. JFK was the only politician I've ever believed in, the only one who got through to me and made me want to be a better person. Harold Macmillan was prime minister here for years and now it's Alec Douglas-Home. How can we relate to cold fish like them? There's no way, but JFK was different.

When he made that speech, a*sk not what your country can do for you, ask what you can do for your country,* I wished I was American. I wanted to be part of his new dream, it was beautiful. Now the future lies broken. When Gray, Shay and Colin came round nobody mentioned the group. We were quiet for a while, didn't know what to say, then we started talking about JFK.

Graham said he was a man you could believe in. Brave enough to stand up for negroes in the States. Sam Cooke just got banned from staying in an all-white motel down in the South. How can you treat *Sam Cooke* like that? Crazy. When Martin Luther King gave his brilliant *I have a dream* speech in Washington in the summer, everyone knew JFK backed every word.

It took courage to stand up to Russia too, when they tried to put bases on Cuba last year.

I remembered walking to school through the park one morning and thinking I might not be coming back. The world could end in the next few hours. As you know, it wasn't crazy talk, we really were that close to the edge. I was only 15, I didn't want to die, but I didn't blame President Kennedy. I'm not big on politics, but I knew he had to make a stand.

Shay came out of school when that crisis was on and saw a headline on a newspaper stand: *Nuclear War Inevitable.* He rushed home to the prefab, where his mum and dad were sitting by the fire. Shay turned on the TV. The old set took ages to warm up and Shay was a bag of nerves wondering if Richard Baker was going to say: *The world will end tonight.*

'What appears to be the problem, son?'

'Mum, mum, haven't you heard?' Shay gibbered. 'Kennedy... Khrushchev.. Cuba... missiles... NUCLEAR WAR INEVITABLE!!'

'Well, you know son, you die if you worry and you die if you don't.'

Shay gave us the punchline in his mum's lovely Irish accent and we all cracked up. Then we felt guilty for laughing at such a sad time, so it all went quiet again and we sat here feeling a bit lost. Colin hadn't said much, then he spoke from the heart.

'When things like this happen, it's not right to give in. You've got to live your life, like President Kennedy did. You've got to keep going.'

He's just a kid, but he was right. JFK was alive this morning, now he's gone. Nothing is certain in this crazy world, so do *what* you can *while* you can. I liked what Colin said, loved Gray's strength and honesty, Shay's warmth and humour. Something happened here tonight... at the worst of times it felt good to be together.

December '63

Thursday 5th

The last couple of weeks have been unreal. First they got a weird guy called Lee Harvey Oswald for killing JFK. He kept saying he was innocent, but he never got the chance to prove it because he was shot dead by Jack Ruby. Now people are asking how that could have happened when there were police everywhere. Nobody knows for sure who killed JFK, but the shockwaves have stopped America in its tracks. The President's funeral was seen all around the world last week on TV, and two haunting images have stayed with me. The first Jackie Kennedy, dressed in black, her pale face lined with sorrow, living through the saddest of days with class and dignity. The second, JFK's little son saluting his father's coffin. Sad, sadder than sad.

Saturday 7th

It's two weeks since that dark day in Dallas. We won't forget JFK but as Colin said *life must go on*, so we got together tonight. Gray had learnt the chords to *Twist and Shout* and written out the words.

Colin sang it, Gray strummed, Shay banged out a rhythm and I sang back-up vocals. We did the the song about ten times and in the end it sounded okay. The good news is, Colin's voice has dropped, so it won't be like having a choir boy as our lead singer. He's very confident and the four of us seem to get on well so, you heard it here first, Colin's in the group. All we need now is a bass guitarist.

By the way, the Beatles were on *Juke Box Jury* tonight. They were quite funny, joking around and voting new 45s a hit or a miss. They didn't rate *Kiss Me Quick* by Elvis, George reckons the song's rubbish but John said he likes those *Kiss Me Quick* hats you buy in Blackpool. The record they really liked was *Hippy Hippy Shake* by the Swinging Blue Jeans. George said the Beatles used to play the song live – bet John Lennon sang it. He loves rock 'n roll.

Friday 13th

Graham lent me his guitar this week with a book called *Play In A Day* by a bloke called Bert Weedon. I tried to play in a day... two days... three days... four days... five days... and got nowhere fast. Uncle Bert's words made no sense to me, then the guitar went out of tune and I didn't know how to fix it. Some of the sounds I made were just plain scary, very Hammer House. Time to face the facts: I'm no guitarist. I told Gray the bad news today and he had an idea.

'Play bass, that's just one string at a time.'

Sounds good to me!

Saturday 14th

Just call me Mr Bass Man.

Colin, Gray and Shay came round this afternoon and we had a good chat about the group in the Inferno. Gray wants to get a 12-string guitar, so with my bass and Shay's drums, we should get a really big sound. Colin may be the baby but he's got his head screwed on. He's been to a music shop in Kilburn called Blank's and he reckons we can get all the stuff we need on HP.

Later I watched that new sci-fi TV show everyone's talking about it. They say kids hide behind the couch when *Doctor Who* comes on, but I didn't think it was very scary, not a patch on *The Birds*. Gray and I saw it last summer (we passed for 18!) and sat there terrified as the birds hit everyone in sight. One old man got it right in the eyes and I've avoided people with budgies ever since.

A good film can play tricks on your mind. When I was a kid, my parents went to see *Them* and when they got home my mum was scared to put the empty milk bottles out, just in case giant ants had invaded Cricklewood.

Silly really, we only get flesh-eating zombies round here...

Tuesday 17th

Picture the scene: Gray and me trapped by a stranger, waiting for the police to come and take us away. We had this great idea you see...

Gray's been doing an extra paper round for a couple of weeks. It belonged to a kid called Kevin Saunders. The shop thought he was ill, but we saw him in school and he told us he'd given up the round coz he was sick of getting cold and wet every morning. We asked if he'd been round to collect his Christmas boxes and he said his mum wouldn't let him. What a drip! Anyone knows the best thing about doing a round is the cash you pick up at Christmas time. I got nearly six quid last year and that's big money. So Gray and I decided to hit Kevin's round and split the cash.

We went out tonight and started knocking on doors in Golders Green, where the posh houses are. Gray had all the numbers written down and the money started to flood in, half-a-crown here, five bob there. A lot of the people were Jewish so Christmas is no big deal to them, but most still gave us something anyway. One lady had definitely had a few drinks and she offered us ten bob if we'd sing a carol, so we gave her *Jingle Bells* at full blast and she loved it. We had a fiver in no time and we were sure we'd double it. Five pounds each would pay the deposits on our guitars.

Then we called at the house of horror. The man who answered the door was quite old, about 30, and when we asked for a Christmas box he told us to come in and we found ourselves standing in the hall by a huge Christmas tree. It was a big family house, but there was no sign of his wife and kids. He started pumping us for information about the paper round, like Dr. No in James Bond.

'Which of you is my paperboy?' he asked.

'Me,' we both said at once.

'Well, make up your minds,' he said.

He was smiling, but we knew he was onto us.

'I do it in the week,' said Gray, 'he does weekends.'

'So you both want money?'

'No, we'll share it,' said Gray.

I have no idea how he stayed so cool.

'Right,' said the man, 'you two stay here, I'll be back in a minute.'

He disappeared and we heard him mumbling thru the door.

'He's calling the police,' said Gray. 'Let's go.'

Before we could move Dr. No was back.

'Thought you'd lost me did you?' he smiled. 'Stick around, I've got a surprise for you.'

We both knew what that would be... police, arrests, handcuffs on wrists, headlines in the local paper, *teenage thugs rob the rich in Golders Green*, I felt the panic rising.

'Well lads, what do you think of *this*?'

Another man burst through the door holding something we weren't expecting in his hands. A tray filled with mince pies, glasses of sherry, and a crispy one pound note.

'Come on,' he grinned, 'help yourselves, don't be shy.'

'Not sure they should be drinking sherry, Sy.'

'Oh, what the hell, it's Chrissy!'

'We both did paper rounds when we were kids,' said Dr. No. 'We like to look after our paper boys at this time of year.'

So we ate our pies, drank our sherry, grabbed our pound note, and got out of there in a hurry. As soon as we hit the fresh air, the drink kicked in.

'I feel really drunk.'

'So do I,' said Gray.

'Do you think they were...'

'Oh yeah, for sure.'

'No problem though.'

'No... and they gave us a quid.'

'Fancy doing another house?'

'Not really.'

'Pack it in?'

'Yeah.'

'Golders Green Wimpy?'

'Definitely.'

We'd had enough thrills for one night...

Sunday 22nd

Had a party at my place last night. All my mates were there, Gray, Shay, Colin, Jem, Podge, Stewart and Tommy. *Johnny Cool* came with his girlfriend and she brought some other girls from school which was absolutely stunningly brilliant. I was a bit nervous before they all arrived, but we had a great time. At first we all stood round feeling like lemons, then I crossed over into the genius zone. I grabbed the red bulb from the Inferno and stuck it in the light socket in the sittingroom/TVroom/dining room/mybedroom. We cleared a space for dancing and didn't look back. The girls brought loads of great records with them like *I Wanna Hold Your Hand* by the Beatles; *Glad All Over* by the Dave Clark Five; *I Wanna Be Your Man* by the Rolling Stones; *I Only Want To Be With You* by Dusty Springfield; and S*winging on a Star* by Big Dee Irwin.

We were all singing along at the top of our voices, except when something naff came on like *You Were Made For Me* by Freddie and the Dreamers, or *It's Almost Tomorrow* by Mark Wynter. Rubbish like that got dumped in a hurry, but I played both sides of my *With The Beatles* album and they loved every song. (That LP is selling so fast it's in the *singles* charts, how mad is that?) The only group to come close to the Fab Four on the night were the Swinging Blue Jeans with *Hippy Hippy Shake,* the record the Beatles liked on *Juke Box Jury.* It was the hit of the night, we played it over and over.

We had to pack up at eleven because my mum and dad were coming home, so one of the girls put on *You'll Never Walk Alone* by Gerry and the Pacemakers. It's dead slushy and in no time we were dancing close and snogging. The girls seemed to know exactly who they wanted to be with, like they had some secret code, and I was happy happy when a girl called Wendy came and danced with me. I walked her home and we did some French kissing on her doorstep. When I got back my best-mates-in-the-world had done a great job of getting rid of the booze and washing out the ashtrays, so when mum and dad came in it was all smiley smiley.

I woke up today feeling good and things got even better when my cousin Peter phoned with some pinch-me-I-must-be-dreaming news. He'd won two tickets for The Beatles Christmas Show in

January. Would I like to go with him? Guess what I said... yeeeeeeeeeespleeeeeaaaassssssseeee.

This could be the best Christmas/New Year ever!

Monday 23rd

I'm writing this on the bus back from Kilburn. We've just been to Blank's music shop to sort out what we need for the group. Gray's getting a Danelectro 12-string electric guitar, made in the USA; Shay's gone for a set of Beverley drums; Colin's chosen a Shure mike and a Watkins Dominator amp; and I've seen a Framus Star Bass with my name on it. Can't believe I will soon be playing the same guitar as Bill Wyman of the Rolling Stones. He's got the deluxe version which costs 60 guineas. I can't afford that so I've gone for the standard at 36 guineas. Bit weird this *guineas* stuff, like something out of Charles Dickens. The cost in real money is 37 pounds 16 shillings.

That's a lot of dough, but I can put down the deposit with my Christmas money and cover the weekly payments from my paper round, so no sweat. Only trouble is you have to get an adult to sign your HP form. Colin, Gray and Shay are sure they can do that, no problem. I left them in the shop fixing up times. I'm going home to ask my parents if they'll do the same for me, but my dad's a bit funny about HP. He comes from a poor family and hates the thought of getting into debt. He's an electrician, works for himself and pays every bill on time. He's got the right to live his life the way he wants, I just hope he doesn't stop me living mine...

Wednesday 25th

I've felt sick since Monday night and now I've honked for real. When I asked about the HP dad said no. Mum stuck up for me and they had a big argument, then dad asked how much the bass would cost and when I told him he went mad. *If you want to waste all that money on a bloody guitar you can go out and earn it first.* He looked really angry so I went up to the Inferno and played *Midnight* by the Shadows. It's an old record I always play when I'm feeling down.

My sister Mavis came over for lunch today with her husband Denis. I tried not to mope around being a pain, but it wasn't easy. Then came another kick in the face for our merry little family Christmas. Dad carved the goose and as soon as we tasted it, we knew it was off. He bought it cheap in Brentford market and it tasted rank. My mum was still on edge from the HP thing and she told my dad he spoils everything, then started to cry. I felt guilty because they wouldn't have argued if it hadn't been for me, so I made out the meat was okay and ate a couple of slices to prove it. Of course, five minutes later I was running up to the bog to chuck up.

And now I'm aching inside, but not because of that honking goose. After all the talk, plans and dreams, dad says I can't join the group. I haven't told the others yet, can't bring myself to do it. I feel so angry, I'm not a kid, I'm sixteen years old. I'll pay for my bass, no problem, all he's got to do is sign the bloody form, but he won't and he's told my mum not to do it either. I don't want to cause any more trouble, so I've just got to face it, the dream is over.

Merry bloody Christmas!

Tuesday 31st

I've hit Gray, Shay and Colin with the bad news. They said the group won't be the same without me, and I felt choked. They even went down to Blank's to ask if their parents could sign for me. The man said no, but it was nice of them to try. I know my mum feels sorry for me, but I'm not talking to my dad. I'm glad he messed up Christmas, serves him right.

I've had the blues all week, but I'm going to a party tonight with Steve. He's this off-beat new kid at school, chalk white face, jet black hair, good writer. Our English teacher wears short skirts and sits on a desk at the front of the class with her very-shapely-bet-she-wears-suspenders legs on show for all of us to see. She's really sexy, but dead strict too. Nobody gives her any lip. She reads out the best essays every week and Podge and I used to grab the glory. Now Steve's her favourite, she loves his *originality,* and I'm not jealous because he is *so damn good*, like he sees everything from a different angle to the rest of us. He's got all these great American records too, Chuck Berry, Bo Diddley, Howlin' Wolf, stuff I've never heard before. Steve can be moody, bit of rebel, and I'm up for some of that right now. It's New Year's Eve and a good time to leave my blues behind.

I might get drunk: watch this space.

January – February '64

With The

Beatles

January '64

Wednesday 1st

Oh God, never again.

I'm crawling into 1964 with my first hangover ever and I feel like death. In fact, death would be welcome if it would stop me feeling this way. My head aches, my body aches, my belly aches, and every time I move I feel like chucking up again, and usually do. It's embarrassing being like this in Steve's house, but his mum's great. *That'll teach you* she laughs, every time I run to the bog. I really like her. She's a journalist, a woman of the world, not like certain narrow-minded people in my family who treat an HP form like it's the work of the devil. If I did get a bass guitar, my dad would probably burn it at the stake.

I didn't ring home last night to say I was staying out. I was too busy having fun at Steve's cousin's party in Hampstead. It was full of arty people and jazz records, everyone smoking, drinking, and eating cheese. You know, *sophisticated*. We were the youngest there by a mile, but after a few wines (I tried the red and white, but liked rosé best) I had no trouble talking to complete strangers about the Beatles, the bomb, *Ready Steady Go!*, teenage sex (yes please!) and how-my-dreams-of-being-in-a-pop-group-have-been-crushed-by-the-tyrant-known-as-my-dad.

I remember a lot of singing at midnight then everything's a blur until waking up at Steve's with this knife through my head. He's feeling a bit rough, but he's doing a whole lot better than me.

'How did we get home Steve?'

'Don't you remember the tube?'

'What happened?'

'Don't ask.'

His earthy laugh says it all. Some kids at school think Steve's a loner, but he looked after me last night, got me back from the party, and I appreciate that. Steve's alright. His mum has asked me to stay for lunch, but right now food is a bad idea. Time to go home and face the flak...

Thursday 2nd

Blimey!

I thought my dad was going to thump me when I got back. He was going on and on about how worried my mum was when I didn't ring. I said I was sorry (I really *was* sorry I'd upset my mum) but he kept shouting and my head felt like it was going to split wide open. I needed peace and quiet, not another drama. In the end mum told dad to stop it and he walked out. The trouble with this place is there's nowhere to hide. I couldn't face climbing up into the loft. I just wanted to go to bed, but we all ended up in the sittingroom/TVroom/diningroom/mybedroom and I fell asleep in a chair.

I felt a bit better after a kip. Dad was out and my mum made me some toast with a glass of milk. I told her I was really sorry about not ringing and she said she knew I was still upset about the group. I gave her a kiss on the cheek and a hug, and if that sounds sloppy hard luck because I love my mum and I don't care who knows it. I tell her all my hopes and dreams and she backs every single one. She's the reason I believe I *will make it* as a journalist, she encourages me, believes in me, and I will make her proud some day.

Mum loves music, I think that's where I get it from, and she said to turn the TV up when *Top of the Pops* came on. It's a brand new chart show on BBC and the deejay, Jimmy Savile, is quite a laugh. The Rolling Stones did *I Wanna Be Your Man*, which the Beatles wrote for them; Dusty Springfield sang *I Only Want To Be With You;* the Dave Clark Five did *Glad All Over;* the Hollies sounded good on

Stay; then the Swinging Blue Jeans belted out *Hippy Hippy Christmas Party Shake.* The Beatles topped the bill with *I Want To Hold Your Hand.*

Good show, we really enjoyed it. Now both TV channels have a weekly music slot, which is great news for pop fans. I turned the set down when my dad got back, then Gray came round and we went up to the Inferno so we could talk. It was freezing up there with only a one bar electric fire to keep us warm, but I'm planning to keep out of dad's way for a while, so I'd better get used to it. I could tell Gray had something on his mind and asked him what was wrong.

'Terry Jenkins went round to see Colin. He's heard we're starting a group and wants to join. His mum will sign the HP form for the bass, but Colin and Shay asked me to come and see you first. Is there any way you can get your dad to change his mind?'

'No, no chance. Thanks for asking Gray, but you'll have to go ahead without me.'

'Right.'

'Don't feel bad about it,' I said, trying to sound like it was no big deal. 'I can be your roadie!' Gray smiled but my act didn't fool him and he left a few minutes later. There was nothing left to say.

Friday 3rd

The Beatles are brilliant and that's official. I've seen it with my own two eyes!

I was feeling a bit grumpy-twitchy-moody on the tube to Finsbury Park. I couldn't stop thinking about the group and me not being in it, sad, sad, sad, then I met Peter at the Beatles Christmas Show and things started to pick up. He'd got tickets for the teatime slot at the Astoria and there were loads of kids in the queue with their young mums, all dressed in their best to see John, Paul, George and Ringo.

Our seats were near the back of the circle, so we didn't have a great view, but nothing could spoil the thrill of being there. Two Liverpool groups got things moving. The Fourmost sang *Hello Little Girl* and *I'm In Love,* then it was Billy J Kramer and the Dakotas with *Do You Want To Know A Secret* and *Bad To Me.* All those songs were written by Lennon and McCartney, so they must be making a fortune.

In some ways the show was a bit corny, like a pantomime. I half-expected Rolf Harris to shout, *Where are the Fab Four kids?* and the Beatles' teeny-weenies to shout back, *They're be-hind you!!* That never happened, but the Fabs did do some sketches, which were quite funny because it was the Beatles and if they sat onstage buttering bread we'd love it. After the break Cilla Black sang the Paul/John hit, *Love Of The Loved,* then her new record, *Anyone Who Had A Heart.* She used to work in the Cavern, now she's a star and there's no way it's gone to her head. Cilla's fab.

THE BEATLES
CHRISTMAS SHOW

THE ASTORIA - FINSBURY PARK
Dec. 24, 1963 - Jan. 11, 1964

Okay, time for the main event. Please welcome... THE BEATLES!!

They open with *Roll Over Beethoven* as teenyscreams bounce around the walls. George is on lead vocals and it's hard to hear him at first, then the kids settle down and the sound gets better. Every new song is greeted by a short burst of squeaky squeals, then we get the chance to listen. Like I said, this isn't a full-on Beatles concert where the noise never stops. This is more like Listen With Beatles, an afternoon treat for the kiddies, and I like it that way coz when you can hear the music they sound *great!!*

All My Loving comes next with Paul hitting the high notes, then *This Boy* is JPG harmony to die for. The Beatles love Ringo, you can tell by the big build-up they give him for his solo spot, *I Wanna Be Your Man,* then the place goes mad for the chart-topper *She Loves You.* Next, Paul melts the heart of every girl in the place with *Till There Was You* from the new album, before they lift the mood again with their current number one, *I Want To Hold Your Hand.* Okay, now get ready for the big finale as John Lennon belts out *Money* and *Twist And Shout* with a voice that lifts you out of your seat and pins you against the back wall. Powerful, exciting, and absolutely stunningly brilliant. The Beatles take a bow and the curtain falls.

I've had such a good time, I feel like screaming myself!

*

I was really on a high coming back from the Beatles' show. There's a big thing going on with their girl fans at the moment, *which Beatle do you fancy most?* I don't fancy any of them, but some of the young mums at the show were quite tasty. I just think the Fabs are the best group I've ever heard. John and Paul are great singers who write amazing songs; George plays guitar lines that get right inside your head; and Ringo may clown around but don't be fooled, he lays down a mean beat on his Ludwig drums. The Beatles are what's happening right now. I'm so happy I saw them... happy I was there... *With The Beatles.*

Saturday 4th

Shay and Colin came round this morning.

Mum and dad had gone out shopping so we all sat in the sittingroom/TVroom/diningroom/mybedroom, drinking coffee and listening to *Saturday Club.* I didn't want to bring them down about the my-dad-no-way-sign-HP-form thing. There was no point going through the whole sad mess again, so I told them about the Beatles show, then we talked about going to see the Stones on Monday. When they left I felt a bit flat... not being in the group still really hurts.

Monday 6th

Tonight should have been happy happy, smiley smiley... but it was bittersweet. Gray, Shay, Colin, Jem and me were all there to see the Stones play live at the Granada Harrow. Peter came too and I paid coz he got those Beatles tickets. Two seats in the stalls cost me 13/- which is a lot of dough, but it was worth every penny. We were surrounded by a rave of screaming girls who were well on the way to a group orgasm. Through the screams we heard the Stones do their two hit singles, *Come On* and *I Wanna Be Your Man*, plus Bo Diddley's *Mona,* Chuck Berry's *Roll Over Beethoven,* and a track from their new EP called *You'd Better Move On.*

I'm a Beatles nut but I have to admit the Stones had the edge on *Beethoven*. Sorry George but Keith's guitar was wilder than yours and Mick's vocals got the whole place jumping. *I Wanna Be Your Man* was the same. I love Ringo's drumming, but when it comes to singing he can't match Jagger. Both those numbers were better by the Stones, but the Beatles show still had more magic for me. Truth is there's no need to choose between them, they're both great bands. We loved the Stones. It would be great to see them play a longer set in a small club like the Marquee. I have no idea why Dave Berry and Marty Wilde were on the bill. Next time give us less padding and more Stones... *that's what we want!!*

Earlier we'd enjoyed the steamy-exotic-thrill of seeing the Ronettes. I've loved them since I bought *Be My Baby* and it was fabtastic to see them live. The follow-up, *Baby I Love You,* is just as good. The three girls ... make that *women!* ... wore skin-tight Chinese dresses and when they swung round to show sexy slits right up to the top of their thighs, an electric shock hit me from head to toe and all parts in between. With their lipstick red lips and beehive hairdos, the Ronettes made the Granada Harrow feel like a sweaty club in Harlem on a steamy summer night.

Hot hot hot.

I loved being at the show with my friends. Shay, Gray and Colin can dream of being up there onstage some day, but I'll be the fool in the wings, wishing and hoping for a chance that will never come. Please don't get me wrong, I'm happy for the lads, wish them all the very best, but it's lonely on the outside. No matter how hard I try, the truth keeps spinning back to hit me in the face. I hate not being in the group more than words can say and nothing will change that. Nothing.

February '64

Tuesday 11th

Sorry I haven't written for a while.

To be honest, I just haven't felt like it. Terry Jenkins has joined the group and they've been practising in Shay's bedroom at the weekends. Shay's got his drums there, but I've heard he's finding it hard to play them. I know I'd be welcome at their rehearsals anytime, but it would rip my heart out to see them play without me. So, I've been living like a hermit, spending most nights in the Inferno, sitting two inches from the electric fire and playing *With The Beatles* over and over and over again. That album is like my comfort blanket – it helps keep the blues away.

We've been having mock exams at school so I've used the time to revise. Got to get good grades in the Summer if I want to go to the grammar. Maths was a nightmare, but I did alright in English Language, English Literature, History, Geography and French. We've got a new French conversation teacher called Michelle. She is dead arty, wears a lot of black and you can easily imagine her sipping wine in some smoky jazz bar on the Left Bank. Yes, this *mademoiselle* is definitely very sexy. Not like the last French student teacher we had who was a real drip. She was asking me about football in a lesson and it went something like this:

Mademoiselle: Aimez-vous le football?

Tony: Oui, j'et adore!

Mademoiselle (face going bright red): No, no, Tony, you 'ave said you love me.

Tony (thinking he is being funny): I do love you, miss!

Mademoiselle: I will not 'ave zis. Get out! Get out!

Great sense of humour... he lied.

I nearly got the cane for that, so I'm glad she's gone back to France. Now we've got Michelle, with her dark hair and smoky eyes. She loves a laugh and we all fancy her like crazy. If I said *j'et adore* to her, I might just mean it.

By the way, the Beatles are in America right now and they're going down a storm. I've seen pictures of fans going crazy in New York and when the Fabs played a big TV show last Sunday 85 billion people watched, or something like that. It's amazing! Think of all those TV sets across the USA tuned to the Fabs. I wonder if tap-dancing Cindy likes the Beatles? They're the first English group ever to crack the States. A month ago I saw them play live in London, now they're kings of New York. Things are moving fast.

Thursday 13th

Newsflash!

Podge went out with sexy/smoky Michelle last night. He took her to a trendy bar in Hampstead called the Witch's Cauldron. I haven't been there yet but it's meant to be really cool, with live music, chess sets, posh newspapers, cheap wine and low lights. Podge kept it all very low-key, but we asked loads of questions like did you hold her hand *à la Beatles,* kiss her, go home with her and make passionate love all night, but he was giving nothing away. All he's saying is they had a good time and yes, he thinks they'll do it again. You know, the old *just good friends* routine. I'm happy for Podge. Good luck, I'm pleased for him. So, jealous? No, you must be joking, that would be very slimy pond life. Okay, the last time I kissed a girl Henry VIII was writing *Greensleaves*, but I'm not getting all bitter and twisted. No way.

Friday 14th

No girlfriend. No group. No bedroom. No happy. No wonder.

Saturday 15th

Got fed up with moping around so I went to see Steve, my off-beat friend. He'd just got back from a record shop in London where you can buy 45s straight from the USA. He'd grabbed a copy of *You Can't Judge A Book By The Cover* by Bo Diddley. It came out last year in the States, real raw sound and I love it. The song fits Steve: he seems quite quiet, but when you get to know him he's a good laugh. He started telling me about a school cruise he went on. There were lots of pretty girls on the ship and the blokes were all boasting about how many they'd screwed. But from what Steve heard in the dormitory at night, there was more wanking going on than fucking! I'm glad I'm not the only one. I can't remember what a girl looks like. Are they the ones with bumps in the front? My sex life is so flat I should move to Norfolk...

Saturday 22nd

The Beatles got back from the States early this morning. Thousands of girls were on the airport roof to welcome them home. They'd been waiting at Heathrow all night in the cold to show the Fabs they love them... yeah! yeah! yeah! John, Paul, George and Ringo were away for two weeks but it was no holiday. As well as TV shows in New York and Miami, they played sold out gigs in Washington and New York, and did about five million two hundred and seventy five interviews and photo sessions. By now they should be Beatlezombies, but they looked great today, standing on the steps of the plane waving and smiling. It all went out live on BBC TV and

I've never seen anything like it before. Welcome home Fabs... we missed you.

Tuesday 25th

Okay, this could be the biggest pop news since the Beatles hit New York!

Gray, Shay and Colin came round tonight and stood on the step looking serious. They said they wanted to talk to me in private. As we walked up the road I asked what was wrong, but nobody said a word. It felt like a scene out of *On The Waterfront* or something, then I saw Terry the bass player standing under the streetlight on the corner.

'Have they told you?' he asked.

'No. What?'

'I don't want to be in the group any more.'

'Right.'

'Do you want my bass?'

'I can't...'

'My mum says you can keep the fiver deposit if you take over the weekly payments.'

My heart skipped a beat, but I had to ask the $64,000 question.

'What about the HP form?'

'You'll have to get someone to sign a new one,' said Terry.

Ice water ran down my spine.

'Can't you ask your mum?' said Colin.

'She might do it,' said Gray.

'Gotta give it a try Tone,' said Shay.

They were right, I can't give up without a fight, can I?

Wednesday 26th

My life's on a knife edge.

I couldn't face asking mum about the HP thing this morning. I felt nervous all day at school and on the way home I kept running through all the things I wanted to say about how dad was holding me back from my dreams but in the end I didn't need to say any of it. Mum knows how much I care about this.

Trouble is, she doesn't want to go behind my dad's back. I can see why she feels that way. If dad ever found out he'd be really angry, so she needs time to think things through. I hate what I'm doing to her and yes, I know I'm a selfish git, but I want to be in the group so much it hurts. Mum has to choose: lie to dad or watch me miss out on something I really want to do. I feel sorry for her, but I hope she helps me. If not, I've told myself not to give her a hard time. I hope I can stick to that.

Thursday 27th

When I got home from school mum was waiting in the kitchen. I told myself again, *if she says no, don't act like a cunt.* But she didn't say no, she said Y-E-S. I gave her a hug and felt like crying. Happy tears, happy happy happy. Wish you could have been there, it was top of the mountain.

Friday 28th

Mum and I catch the bus to Kilburn, feeling like spies. She signs the HP form for the bass and all I need to do now is pay 7/6d a week. I can do that for sure. We walk out into the noise of the evening rush hour on Edgware Road. I'm buzzing and mum looks as happy as me. I buy us both a bag of chips and we eat them out of the paper on the way home.

We've got our story worked out. I'm gonna say Terry's mum did the HP stuff ages ago, so I'm just taking over the payments. My heart's thumping when I speak to dad, but all he says is *make sure you pay on the nail.* No big fuss. Maybe he's sorry for giving me a hard time, I don't know, I just get out quick, jump on my bike and ride round to

Gray's to tell him the good... no make that *absolutely stunningly brilliant...* news!

Saturday 29th

Went to see Terry this morning to pick up my guitar. I love the sound of those two words: *my guitar.* The Framus Star Bass looks so good I might even sleep with it tonight. We all know we've got to work hard to get our group moving, Steve calls it *paying your dues,* but someday soon we could be *With The Beatles* in New York or rolling with the Stones on *Ready Steady Go!*

Now, wouldn't that be nice...

March 1964

Freewheelin'

Sunday 1st

On a scale of one to ten, our group rates a big fat zero.

I went round to Shay's today with my new bass guitar, full of shiny hopes and dreams. Two hours later we were still bashing away at *Twist and Shout* and it was driving us round the *twist* and making us *shout* with frustration. If we carry on like this we'll be done for murder. Murdering a song, murdering each other, murdering something. Gray and Colin are fine, the silly boy lemons are Shay and me. He's got to learn how to move his hands and feet at different times to give one solid driving beat. It's tough being a drummer, but I've got no real excuse. Bass guitar should be easy, but I'm finding it hard to know which string to pluck with my plectrum, or is that plec with my plucktrum? I'm like a kid learning to ride a bike. I'm going along okay then I lose it for a second and *wham!* I crash in a heap. Once in a while Shay and I get it together, but the music still sounds crap. I don't know why. We bought a good amp to share between Gray's guitar, Colin's mike and my bass. It's got four inputs so we can plug another guitar or mike in there if we want. We spent a fortune at Blank's music shop, so how come we sound such a fuzzy mess?

Question: how do people sing and play at the same time? Like Lennon with his guitar or McCartney with his bass. I mean, these guys are my heroes, but what's the real story here? Were they weird kids who sat in their bedrooms learning to sing as they played, instead of going out and having fun? I don't see how you can learn that stuff and still have any kind of life in the real world. I'm starting to think this group thing's not for me: I might tell Terry he can have his bass back!

Friday 6th

Violins are playing, rays of light burst from the sky, on this magicalious day... I AM FREE!!

My parents have bought a caravan in a holiday park at a place called Leysdown on the Isle of Sheppey in the mouth of the River Thames. Don't ask me what it looks like because I've got no idea. I've been in the dark on this. Totally. Mum told me they didn't want to say anything about the caravan until they were sure they'd got it and now it's all sorted the plan is for them to go away every weekend from now until October and she'll leave me plenty of food which she knows I can cook and yes I can have my mates round but no late night noisy parties or I will be in trouble with my dad and how does all that sound to me?

Answer: I like it!

In fact, I *love* it. I've spent my whole life so far in a house full of people... my family people... *feudin'* type people... and suddenly I'm being told mum and dad will be in caravan heaven every weekend for the next seven months. Add to that the happy fact that the Piles go away every weekend too and that gives the following equation:

Empty house + Tony = FREEdom with a capital FREE.

When mum told me the jaw-dropping news I felt like dancing but I thought she might get edgy if I looked too excited, like I was already planning my first all-night orgy, so I just said I'd be fine and not to worry about me. When dad came home he told me not to act like a drunken drug-crazed sex maniac while they're away. Well, he didn't use those words, but that's what he meant. He said *mum thinks we can trust you to look after the place* which made me feel guilty before I'd done anything wrong.

But the way I see it, as long as I steer clear of playing the Stones full blast at midnight, things should work out fine. I mean I'm 16, so I won't be like some soppy kid kicking up a fuss the minute mum and dad are out the door. That would be dumb. I've got my chance for freedom and I'm going to make the most of it. This is how it will work: I'll go to school Friday morning and come home in the afternoon to an empty house where I can do what I like until Sunday night. That's *what* I like *when* I like: eat, drink, smoke, play music, hang out with friends and (if I get lucky) girlfriends, go to bed *when I like*, get up *when I like*, do *what I like* for two absolutely stunningly brilliant days every week from now to October.

Amazing!

The first thing I did when I got the weekends-mean-freedom news was get in touch with Shay. We need to talk about the group. His family don't have a phone so I went on my bike. Asking a friend round for a bite to eat felt good. He'll be here soon and the menu will be Tony's *spaghetti special* washed down with a few glasses of cider. Then we need to get down to some serious talking about his drums and my bass. We got off to a bad start last Sunday and we've got to fix things in a hurry...

Saturday 7th

It took Shay two minutes to sum up what we need to. He told me he was moping around last Sunday after we'd left and his dad pointed to his drum kit and said *get on those things and learn 'em!!* Shay knew his dad was right, it was time to stop moaning and start working, and that goes for me too. Shay's been playing along to records every night and little by little things are getting better. I said I'll try the same with my Framus, starting with *Twist and Shout*, and that was it, end of chat about the group.

I left Shay in the sittingroom/diningroom/TVroom/mybedroom watching *Ready Steady Go!* while I went to cook our Italian meal. How come I know how to cook spaghetti? Well, my Uncle Ted lives in Rome with his wife Giuliana and their five daughters, who should all be in TV ads for shampoo and toothpaste coz they look like little film stars. They chat away in Italian at about a thousand words a minute, but they have very English names, Elizabeth, Sylvia, Mavis, Shirley and Jacqueline. Little Jacqui is a real surprise with her long blonde hair. Uncle Ted says Giuliana must have made friends with the milkman. That makes her laugh, in fact they laugh all the time and it's easy to see they are still very much in love. I like being around them.

They all came to stay for a week last year and it was a real crush to get everyone in our two rooms, but it didn't matter because the flat was full of life and fun. Giuliana shone like Italian sunshine: I loved the smell of her fresh ground coffee and the hot loaves she bought for her kids every morning. She always tried to speak English but sometimes it went a bit wrong. Like the day I came in from school and said I was very hungry. Next thing I know my uncle's asking what's wrong. I didn't know what he was on about, then Giuliana came in and said, *Tony, you tell me you very angry.* No, not angry... *hungry!!* She roared with laughter and it gave us an instant catch phrase before every meal. *Tony, you hungry or angry?* I was mostly hungry.

I had to be careful not to go on about how great Giuliana's food was because I didn't want mum to get jealous, but I couldn't get enough of her pasta dishes. I'd never eaten that kind of food before. We're like most English families, we stick to meat and two veg, never tried curry, never tried Chinese, never tried anything really. That's just the way it is. So, eating big bowls of pasta was some kind of heaven. Mum and dad weren't too keen, especially when Giuliana put garlic in the sauce, but before she left I asked her how to cook spaghetti so I could make it when she was back home in Rome.

Giuliana took me to shop in Golders Green that sold food from all over the world. She showed me the best spaghetti to buy. It comes wrapped in blue paper and costs 2/6d so it's not cheap, but it's dead easy to cook. Just boil it for 12 minutes in a big pan of salty water and you've got a great meal for at least four people. How do you make a lovely pasta treat? Easy: 1) shut the kitchen door so nobody can see you, 2) drain the spag, put it in a big bowl and leave to cool down a bit, 3) have a pee in the sink and don't wash your hands, 4) put a very big glug of Heinz tomato sauce on top of the spag with some salt and pepper, 5) add a huge heap of grated Cheddar cheese, 6) roll up your sleeves, stick your hands in the bowl and mix like crazy for one whole minute, 7) use your hands to put the spag out on the plates (forget doing it with a spoon, I've tried and it's a nightmare), 8) wash and dry your hands and serve your mates with a meal they will love the way Lady loves Tramp when they eat spaghetti in the moonlight as their Italian friends serenade them with that supercute song *Bella Notte*.

You're probably wondering why the pee-in-the-sink bit, right? Well, it's an old Italian peasant thing that goes back years and years to when the chef always had a pee before serving dinner and since washing your hands meant walking down to the local mountain stream, the chef would just mix the pasta with his wee wee fingers and … no, sorry, I'm just joking with you. There is no pee-in-the-sink bit, that's rubbish. What you really do at stage 3) is wash your hands until they're as squeaky clean as a Disney cartoon, then get busy mixing your *spaghetti special*.

Shay loved it. He was really impressed I could cook. He said he had a misty memory of boiling an egg once when he was about seven, but that's his cooking career in a nutshell. I've always enjoyed messing about with food… probably because I eat so much of it!

Shay said *Ready Steady Go!* wasn't much cop. We want to see exciting new groups on the show every week, but tonight it was Adam Faith and Johnny Kidd & The Pirates. They've both been knocking around since the early days of British rock 'n roll with Billy Fury, Marty Wilde, Tommy Steele and all that crowd. And British rock 'n roll was never American rock 'n roll. It was like they took a wild cat and turned it into a pair of fireside slippers. I hate to sound mean about Faith and Kidd, but what were you thinking *RSG*?

It's a weird time for music right now with fabtastic new groups like the Beatles and the Stones sharing the charts with corny stuff like Jim Reeves. Shay ran through all the records he likes and hates, telling me the reasons why. If you like satire forget *TWTWTW,* come round to my place and see Shay's send-up of Freddie and his dopey Dreamers singing *Over You* complete with a Spike Milligan type *Freddieshouldbeinafunnyfarm* dance routine. Wild!

Shay loves talking, loves joking, loves laughing, loves music and he loves drinking, which is what we did 'til gone midnight. We talked about Gray and Colin, but mostly we talked about girls and how we're sure to meet more when we're up there in the charts. The Beatles started work on their first movie this week. They've been filming on a train, so we made up our own nutty version starring our group. The more we drank, the madder it got. In the end Colin and Gray were driving the train through Cricklewood at 500 miles per hour, Dr. No was in a shoot-out on the roof with James Bond and the Saint, and Shay and I were eating *spaghetti special* with Ursula Andress in her supersexy white bikini, while the Spike Milligan sang *Bella Notte* by the light of the silvery moon.

Shay's great, if he's going to work hard on his drums I'll do the same on my bass. By the way, I heard the Beatles had fun on their train... bet it wasn't as crazy as the Shaytone Express!

Sunday 8th

Rehearsed with the group at Shay's today. *Twist and Shout* is getting better. Give us a few more weeks and we might even start a new song.

Saturday 14th

I'm writing this in the Witch's Cauldron in Hampstead where arty student types sit at tables in gentle light, drinking, smoking, talking and listening to music from two young guys with acoustic guitars. Their voices blend in perfect harmony as they sing a stream of songs I've never heard before. It's the kind of place you try to look cool and intelligent, like you're a poet or something.

I'm here with Podge, Steve and our supercool French teacher Michelle. I think Podge was getting fed up with us asking him if he was sleeping with her, so he asked us along to prove they really are *just good friends*. I know we've been childish, bit pathetic really. Still, it was great walking in here with her tonight, even if we were all trying a bit too hard. The others were soon talking politics and I'm not into that so I got my notebook out and started writing, while trying for that angry young man look.

I felt a bit hungry so I ordered a bowl of soup called *witch's brew* and the waitress laughed when I said I'd like it shaken not stirred. I started to relax a bit and asked Michelle if she knew any of the songs we were hearing. The ones she liked best were by a folk singer called Bob Dylan. I've heard the name, but don't know much about his music. Michelle's got his first two LPs and she's going to lend them to me which is very *très bon pour moi*.

The musicians take a break and one of them comes over to sit with friends at the table next to ours. I really liked a song he sang about greenback dollars and ask him who it was by. He says The Kingston Trio and they've been playing numbers by Peter Paul & Mary and The Highwaymen too. He tells me Dylan's third LP has just come out and it's brilliant. He's learning some of Bob's new songs so watch out for extra magic in the Witch's bubbling Cauldron soon.

The singer starts chatting to his friends, and I get back to my notebook. When he stands up to play again he says to listen to the words of the first song. *Blowin' in the Wind* is beautiful and when you focus on the lyrics they really hit home. If all Dylan's songs are as good as this, I can't wait to hear Michelle's LPs.

I'll stop writing now because I want to listen to the music and Michelle just gave me one of her French cigarettes which was so strong I feel like I'm on drugs. It says *Gauloises* on the pack next to the ashtray. If anyone ever offers you one, please give the following answer... *non merci.*

Midnight. I'm home. I'd built going out with Michelle, Podge and Steve into a big jangly thing, but it was great. No sex, no orgies, just great live music and good times. It's weird, I live in a man's body but in many ways I'm still a kid. I need to grow up a bit, definitely. I really enjoyed those folk songs tonight. Trouble is, you never hear that stuff on the radio.

And now on Workers' Playtime... Blowin' in the Wind by Bob Dylan.

Can't see it happening, can you?

Friday 20th

I've been playing Michelle's LPs all week, *Bob Dylan* and *The Freewheelin' Bob Dylan.* His voice would drive a lot of people crazy, but I love it. Dylan is like the Beatles, he's got his own sound. He sings every song from the heart and his acoustic guitar fits the mood, from love songs to protest. The red light glow of the Inferno is the perfect place to hear him. Remember what the singer said in the Witch's Cauldron? *Listen to the words...* that's what I've been doing and to be honest, it's been quite depressing. Songs on the first LP include *In My Time of Dyin', Man of Constant Sorrow, Fixin' to Die* and *See That My Grave Is Kept Clean.* It's a long long way from *Hippy Hippy Shake.*

The second LP, *Freewheelin',* has more of Dylan's own songs and they have an honesty that cuts to your soul. *Blowin' in the Wind, Masters of War* and *A Hard Rain's a-Gonna Fall* get you thinking about dark forces that could destroy our planet. *Girl from the North Country* is a lonely song for a lover Dylan once knew and *Bob Dylan's Dream* is about good friends he has lost along the way. It's all a bit gloomy, but his songs put a spell on you and leave you feeling kind of sad, thoughtful and excited, all at the same time.

I guess you could say the same about two books Michelle lent me with the records. They're by an American guy called Jack Kerouac. She reckons he's a bit like Bob Dylan without a guitar and she's right. I love the way he writes in a crazy flood of ideas. *On The Road* is about criss-crossing the States with friends who share the thrill. *Big Sur* is more scary with Jack going crazy in California. I've only read bits of the books so far, but I've seen enough to know he's a great writer. I love the way he spells words the way they sound, makes up his own rules. I'm gonna try a bit of that too.

Like I said, I need to grow up a a bit. Reading Kerouac and listening to Dylan is sure to help, but after three red light nights in the Inferno I was up for a bit of *Ready Steady Go!* and tonight's show was smack back on form. Mum and dad are away at their caravan so I turned the TV up good and loud. The Beatles sang *It Won't Be Long* from *With The Beatles*, plus both sides of their single *Can't Buy Me Love* and *You Can't Do That* with its guitar solo *à la Lennon*. There was plenty of funny chat from the Fabs and John was out to plug his new book every chance he got. I don't know what's in it, but I do know I'll buy it.

There was another good group on *RSG!* tonight. They're called the Animals, they come from Newcastle, and they're great. They play R&B, the music Steve loves, and if you shut your eyes you'd swear the lead singer was a black man from the Deep South, not a white man from the North-East. Their new single is *Baby Let Me Take You Home* and I felt very finger-on-the-pulse coz I knew the song already

– it's on Bob Dylan's first LP. They've changed the words a bit, but it's the same tune with a new driving beat that builds to a big climax. They do it better than Dylan... sorry Bob!

Sunday 22nd

Something really scary happened last night and I think I'm cracking up.

I watched the Eurovision Song Contest live on TV all the way from Denmark and here comes the really bad news... *I liked the winning song!!* Do you know what this could do to my cred with the boys in the band? Eurovision is a bingy-bongy-silly-songy joke, everyone knows that. So I'm sitting there with an I'm-too-smart-for-this-crap cynical smirk on my face, when this Italian girl with long dark hair walks out onstage and knocks my socks off with her pretty song, *Non ho l'eta.* She's 16, same age as me, and she looks lovely in her little black dress. Not sexy, *lovely*, the kind of girl you'd be proud to take home to tea.

Her name is Gigliola Cinquetti and when the votes start rolling in I'm with her heart and soul. I wonder if my family in Rome are watching as *la bella senorita* wins for Italy. I'm happy for her and I don't feel bad about Matt Monroe only coming second for GB with his corny effort, *I Love The Little Things.* It's real tripe, the kind of rubbish that fills our airwaves when we'd rather be listening to the Beatles or the Stones. If Lennon and McCartney wrote a song for Eurovision they'd win hands down, but they wouldn't touch it with a bargepole coz they know it's as uncool as an unplugged fridge. That's why this thing with me and Gigliola *must stay a secret.* Don't tell a soul, okay?

Right, I'm off to Shay's place and if the group say anything about *Non ho l'eta,* I will s-w-e-a-r I've never heard it, didn't s-e-e it, know n-o-t-h-i-n-g about it, cross my heart and hope to spy, as James Bond said to Ursula Andress and her supersexy white bikini on the Shaytone Express to Cricklewood.

Monday 23rd

When I got to rehearsals yesterday, the group had already learnt how to play *Non ho l'eta* and Colin was singing it in a high voice like Frankie Valli off the Four Seasons. I thought it sounded great, then I realised it was just my imagination and they were doing *Twist and Shout...* again. The truth is we're getting nowhere fast. We're all off school next week for the Easter holidays, so I've asked mum if we can go down to their caravan for a few days to really work on our music. She looked a bit nervous, but I don't know why. It'll just be Colin, Gray, Shay and me, singing, playing guitars, cooking our own food, doing our own washing up, and trying our best to keep the place neat and tidy. Can't see anything to worry about, can you?

Tuesday 24th

The lads all came round tonight. We went up into the Inferno and I told them the good news. Mum's persuaded dad to trust us. One week today we're on the road... Leysdown here we come!

Wednesday 25th

The Beatles were on *Top of the Pops* tonight with *Can't Buy Me Love* and *You Can't Do That.* The Fabs were gear, as usual. John, Paul, George and Ringo are still working on their new film, but they took time last week to pick up some show biz award from a politician called Harold Wilson. It felt weird seeing them with him, like they didn't fit in the same photo. Pipe man is just another of those dusty old men who mean nothing to me. Everywhere you look oldies are running the show and it gets on my nerves.

Take TV and radio, *please* take them coz we don't want them. The bosses are yesterday's men who see teenagers as an alien force from the Planet Problem. They don't understand us: when they try to make pop shows they always get it wrong. Did you see *It's The Beatles!* on BBC TV last Christmas? Question: was the cameraman kinky? He spent more time looking up the skirts of the screaming girls than he did focusing on the Fabs. Was John Lennon there? I didn't see him, did you? The sound was terrible too. Old men, old men, messing things up again and again. The Beatles playing live in Liverpool: it should have been heaven but it came out as hell. *Ready Steady Go!* is my fave TV show, but Keith Fordyce looks like a posh dad who's walked into a teenage party. *Top of the Pops* has all the latest hit records, but old-time deejays who just don't fit the scene. Jimmy Savile is zany and different, the way a deejay should be, so why not let him do *Pops* every week? Brian Matthew is another deejay I like coz the Beatles have sung on both his radio shows, *Saturday Club* and *Easy Beat,* and the Fabs even rang him from New York to tell fans back home how things were going in the USA. You get the feeling most people at the Beeb have no idea what's happening in music today, but Brian Matthews is different. The Beatles think he's fab and that's fine by me.

Okay, time to get off my chip-on-the-shoulder soapbox. Those *DylanBobKerouacJackredlightInferno* sessions have left me feeling a bit like a rebel, so when Steve asked if I wanted to go on the Aldermaston March I said yes right away. Ban The Bomb! After Cuba, I'm all in favour of scrapping each and every nuke on the planet. It doesn't take a genius to see it makes sense. It should have happened years ago after the horror of Hiroshima and Nagasaki. If joining the march will help, I'm there. And that scary *Eurovisionisfab* night proved I'm close to a *Big Sur* type crack up, so it'll be good to get out and hit the streets with Steve.

By the way, this has got nothing to do with the stuff we read in the paper about sex parties on the march. Okay, maybe we *are* hoping for an orgy or two with some long-haired ladies with baggy sweaters and skin-tight blue jeans, but that's not the only reason we're going.

Honest.

Easter Saturday 28th

Well, we found the march in east London yesterday and we saw plenty of blue jeans and baggy sweaters, but they were mainly on grey-haired men with beards and thick glasses. Most of the people were much older than us, but there were a couple of young guys with guitars singing Aldermaston anti bomb songs. Steve and I would have joined in, but we didn't know the words. I asked if they knew any Dylan and they tried a bit of *Blowin' In The Wind* but it wasn't great, so they went back to the stuff they knew. It was good to have some music to keep our spirits up as we trudged thru the breezy streets, but some of the oldies looked like they wanted to shove those guitars where the sun don't shine.

I'd been expecting a bit of angry chanting and shouting, but there was a lot of trouble on last year's march and nobody wanted that again so things were peaceful, which was good but a bit boring. After a couple of hours I was bursting for a pee: mid-afternoon Good Friday and of course everything was shut, pubs, shops, cafes, everything. I told Steve I'd see him later and headed off down a sideroad. I don't know what I thought I'd find, public toilets in the front garden of 47 Convenience Avenue maybe? I was getting desperate and trying not to think of waterfalls and fountains, then I saw an alley beside some terraced houses and went for a nervy wee. I half-expected one of the neighbours to look over the fence and tell me to fuck off. That's what I'd do if someone pissed outside my house. I wasn't proud of what I'd done, but boy it felt good. On the *Thank Your Lucky Stars* Janice scale, I'd give it *foive*.

I ran back up the road to the march.

'Exciting, isn't it?'

I realised I was walking next to... wait for it... a girl in tight blue jeans and a baggy sweater. She had short black hair and green eyes that burnt bright with the passion she felt inside. She looked hungry to hear what I had to say, but my mind was still in the alley.

'Sorry?'

'I said it's exciting, all marching together for what we believe in.'

'Yeah, Ban the Bomb, they should have done it years ago.'

That's all I needed to say and Tasha was off and running with her thoughts and opinions on the Cold War, Cuba, Khrushchev, Aldermaston and all points east and west. Blimey! Did this girl want to ban the bomb or did she want to ban the bomb? I felt like I was under attack myself, smack bang in the path of a rushing, flooding river. The only time I cut across her flow was when she started to have a go at JFK and I don't want to hear that from anyone, not even a pretty girl with flashing green eyes. I said if Kennedy hadn't stood up to the Russians over Cuba, Americans would be living with the fear of being nuked every day of their lives. Tasha thought hard and said *maybe* I had a point, then she smiled and asked if she'd been going on a bit about the bomb and I said maybe just a little.

We started talking about other things, like doing '0' levels, and she told me she got nine last year. I said she must be brainy coz I'm only taking six and that's a sweat. She looked pleased and I was happy she couldn't read my mind because in there we were lying naked on satin sheets and I was kissing her beautiful big *wangzangaroonies*. She talked A-levels and I thought... *wang*. She talked friends and I thought... *zanga*. She talked Uni... and I thought *roonies*. Sorry if I sound pervy, but that's the way it was. After a while she started to notice I wasn't really listening: time to go.

'I'd better find my friend.'

'Okay, maybe see you tonight when we stop?'

'Yeah, thanks.'

I hurried away kicking myself, well not really or I would have fallen over, but you know what I mean. Why say *thanks*, like I was *grateful* she'd spoken to me? I know I need to get better at playing it cool, look at Dylan, he lives like a man of mystery and the less he says the more people want to know him. I bet he has loads of women in his life, like that pretty girl on the *Freewheelin'* sleeve, hugging him tight as the two of them walk thru the snow looking cozy and happy. Good luck to you Bob: I hope to be just like you someday. A cool dude, not an awkward teen, which is what I feel most of the time. Ah well, no point beating myself up, but I'd blown it with Tasha that was for sure. I headed on up the line, listening for those kids with guitars, and pretty soon Steve and I were side-by-side again.

We sang *We Shall Overcome* as we walked together and it felt good. Two hundred thousand Americans brought that song to Washington last year, when Martin Luther King spoke of his dream that one day little children of all colours and creeds will live as one. His words were beautiful and so was the message of our march, which made me feel even worse about not listening to Tasha when she was pouring her heart out.

I felt exhausted by the end of the day, but not from the walking. It was all the stuff swirling around in my head that wore me out. We trooped into a big dusty hall where the marchers found a place to sleep, quietly, politely, peacefully. I looked at Steve, he looked at me, our minds met as one, no orgies here tonight, no way, no how.

'Have you lads got sleeping bags?'

A jolly-hockey-sticks type was staring at us. We shook our heads.

'Oh dear, this floor's jolly hard you know.'

Jolly hockey gave us a sad smile, but there was no need for her to worry. Sleep on a hard wooden floor when we were ten minutes from the nearest tube... did we look crazy? We were heading for the exit in a drumbeat and as we walked out into the street I came face-to-face with Tasha. I thought she'd cut me dead, but she gave me a golden harvest smile.

'Hi! Mummy got a bit tired, but we've made it.'

'I've got to go now.'

She looked disappointed and I took a chance.

'Can I write to you Tasha, you know, keep in touch?'

She grabbed a pen from her mum and pushed a piece of paper into my hand.

'Write soon,' she said, her voice as soft as a kiss.

'Who was that?' asked Steve.

'Just someone I met.'

Believe it or not, I played it cool for once.

We were amazed to find a little corner shop open on our way to the tube. After walking all afternoon we were ready to treat ourselves, so we bought chocolate, drinks, cigarettes and Steve's favourite music paper. We felt like kids who'd skipped out of school early.

'Fancy this?' asked Steve, as we sat on the platform enjoying our choccy fix.

It was an ad in the *Melody Maker* for the Yardbirds at the Marquee. I said no, I didn't fancy seeing Eric 'Slowhand' Clapton live at one of the coolest clubs in London. We laughed a bit then took the tube to Tottenham Court Road, walked down Oxford Street, turned left into Wardour Street, and found ourselves standing in line before the doors opened. The next few hours flashed past in a dream.

The Marquee feels good as soon as you walk inside. Everyone stands to watch the bands who play on a low stage at the top of the room. A long mirror covers one of the walls which makes the place look a lot bigger than it really is. Have you heard of Mods? They've been around a while, a sort of cool clique, and there were plenty in the club last night. Guys with short hair, smart suits, button down shirts and shiny shoes. The girls had short hair too, cool shirts and sweaters, skirts down to their knees. American R&B records played before the Yardbirds came on and the Mod girls danced up a storm, moving with an easy jazzy sway, while the guys stood in packs looking relaxed and tense at the same time.

Steve caught me staring at the girls and quietly told me to look elsewhere if I wanted to keep my head on my shoulders. He's streetwise and he'd picked up on a get-on-the-wrong-side-of-us-and-we-will-beat-you-to-a-pulp vibe coming from the Mod blokes, so I focused on the stage until the Yardbirds walked out to a big cheer. They recorded a live LP here a couple of weeks ago, so it was a bit like Arsenal playing at Highbury, they had the crowd on their side.

I've never seen an ace group in a top club before and the first thing that hit me was the power of the music. It was loud... exitingly, ear-bashingly, knee-shakingly, L-O-U-D. I thought I'd spend most of my time watching Slowhand, but this is no one man band. The Yardbirds took over from the Rolling Stones as the house band at the Crawdaddy in Richmond a while back and now they're carving out a big name for themselves across the UK with their hot live shows.

The drummer, Jim McCarty, reminds me of Charlie Watts coz he delivers a driving beat without breaking sweat. Chris Dreja holds the sound together with his crisp rhythm guitar and Paul Samwell-Smith's flowing bass runs leave me knowing I've got a helluva lot to learn. The singer is a slim fair-haired guy called Keith Relf and like the rest of the band he looks neat in his smart shirt and tie. Nearly all the songs he sings were written by black R&B stars in the States, but Keith doesn't try to copy them. He sings like a kid who grew up by the Thames, but his harmonica playing is pure Mississippi delta.

Clapton was brilliant, of course, but so were the rest of the band. I stood there thinking maybe this was the kind of music our group could make... I only said *maybe*. Steve's was buzzing on the tube back to Golders Green. He knew nearly every song the Yardbirds played and he'd got most of the original versions too. Some were made years ago, but we've never had the chance to hear them in the U.K. That's all changing now, R&B is here to stay!

I crashed out at Steve's place and this morning he treated me to a string of great records from the Yardbirds' set: *Too Much Monkey Business* by Chuck Berry; *Smokestack Lightning* by Howlin' Wolf; *Boom Boom* by John Lee Hooker and two great songs from Bo Diddley, *I'm A Man* and *You Can't Judge A Book By Looking At The Cover*. When I think of all the wonderful music we've been missing out on, while the BBC has been serving up slop like *Sing Something Simple*, it makes me want to cry.

I'm not sure how EC got his nickname, maybe for the same reason the giant in Robin Hood is called Little John. When he's playing guitar, Eric is anything but slow, his fingers bounce around the strings like they're made of *flubber*. When it comes to quickfire rat-a-tat-tat solos he's king of the west (end), but he's got this other thing going with the Yardbirds, on songs like *Who Do You Love?*, where he builds a roaring chunk of sound by strumming chords so fast his right hand seems to go into slow-motion. Is that where he got the Slowhand tag? Don't know, but maybe...

When Steve and I walked out of the Marquee last night, I told him I thought we'd just seen the best guitarist in London, England, Great Britain, the World and the Universe. I know I was high on the thrill of the show, but I still feel the same way today. Who can hold a light to EC? Maybe some alien guitar hero on Saturn or Venus, but I doubt it. When he's driving a thumping song like *Pretty Girl* he sets the place alight, then on a slow blues like *Five Long Years* his guitar cries the saddest tears.

You can't learn to play guitar like Eric Clapton, that's a gift from the gods, but maybe I can take something from the treasure chest we opened last night and bring it on home to our group. We need more gear from Blank's music store that's for sure. The Yardbirds had different amps for every guitar and Keith Relf's voice and harmonica boomed out of huge speakers at both ends of the stage. Now let's take a snapshot of what *we've* got: one little Watkins Dominator amp for Colin's mike, Gray's guitar and my bass.

No wonder we sound fuzzy!

Steve's getting a bass guitar too and he already knows a lot about the music he wants to play. Have you heard of 12-bar blues? It sounds like a pub crawl but it's the secret link to all kinds of great music from blues and rock 'n roll to R&B. Hundreds of hit songs have been written using the same simple chords. Steve lent me a record he just got from the States called *Hi-Heel Sneakers* by Tommy Tucker. It's a 12-bar in the key of C and you time each bar to a count of four. Steve wrote down the chords, *C C C C F F C C G F C G*, and said if we learn that song we'll be able to do a hundred more like it. This could be our *Open Sesame* moment. Learn to play those 12 bluesy bars and our world could change forever. We've got plenty to work on in the caravan next week. Roll over Bo Diddley and tell Chuck Berry the news...

Easter Monday 30th

Steve was right about Mods liking a punch-up. There was a riot going on in Clacton today: Mods and Rockers smeared across the news headlines, Lambretta kids fighting motorbike leathers, running battles on the beaches, angry gangs chucking stones at the police, scuffles and arrests on the seafront. Hope we don't run into any riots on the Isle of Sheppey... I've just been marching for peace!

April '64

Cathy & Caroline

Wednesday 1st

It was dark when we got to Leysdown. We split up to look for *Clovelly* coz mum and dad have named their caravan after a place in Devon where donkeys carry fat people up a steep hill. Our plan was simple: find the caravan, shout the code word *Inferno!* and the rest of the lads would come running.

It felt quite creepy walking round the site on my own. I found some toilets and went for a waz but the lights didn't work. I told myself it was stupid to feel frightened: what was I a man or a mouse? I nibbled on a bit of cheese as I tried to make up my mind. (© Acme Cheesy Jokes Ltd.) Then I had a brilliant idea: whistle. When you whistle you feel happier and braver, it's a well-known fact, so I tried a burst of *All My Loving* but the tune came back with a scary echo that made me think of graveyards and open coffins, so I gave up and tried to finish my wee in a hurry.

'What you doin'?'

The angry voice gave me such a fright I let go of my willy and peed my pants. I spun round and the glare of a torch hit me in the eyes.

'I've been watching you and your mates. What you doin' on this site?'

'Looking for a caravan.'

'So you can smash it up?'

'No, it's my mum and dad's.'

'What's it called?'

'Clovelly.'

'What are your mum and dad called?'

'Lily and Cyril.'

'Where do they come from?'

I was over the shock by now and getting fed up with his questions.

'Cricklewood, if that's alright with you mate.'

'Okay, keep your shirt on son. I know who you are now.'

'Who are *you* then?'

'Stan, pleased to meet ya.'

He pulled his torch away from my eyes and I saw the man of mystery for the first time. He was short and tubby with a bald head and big grin.

'Sorry mate, can't be too careful these days. Hear about those Mods and Rockers?'

I didn't want to talk so I walked out, but Stan was right beside me, all smiles.

'Nice people your mum and dad, me and Doreen went for a drink with them last Saturday.'

'Know where their caravan is?'

'Course, come on I'll show ya.'

When I heard those magical words I realised I didn't *hate* Stan, in fact I *loved* him and wanted to have his babies. A couple of minutes later we were outside *Clovelly* and Stan thought I'd cracked when I screamed *Inferno!* but he was soon chatting with the rest of the lads and showing us how to hitch up the Calor Gas container so we could cook some food. He was a nice guy, pity he made me piss myself. It took the lads about point-five of a second to spot the dark patch on my jeans before I had a chance to wash and change. Gray and I have been chatting a bit in French to get ready for the exams, so I soon had a new nickname, *Monsieur Oui-Oui*. And talking of wee-wees, I need to go toot sweet so I'll see ya later...

*

Midday. When I got back to the caravan after a long hot shower the lads were all up and about, so I started fixing breakfast coz as you know I love to cook. When I first went to Whitefield I didn't want to do woodwork (boring) or metalwork (even worse), so I asked if I could do domestic science with the girls. Blimey! You'd think I'd asked if I could strip them all naked and make love to them one by one. I thought it made sense to learn how to cook shepherd's pie and maybe bake a loaf or make a cake, but my idea was *shockwave city* and they turned me down flat. Instead they taught me how to make a mortise and tenon joint and that's a skill I plan to use every day of my life, rain or shine... I don't think.

I've picked up how to cook along the way... *et la cuisine de Monsieur Oui-Oui est très bonne.* I made bacon sarnies for brekkie and they went down a treat. After last night, one thing was for sure, no more beans. We were all tired and hungry after Stan left, so I got our carrier bag of food out and toasted a whole sliced loaf and put it on the table with half a pound of butter. At the same time I heated up three tins of baked beans and fried five eggs, while Jem and Colin sorted out *whowantedhowmanysugarsintheircoffee.* Then Gray put the Stones EP on his portable record player and we got stuck into our feast to the sounds of *Bye Bye Johnny*. That meal really hit the spot and by the time we'd finished there were no patterns left on the plates, which wasn't surprising coz they were white to start with. (Pause for hysterical laughter from reader... that's you!)

Around midnight we started to feel tired. The caravan had one double bed, which Jem and I were sharing; two long seats that turned into beds, which Shay and Gray were using; and a strip of floor by the door where Colin was sleeping like a watchdog. That started a silly joke - every time Col spoke we all barked. He could have got cheesed off with that in a hurry, but he just laughed. Col's that kind of guy, he's only 13 but he's got his own way of doing things. He doesn't swear, instead of saying fucking he says *flippin'*, instead of bloody he says *blinkin'*. He gets his *flippin'* leg pulled all the *blinkin'* time, but it doesn't faze him. If there was an award for laid-back lead singers, Colin would win first prize. When Jem asked if he could come with us this week I knew we'd be short of beds, but Colin offered to bring a Lilo and sleep on the floor. That's our singer: Mr Nice Guy. Mind you, he did go on a bit last night. We were just dropping off when a voice rang out in the darkness...

Colin: How did you do it Tone?

Tony (sleepy): What?

Colin: You know... your jeans.

Tony: Stan made me jump.

Colin: How?

Tony: Crept up behind me in the bogs.

Colin: What did you do?

Tony: Wet myself.

Laughter from the lads.

Gray (French accent): A *terrible zing* for *Monsieur Oui-Oui!*

Shay: In fact, you could say he was pissed!

More laughs in the dark, followed by a loud f-a-a-r-r-t!

Jem: Phew! Who was that?

Colin: He who smelt it dealt it.

Jem: It wasn't me.

Gray: Don't look at me.

Colin: How can we look at you... it's dark in here.

Shay (B-movie scary voice): Beware the Ghost of Baked Beans Past!

Ghostly noises from the lads.

Gray: Not scared are you Tone?

Tony: You lot really know how to take the...

Colin: Piss?

Shay: No thanks, he's just had one!

And so it went on: jokes, farts, laughs, giggling in the dark like a bunch of silly boy lemons. Anyone would think we were on holiday! Mind you, I hope it's not the same tonight, I feel knackered.

*

6.30pm A-goo-goo, a-gee-gee, brill-fab-wop-bop-a-go-go-go...

Can't speak, hand still shaking with excitement, hard to write, must tell you the good news, the great news, *strapmetoastar andraceacrossthesky* news. We found Radio Caroline this afternoon. It's a brand new station coming live from a ship in the North Sea and we're in the perfect spot to hear it loud and clear. The Light Programme was dishing out the usual rubbishy granny music, so Jem started flicking round the dial and came up with 199 on the medium wave, our new slice of heaven.

We knew he'd found something special the minute we heard it. They were playing a brilliant new song, not pop but classy and cool. The kind of record you *never* hear on the Beeb.

'What's that Jem?

'Don't know, just found it.'

We listened in silence, like we were in church. A young American voice came in over the end of the record. 'That was *Walk on By* by Dionne Warwick and this is Radio Caroline on 199, your all day music station. Here come the Rolling Stones!'

Just like magic another great record blasts out of the radio. Jem turns it up to max and fills the caravan with the sound of Caroline. We've only just met her but we're already in love. The Stones *do* fade away but we're straight into *Can't Buy Me Love* by the Fabs. We stare at each other with wide eyes, frightened to move in case we break the spell and fall back into the dark ages BRC... Before Radio Caroline.

But this is no dream. The music flows like a golden river in the sun: the Animals, Dusty Springfield, the Searchers, the Dave Clark Five, the Merseybeats, Manfred Mann, the Ronettes, the Hollies, Gerry & The Pacemakers, the Mojos, plus more Stones, more Beatles, songs from LPs and fab golden oldies like *Louie Louie* by the Kingsmen. This is a brave new world and we're loving every minute of it.

It's quite cold out so we stay in the caravan all afternoon listening to the music. Caroline seems to have a hotline to our heads, it's *for us*, on *our wavelength* and it thrills and chills us to the bone. We've never heard anything like it before, not even in our wildest dreams. At six o'clock a deejay called Simon Dee tells us Caroline is closing down for the night, but they'll be back at six in the morning. We hope Simon's as good as his word: we want more Caroline...........moremoremoremoremoremoremoremoremore moremoremoremoremoremormoremoremoremoremoremoremore moremoremoremoremormoremoremoremoremoremoremore

moremoremoremormoremoremoremoremoremoremoremoremoremore
moremoremormoremoremoremoremoremoremoremoremoremoremore
moremormoremoremoremoremoremoremoremoremoremoremoremore
mormoremoremoremoremoremoremoremore... they crid!!

And then... silence.

We feel ourselves being sucked back into the bleak evening choice
between the Light Programme, which is fab for anyone over 85, and
Radio Luxembourg which fades in and out on 208 and teases like a
pretty girl who lets you look but not touch. Jem flicks the dial to the
Beeb, dopey voices, dopey music, dopey everything. The let-down
after the thrill of Caroline hits us like a kick in the balls.

'For fuck's sake turn it off... it's crap!'

Gray has spoken and nobody's arguing. He picks up his guitar, *Hi-
Heel Sneakers,* 12-bar blues in the key of C, let's get it right now,
learn more songs, work hard on our music, make our group great,
chase a new dream, make a record, hear it on Radio Caroline, your
all day music station...

Thursday 2nd

What's that smell?

Bad news: we've had a fire. I did sausage, chips and tomatoes for
dinner last night, followed by tinned fruit and a can of evaporated
milk. The second part was good, I opened those tins like a top chef.

But the first part, well, shall we say not great? I had two frying pans going with loads of butter. The chips and sausages cooked in no time and they looked really tasty until it came to the knife and fork bit. The tomatoes were alright but when you cut the chips they were raw and the bangers were a dodgy shade of pink inside. I asked the lads to stick their food back in the pan. Then I fried the splodge too long and it came out as a lumpy grey mess with red spots on top.

So, it came as no surprise when Shay and Gray said they'd cook breakfast this morning. Colin, Jem and I decided to walk into town to buy some papers. We got some crispy rolls too and crunched them on the way back. It was a bit cold but the beach looked great, big fried egg sun, bright blue sky, sparkling sea. A good-to-be-alive kind of day... *then* we saw smoke coming out of the caravan window... *then* we saw Gray coming out of the caravan window... *then* I saw myself running across the field but it felt like I was standing still. For a second I thought it must be a bad dream, but the shock on Gray's face told me this was for real. In my mind I saw flames leaping in the caravan and the whole place going up in smoke. What would I tell mum and dad? Goodness gracious, bloody great balls of fire!

'Sorry Tone,' said Gray.

'What happened?'

'We burnt...'

'Shay,' I screamed, 'where's Shay?'

'Slight cock-up on the grub front.'

Shay stood smiling at the caravan door, looking cool in his white shorts.

'We saw the smoke,' said Jem.

'Thought the place was on fire,' said Colin.

'Blame Lynchy,' said Shay. 'He was meant to be watching the toast while I boiled the eggs, but he got bored and started playing *Hi-Heel Sneakers* and it sounded good so I came out to listen. Next thing we know the toast is on fire and there's smoke everywhere. Gray runs in and sees there's a knife on fire too, so he grabs it and jumps out the window.'

'Why didn't you just walk out the door?' asked Colin.

'He's been reading too much James Bond,' said Shay.

It wasn't like Gray to panic, he's one of the toughest guys I know, but it was early, he was still half-asleep, he saw danger and he sorted it in his own fearless way. See Double-O Lynchy in his new hit movie, *From Leysdown With Love!!*

We all got busy sorting out the burnt toast, cleaning the cooker and opening the windows to get rid of the smoke. By the time we'd done all that the eggs were rock hard, but Shay chopped them up and put them in buttered crusty rolls with a dollop of Daddies brown sauce and they were dee-lish. A couple of coffees later it was like the fire had never happened.

'I've just thought of a name for your group,' said Jem.

'What's that?'

'Well, after this morning... the Infernos!'

Laugh? I nearly put some toast on! Then we thought a bit... and talked a bit... and nodded a bit and said... no smoke without fire... great name...all the way from our attic hideaway... the Infernos... we like it!

*

Midday. We're all on the beach. It's quite cold but the sun's still shining, Radio Caroline's playing and the records are just as good as yesterday. Every now and then a sexy woman says: *This is Caroline on 199 your all day music station, the sound of music all day every day on 199 meters medium wave.*

After a lifetime in the radio wilderness, we can't believe our luck. Gray, Shay, Jem and I start a kick-about with the Frido, but every few minutes Colin shouts *Beatles!* or An*imals!* or *Rolling Stones!* and we come running up the sand to listen. In the end we give up on the football and let the beautiful sound of non-stop pop wash over us.

Radio Caroline .... your all day music station.

'There's a new girl on *Ready Steady Go!* this week,' says Colin, looking up from his paper.

'Who?'

'Cathy McGowan, she's only 19, never been on TV before, beat six hundred other girls to get the job.'

'Photo?'

'Yeah, she's nice,' he says, holding up the paper so we can all have a look.

Long dark hair, lovely smile, laughing eyes... and that's just Colin!

'It says she loves pop music and fashion and she feels like any other fan.'

'Not flash then.'

'No, pretty too.'

'Definitely.'

'We've got to see her.'

'Need to find a telly by tomorrow night.'

'Let's ask Stan.'

Friday 3rd

Good news!

Stan came round this morning and his mate in Leysdown said we can go to his place at six to see the show. The Stones and Manfred Mann are on tonight. Can't wait. Stan stayed for a coffee and fried egg sandwich from today's brekkie chefs Colin and Jem. I think Stan really enjoyed chatting to the lads about music. He said the Beatles are alright, but the Stones belong in a zoo. He loves rock 'n roll and he's got every record Buddy Holly ever made. He saw the Crickets live at the Palladium in the Fifties and reckons it was the best show ever. I love rock 'n roll too. I may be into the Beatles and the Stones but I'm not gonna turn my back on the music I grew up with, that wouldn't be right.

My sister Mavis is a bit older than me and she started buying 78s when I was a kid. She had great taste in music so I grew up listening to American classics like *Jailhouse Rock* and *Heartbreak Hotel* by Elvis, *Tutti Frutti* and *Rip It Up* by Little Richard, *Why Do Fools Fall In Love* and *I'm Not A Juvenile Delinquent* by Frankie Lymon & The Teenagers and *Diana* by Paul Anka. Mavis used to stay in with me every Tuesday night when mum and dad went to the pictures and the minute they walked out the door she'd tune the radiogram to Radio Luxembourg for all the latest hits, plus adverts from a man called Horace Batchelor who wanted people to write to him in *K-e-y-n-s-h-a-m*, that's *Keynsham, Bristol*. I saw Mavis and her boyfriend Denis jive at a party and asked if she could teach me how. A couple of years later I shone with pride when Mavis jived with me on her wedding day and rock 'n roll music rang out like church bells as we danced on the shiny wooden floor... *wopbopaluma-dingdangdong!*

*

Okay, what else has been happening? Here are the headlines on Radio Inferno...

Monsieur Oui-Oui Bounces Back!

After the *greysludgewithredspots* disaster I had to win back a bit of pride, so I gave the boys my five-star dish for dinner last night, *spaghetti special.* Shay, Gray and Colin were outside working on *Louie Louie.* Gray says it's easy, just three chords: he strummed his guitar while Shay smacked out a rhythm on his tambourine and Colin sang along. Jem helped me in the kitchen, frying sausages over a very low heat and turning them every few minutes so they wouldn't burn. (Top tip: take your time cooking bangers, slow and easy is the way.) Next we grated a pound of cheddar cheese, then boiled and drained a whole packet of blue paper spaghetti. While that was cooling down we cut up the sausages and sprinkled them with salt and pepper.

Now it was crunch time and we were ready. Jem stood by the door to make sure nobody came in. I washed my hands, gave the washing-up bowl a good rinse, then used it to mix the spaghetti with Heinz tomato sauce, sausages and cheese. I'm not saying the way I do pasta is pretty, but the lads were soon tucking in and asking for more. *Monsieur Oui-Oui* was back!

Colin's Late Night Chat Show.

Thursday night. Darkness in the caravan. The lads are trying to get to sleep.

Colin: What was the first record you ever bought Jem?

Jem: Tell ya in the morning.

Colin: Now is the time for conversation.

Gray: Now is the time to belt up.

Shay: Right.

Colin: Okay.

Silence... but Colin's got everyone thinking.

Tony: What *was* your first record Jem?

Jem: *The Young Ones* by Cliff Richard.

Groan from the lads.

Jem: I got it for the flip-side... *We Say Yeah*.

Colin: I liked that.

Gray: Hank Marvin... great solo.

Tony: Remember when you got *Apache,* Gray?

Gray: First Shadows number one! We took it over the park with the portable and played it about fifty times on the spin.

Tony: I've just got their new one, *Theme For Young Lovers.*

Colin: Corny title.

Tony: I know, but I still love their sound.

Gray: *Apache* wasn't my first record. I got a few for my parents before that, but they were those bloody awful Embassy covers from Woolies.

Tony: They were rubbish.

Colin: Yeah, but that's all we could afford on our pocket money.

Gray: Right, then when I got my paper round I started to buy some decent stuff... like *You're Sixteen* by Johnny Burnette... and I remember thinking sixteen sounded really old.

Tony: (Peter Sellers old man voice): Don't worry about it mate...

Shay: (mum's Irish voice): You die if you worry and you die if you don't.

Laughter from the lads.

Colin: My first proper record was *Love Me Do* by the Beatles.

Tony: Blimey, that's only last year.

Shay: (mum's Irish voice): He's just a wee one to be sure...

Jem: Don't talk about wee... you know what Tony's like.

Tony: I'll jump out of the window.

Gray: No you won't... that's my job!

 Laughter from the lads.

Gray: What was your first, Shay?

Shay: Jayne Mansfield in Hollywood...

Gray: Not who... *what*?

Shay: *Oh Carol* by Neil Sedaka, bought it for my brother.

Tony: Mavis had that too.

Shay: I got it on a 78 in that record shop by the roller skating rink.

Tony: I fell over there and smashed my head.

Jem: In the record shop?

Tony: No, the roller rink.

Shay: (Henry Crun *Goon Show* voice) He's never been the same you know...

Gray: Remember when you asked for a Perry Como?

Jem: In the record shop?

Tony: No, the barber's.

Jem: Is anyone following this?

Gray: There was a barber's shop down by the rink. They used to do boys' haircuts on Mondays for sixpence a throw. Shorn like sheep we were, short back and sides, cut the fringe, lob some Brylcreem on top, comb your hair into a parting and quiff and that was it... next one please.

Colin: What happened Tone?

Tony: I'd seen Perry Como on TV and asked if I could have my hair like his. The barber said to his mate, *this lad wants a Perry Como,* and the other one laughs, *we do 'em all the time son.* I was chuffed, then I got the exact same haircut as all the other kids. I said, *that's not a Perry Como, a*nd the barber said...

Gray: *When Perry Como comes in 'ere son, 'e has it done just like that!*

Laughter from the lads.

Tony: Right, I need some kip.

Shay: 'Night Perry... got your hair net on?

Laughter. Silence falls... but not for long.

Colin: What was your first record Tone?

Tony: Can't remember.

Colin: Bet it was on Embassy.

Tony: No, my mum bought *Tell Laura I Love Her* on Embassy and that put me off for life. It was c-r-a-p... worst record in the world award.

Gray: So what was it then?

Tony: It's a bit embarrassing.

Jem: (mischievous) Come on Tone.

Expectant silence: there's no hiding place.

Tony: You know Mavis had all those great rock 'n roll records? Well, when I was about nine I used my birthday money to buy one for myself. I knew about Elvis, Little Richard, Jerry Lee Lewis, all that crowd...

Shay: So what did you get?

Tony: *Bugs Bunny Meets Hiawatha* by Mel Blanc.

Laughter from the lads.

Shay: (Bug Bunny voice) What's up doc?

Laugh... I nearly had a carrot!

*

And now we're lazing around on the sand coz it's the warmest day so far. You still need a jumper, but there was snow around last week so we've been dead lucky with the weather. The Beach Boys are playing on Caroline and Jem gets a bit carried away with the sunny afternoon.

'Bet there'll be a few in swimming this weekend,' he says.

'You're joking,' says Shay, 'didn't you see those penguins?'

'Nuns?'

'No, real penguins with woolly hats on.'

'Bet the water's not that cold.'

'Go and try it then.'

I start to get a bit worried about my 'kid brother'. He has been known to do crazy things... like trying to dig to Australia with me!

'It will be cold, Jem.'

'I'll just go for a paddle.'

'I'll come with you,' says Colin 'Mr Nice Guy' Green.

They take off their shoes and socks and walk down the sand. They know we're watching them and try to make out the sea's warm, but they can't keep up the act for long.

'What's it like Jem?' Shay shouts.

'Bloody freezing!'

We all crack up laughing as they run back up the beach with big grins on their faces. As usual there's a great record playing on Caroline and the timing's just right for two kids with cold feet.... the Searchers, *Needles and Pins!!*

*

5.45pm Funny how time runs on a holiday. That first scary night with Stan and his torch seems years ago. No probs in toilet block number nine this evening, plenty of hot water as we all hit the showers. Stan says Leysdown comes alive at the weekend, so we're soon in our best gear hoping to get lucky. Okay, they're calling me, ready, steady, gotta go...

Saturday 4th

Stan's mate Bob was a nice bloke. We took him a couple of bottles of Guinness and he seemed well pleased. We all loved Cathy McGowan. She uses words like *smashing* and *super* but they don't sound corny when she says them. You can see she loves being on the show and it's great to have someone so young on our TV screens. *RSG!* is like a weekly guide to what's happening in music, dance and fashion. I like the new theme music, *5-4-3-2-1* by Manfred Mann. It used to *Wipe Out* by the Surfaris but that surfing stuff is a bit old hat now. Even the Beach Boys have left the waves behind, they're singing about cars these days. *RSG!* is *now* and the Manfreds' countdown fits like a glove.

Ready Steady Go! ended at seven so we thanked Bob and walked into downtown Leysdown. (In other words, the bit with lights!) Stan was right about things coming alive at the weekend. Where did all these people come from? Mums and dads, little old grannies, excited kids, running, walking, laughing, talking, filling the place with noise and good times. The fish and chip shop on the corner was doing a roaring trade. There was a big sign in the window, *OT PIZE 'N CHIPZ*, and that's what most of us had. The red hot food came in big paper bags and we sat on the seawall to enjoy it.

'Got a chip then?'

A girl with short blonde hair and a cheeky/sexy smile was looking at Gray.

'Come and get one.'

She sat close to Gray, very close. He's a good-looking guy, the girls always go for him.

'Want one?'

Shay held up his bag of chipz to a shy-looking girl with long brown hair. She nodded and smiled. Colin, Jem and I didn't say a word, but we were watching every move like hawks. At first the four of them sat there munching chipz not knowing what to say, then the blonde asked if Gray and Shay were on holiday and they were soon chatting away about the caravan, the Infernos, *Ready Steady Go!* and Cathy McGowan. (The girls thought she was fab too.) There's an unwritten law that says if your mates pull you don't hang around to cramp their style, so we left Gray and Shay to it.

Leysdown had been dead all week, but now neon lights and pop music spilled from the brightly-lit amusement arcades. Jem and Colin went to play the slot machines but I needed to make my money last a bit longer. I'll tell you what I did if you promise not to laugh: I played Bingo. I know... I know... a week ago I was watching the Yardbirds at the Marquee with Steve. Now it was *two fat ladies...88!!* My street cred was in a tailspin but I'd seen a cute teddybear I wanted to give Tasha next time we meet.

The Bingo cost sixpence a game and I blew two bob without winning a thing, so I went to find Jem and Colin and guess what? They were laughing and joking with a couple of pretty girls their age or maybe even younger. There was no point staying there on my own, so I left the bright lights behind and walked back to the caravan along the seawall. It was a lovely *Bella Notte* night, big yellow moon in the sky and a gentle breeze kissing the waves beneath the stars. I suddenly felt very sad: my friends were having fun with the girls they'd met and I was all alone. I sat down and stared out to sea, soon tears were stinging my eyes.

Just joking! I didn't feel like that at all: I was happy for the lads and happy to have some time on my own. I need that once in a while, time to think, time to dream, just drift off into my own little world where the Infernos are number one. I had my evening all planned out. There was some cider left in the bottle from last night, so I'd tune the radio into 208 and find something brilliant to say on my postcard to Tasha. I'd been thinking about her all week and I really wanted to see her again, with her flashing green eyes and beautiful *wangzangaroonies...* she's really got a hold on me! I bought the card yesterday but it's tough to come up with a cool *Ban The Bomb* type message in a place like Leysdown... everyone's too busy having fun fun fun. I'd just poured a glass of cider when there was a loud knock on the caravan door. It was Stan.

'TV show alright?'

'Great thanks.'

'You lads coming for a drink?'

'They're all out Stan.'

'On the pull are they?'

'Something like that.'

'Well Doreen's waiting, let's go.'

'Where to?'

'Boozer up the road, bit of music, you'll love it.'

'Thanks but...'

'No buts mate, don't want your mum and dad thinking I left you all on your lonesome.'

Stan wasn't taking no for an answer. Ten minutes later we were in the pub and it was great, loads of smiling faces all talking at once. I fancied cider but some people think it's a woman's drink so I had a pint of bitter instead. Euugghh! How do people drink that stuff? One pint lasted me the whole night and every sip tasted like medicine.

There was meant to be a group playing but they hadn't showed, so after a few drinks the smiley smiley faces started their own singsong. Loads of people come down to Leysdown from the East End and they sure know how to enjoy themselves. I knew most of the songs they were singing, I'd heard them at parties round my nan's house, *My Old Man Said Follow The Van, Roll Out The Barrel, Maybe It's Because I'm A Londoner*. I was right in there with the rest of them, then Stan put me on the spot.

'Tony's in a group, he'll give us a song.'

'Will I?'

'Course you will... what about a bit of Beatles?'

Everyone was smiling and staring at me. I knew if I bottled it I'd look a right prune, but have you ever tried singing a Beatles song? I love their music, but they've got a sound all of their own. No Beatles from me, that was for sure. Panic time, then I thought of Buddy Holly. When I was a kid I won a prize at a party singing *It Doesn't Matter Anymore.*

'This one's for Stan and Doreen,' I said feeling like a Caroline deejay, then I just went for it, singing at the top of my voice, waving my hands in the air, enjoying the song and loving it when people joined in. I sat down to handclaps and a couple of cheers, mainly from Stan, and it felt great. Not quite *Ready Steady Go!* but I'd had a good laugh and now it was time to *frappé la rue.* I didn't want to leave the lads hanging round outside the caravan and sure enough, when I got back Jem and Colin were sitting on the step waiting to tell me all about the girls they'd met... walked home... and snogged.

Shay and Gray came back around midnight and they'd had a nice time too, but I don't think their thrills stopped with snogging. When we got into bed and turned out the lights it was time for...

Colin's Late Night Chat Show.

Colin: We were snogging those girls for ages weren't we Jem?

Jem: I'm seeing mine again tomorrow.

Shay: We went way past snogging, didn't we Gray?

Gray: Yeah.

Jem: Why were you snogging Shay?

Gray: Piss off.

Colin: How far did you get then?

Shay: I was up to five or six.

Gray: I was at seven, maybe eight.

Tony: What does that mean?

Shay: It means he was having a bloody good time!

Colin: I get lost with all that one to ten stuff.

Shay: Well, five is when she lets you feel her boobs.

Gray: No that's six.

Jem: I thought that was seven.

Colin: No, that's when you put your hand up her skirt.

Confused silence.

Tony: That crap's for schoolboys.

Colin: We *are* schoolboys.

Tony: I know but...

Shay: It's just a way...

Gray: ... to say how far you got.

Shay: Right.

Colin: But nobody knows...

Jem: ...what the numbers mean.

Tony: So the whole thing's pointless.

Jem: Let's make up our own.

Colin: All the steps...

Gray: ...to happy sex.

Shay: Fugg me, fugg me, she crid!

Laughter from the lads.

Colin: So where do we start?

Jem: When you get nothing at all.

Tony: That's an **Embassy**... complete waste of time.

Graham: Snogging...

Shay: That a **45**... enjoyable but over too soon.

Colin: Feeling her boobs...

Gray: **EP**... extra pleasure.

Tony: Feeling her fanny.

Gray: **LP**... luscious pleasure.

Shay: *Luscious*... like it Lynchy!

Colin: What about going the whole way?

Jem: Only one thing it can be...

Shay: **Exeter!**

Laughter from the lads.

And so here it is... *The Infernos' Code d'Amour!*

1. **Embassy** when you draw a big fat zero
2. **45** when the fun stops at snogging
3. **EP** feeling the girl's boobs (wangzangaroonies)
4. **LP** feeling the girl's fanny
5. **Exeter** going all the way

You can use our code if you want, just send a small donation to: The Auntie Rotter Home For Sex Maniacs, Cricklewood Broadway, London... *North-West 2 mate!!*

*

'Still lazing about?'

My dad's voice drifted in thru my dreams and there he was smiling at the caravan door.

'It's like a den of thieves in here, mum,' he called back over his shoulder.

A sleepy chorus of *Morning Mister Norman, Sorry Mister Norman, We're getting up Mister Norman,* echoed from the chaos of sheets, blankets, pillows and crumpled clothes.

'We'll be be back in half-an-hour,' said dad, 'I want you lot up and about by then.'

I heard him speak to mum outside.

'They're still in bed. Let's go down the beach, give them a chance to wake up.'

Seconds later the caravan was a blur of action. We sorted out the beds first, then packed our bags and put them out on the grass. Jem and Colin did a great job of cleaning the cooker, while Shay and Gray wiped everything in sight with damp cloths and I swept up two loaves of crumbs and five beaches of sand from the floor. By the time mum and dad came back *Clovelly* was looking spick and span.

'Everything alright?' asked mum, as she kissed me on the cheek.

'We did burn a knife.'

'Right, no pocket money this week,' laughed dad. He was in a good mood, probably relieved the caravan was still in one piece, plus he likes my friends. They're always polite, *Mr Norman* this, *Mrs Norman* that. We're all the same with each other's parents, maximum respect because they're nice people. It may all sound *fuzzycornyhollywoodmovie,* but it's true, we're lucky like that.

'Can we cook you some breakfast Mrs Norman?'

'No it's okay Jem, I'll do it.'

The only food we had left was a couple of onions and a tin of Spam, so the lads walked into Leysdown to buy some brekkie bits, while dad got busy planting some bulbs round the caravan and I told mum what we'd been up to, well most of it. Gray, Shay, Colin and Jem were soon back with the eggs and bacon, plus a bunch of daffodils and a box of Milk Tray for mum. She was pleased, dad was pleased, and I was pleased... have I got great mates or what?

Mum cooked a smashing (©Cathy McGowan Catchphrases) breakfast and the jokes and chat were soon flying as we sat eating in the sun. Jem and I are here for the weekend, but Colin, Shay and Gray are headed home today. When they left to catch their coach the caravan seemed very quiet. They've been gone a few hours now and it's not the same without them, but it's our last night and we can't waste it. Jem's meeting his pre-teen queen and I've got a hot date at the pub with *Peggy Sue...*

Sunday 5th

Midday. Last night was a lot of fun. Stan sang some Holly hits with me and *ravedonlikeareal wildchild!!* Jem came home with a love bite on his neck, so he'd had a good time too. He was still asleep when I woke up, so I went for a walk with dad to pick some mushrooms for breakfast. I'm sad to say I often feel a bit on edge when we're one-to-one, he seems much more relaxed when my mates are around, but today we had a really good talk. He said I'd have my own bedroom by now if we'd won that court case, but as there's no sign of the Piles moving out (he used their real name) he's decided to build an extension in the back garden so the *sittingroom/TVroom/diningroom/Tony's bedroom* will soon be just the last one. My own bedroom after all these years... how cool is that?

I started to jabber my thanks, but there was more.

'How are you getting on with your group?'

'Okay.'

'Mum said you rehearse at Shay's?'

'Every Sunday.'

'What do his mum and dad think?'

'They've never said anything, but it is quite noisy.'

'What about using the loft?'

'The Inferno?' I heard the surprise in my voice.

'You can give it a try... I don't think we'll hear much downstairs.'

I felt like hugging him, but that's not dad's style, so I thanked him about a million times on the way back to the caravan. The Infernos playing live in the Inferno... it's gonna be great. My own bedroom, rehearsals in the loft, Caroline on the airwaves, Cathy on *Ready Steady Go!* It's all too much and suddenly I hear Ringo thumping a jumping solo in my heart.

Perfect end to the holiday, or what?

All we are saying... John and Yoko, Heathrow, April '69.
Chris Walter took this photograph on the day we met the Lennons.

I interviewed Mick Jagger just days before the death of Brian Jones.
The Stones in The Park concert on July 5th 1969 became a tribute.
'He is not dead, he doth not sleep, he hath awakened from the dream of life.'

The Fabs inspired the birth of the Infernos, who soon became... The Rest!
(l to r) Graham Lynch, Colin Green, Shay McKeown and me.

*'Ask not what your country can do for you,
ask what you can do for your country.'*

JFK's famous words made me wish I was American.
I wanted to be part of his new dream, it was beautiful.
Then came Dallas. Sad, sadder than sad.

Cathy McGowan with Paul Jones, lead singer of Manfred Mann.

As the new star of *Ready Steady Go!* Cathy was at the heart
of the British music scene at a fantastic time. We loved her.

The arrival of Radio Caroline in '64 changed our world forever.
Non-stop hits live from the North Sea... *absolutelystunninglybrilliant!!*
I even liked Tony Blackburn's jokes. They were almost as corny as mine!

April - May '64

Better

Move On

April '64

Sunday 26th

Am I wearing a bright green wig and a shiny red nose?

I should be coz I feel like a clown. I'm sitting on a bench in Oxford station waiting for the train back to London. I nearly had a great time with Tasha today: nearly but not quite. Like I told you, I hate woodwork and metalwork. Instead of mortise and fucking tenon joints why don't they teach us something useful? Like *O-level Bra Removal*, for example. How are you supposed to know how to do that stuff if nobody teaches you? I've been in school since I was five and I've never been given one word of sex education. It's crazy, I'm jumping with desire but I have no idea how to make the most of it.

145

A little advice would be nice... starting with how to take a girl's bra off without feeling like a prat with chipolata fingers.

Let's start at the beginning...

On our last day down at the caravan I heard the title track from Bob Dylan's new LP, *The Times They Are A-Changin'*. It hit me like a bolt of lightning and thrilled me to my soul. The words say everything I've been thinking these past few months. It's about being young and telling old people to step inside if they can't help the world find a brighter future.

I wrote to Tasha, asked if she'd heard *Times* coz I knew she'd love it too. After raving on a bit about Radio Caroline, there was just room to squeeze my address on the bottom of the card before posting it on our way out of Leysdown. I got a letter back a few days later. Tasha said she loved Caroline, had bought the Dylan LP, and would I like to come to Oxford sometime coz she'd really like to see me again.

Skip to this morning and this is how my day went slowly downhill...

Bustopaddingtonandtraintooxford: feeling good, adventures ahead, bit nervous, but happy.

Oxfordstation: big smiles from Tasha, no kisses but her warm hug feels nice.

Sundaylunchwithhermother: Tasha's dad died three years ago, sad sad sad, but it's easy to see she's close to her mum. They both smile when they talk about Tash's sister Monica who is studying to be an actress up in London. They say she's *a bit of a wild child* which means I'd like to meet her sometime. We end up talking about exams (time to go time) and I tell them I'm hoping A-levels will help me become a writer. Tash says she dreams of going to St Anne's College in Jericho and her mum cracks up when I say it'll be great to study abroad. How was I to know there's a Jericho in Oxford? Her mum reckons the other one would be *a bit too hot for comfort* but I like a bit of sun myself.

Puntingonthethames: It's a bright afternoon and we watch students trying not to fall in as they stand on the back of their boats poking long sticks into the water. Punting's been around for years and it's supposed to be a lazy trip down the river, gliding along in the sun, but there are so many punts out on the Thames today it looks like the North Circular. I'm happy on dry land, walking along the bank with Tash. It feels nice being with her, like we've known each other forever.

Overthegrassandunderthetree: We head further out of town to a quieter place Tasha knows. We walk across the emerald grass and lie down together under a big tree. Seconds later we are lost in a sizzling kiss. Her mouth is full and warm, sweet and wet. At first we kiss with our lips, then I feel her tongue slowly turning around mine. My mind flashes back to that *threeonabedfrenchkissingsession* with Gray and the luscious Judy. I enjoy the thrill of the game and feel Tasha's passion rising as she pulls me closer to her. My right hand seems to have a life of its own - like my willy which is rock hard in my jeans - and I'm soon exploring inside her jumper. I've never felt a girl's bra before: I've seen photos but this is different, like a whole

147

new universe. It's made of something silky and it plunges down in the middle so Tasha's *wangzangaroonies* are almost naked...

And that's where our riverbank passion session hits a brick wall. I swear I searched every inch of that bra but could I get it undone? Could I fuck! Every second I spent fumbling felt like an hour walking over hot coals. The heat fell away from Tasha's kisses and *I* knew *she* knew I wasn't the dream lover she'd been expecting.

Benchatoxfordstation: Nothing was said as we walked back, but our smiles had faded with the afternoon sun. We kissed goodbye and said it had been a great day, but we didn't mean it. An awkward stranger called embarrassment had gatecrashed our party and the magic was long gone. I walked away from her feeling like a fool and a complete loser. I've been sitting here on this bench ever since, running the nightmare over and over in my mind. Can't wait to get back to London.

*

I'm on the train but you know what it's like when you've made a complete prat of yourself. You can't shake the tentacles of memory, they cling to you wherever you go. I keep seeing my chipolata fingers searching for the clip on that sodding bra and the same question echoes over and over in my mind: *where the hell was it?* It's driving me nuts. I need to think about something else, do something else, write about something else, so here's what's been going on since we came home from the caravan...

Announcement: Good evening ladies and gentlemen, our journey to London will now be a Tasha-Free Zone!

Getting up at 6:30 for my paper round on the first morning back from Leysdown was a shock. First thing I did was tune the kitchen radio into 199 to see if we could get Radio Caroline in Cricklewood, and there she was in all her glory, playing a bouncy song called *My Boy Lollipop* by someone called Millie. What a great way to start the day. We couldn't wait to tell all our mates at school. They were wide-eyed with wonder, just like we'd been a few days before. An all day pop music station? Amazing!

While we've been away the Mop Tops, that's what they're calling the Beatles these days, have been hitting it big. They've got the Top 5 singles in America plus nine more in the Top 100. Those five chart-toppers are *Can't Buy Me Love, Twist And Shout, She Loves You, I Want To Hold Your Hand,* and *Please Please Me.* Americans know great music when they hear it, they gave us rock 'n roll and now we've given them the Fabs. The papers are saying that after JFK was killed, Americans wanted something new and fresh in their lives, and the Beatles came along at just the right time. If that's true, good luck America... you deserve to smile again. Back in London the Fabs have made it into Madame Tussauds and the waxworks of John, Paul, George and Ringo look amazingly life-like and real... he lied.

Pop music is everywhere and things are moving for the Infernos too. Graham just got the new Rolling Stones LP and we've been playing it over and over to see if we can cover any of the songs. Steve was so right about 12-bar blues, it's the key to a goldrush of great records. Okay, you might need to juggle the chords around a bit, but say you sing in the key of C, just learn C, F, G, G7, then add a little A minor to the mix, and you'll be playing from now 'til Christmas and never need to sing the same song twice.

I gave Steve *Hi-Heel Sneakers* back and he lent me two more hot 45s, *Walking The Dog* by Rufus Thomas (it's on the Stones LP) and *Road Runner* by Bo Diddley. I played them when the lads came round and Gray sorted the chords in no time coz they're both 12 bars, so our song list is growing fast. The Inferno is a great place to make music, we keep all our gear up there now including Shay's drums. With its soft red light it feels like a jazz club or something. The weather's getting warmer too, so our fingers don't freeze and the sloping wooden roof gives us a nice twangy sound. Strips of old carpet cut a crazy mosaic on the floor and the cider and menthol cigarettes we share make us feel cool and bohemian. (We smoke menthols coz if dad sticks his head thru the hatch he won't know we've been smoking... he'll just think we eat a lot of mints!)

Shay and I are starting to click in the band. His drumming is getting better all the time and I just keep my bass lines simple and hook in with him. We haven't done any gigs yet, but we've got a roadie. Mick's been Gray's mates for ages and he enjoys sitting round listening to us play and helping any way he can. The thing Mick really loves to do is play the drums. Shay lets him sit in on a couple of numbers at the end of the session and he's really good. Mick would love to be in a group himself, but he can't afford a kit. I feel sorry for him: I know how it feels to be on the outside looking in. But Shay's our drummer and nothing's gonna change that, so Mick sits and waits for his burst of glory at the end of every night.

We've been getting together two or three times a week since Leysdown. That trip did us good, we really feel like a group now and we're getting better. Colin's mike, my bass and Gray's guitar still go thru one amp, but that will change. Gray and Shay start work soon and the plan is to splash out on some new gear. I'm hoping to do another two years at school and have no idea where my share of the money will come from, but I'll worry about that when the time comes.

*

We're here! Paddington, home of the marmalade loving bear. Where did that journey go? It was good writing about my mates, took my mind off things. I still feel bad about today, but I guess I'm not the first bloke to struggle with a girl's bra. Think I'll ask Shay and Gray if they've got any tips: they're men of the world. And who knows, maybe I'll see Tasha again sometime. I hope so... and not just because I want to get inside that sexy lacy bra. There's something about her smile that makes me wish she was sitting here beside me right now...

May '64

Sunday 17th

The water-splash is my favourite ride at Battersea pleasure gardens. It takes you high then plunges you down into a soaking cloud of cold water... just like a date with Tasha!

I really didn't think I'd be hearing from her again after the *manwithchipolatafingersfailstoopenbra* shock. I sent her a letter saying it had been great to see her, which it had in many ways, and didn't mention the embarrassing bit under the tree. One week, two weeks, three weeks, no word, nothing. Then on Friday a postcard from Oxford with a picture of a library and a number to call Tash in London.

First time I rang there was no reply, then I spoke to her sister Monica who sounded nutty but nice. She said they'd just had a *fabulous* time at Portobello Road market and was I coming to Ricky's rave in Chelsea coz she was *dying* to hear all about my group and tell me about the time she met Paul McCartney. It was like a mad rush of friendly energy and Tasha sounded a bit dull when she came on the line. I didn't get an invite to Ricky's rave, but Tash said she'd meet me today.

*

London Zoo. I've loved this place since I was a kid, but when we arrive the queues are just plain scary. Bank Holiday + Sun = Crowded

Zoo. So we skip the animals and head for the park where we sit on the grass and eat ice cream in the hot sun. Tasha's got a radio with her and it's tuned to Caroline. Tony Blackburn's on the air and he tells us the station now has four million listeners and I'm not surprised coz we've been starved of great music and that's what they serve up every day.

I sing along with the Stones on *Route 66* and Tash smiles as I pout my lips like Jagger. Three seconds later it's Tasha's lips I'm kissing and they're hot and sticky with the taste of vanilla ice cream. We move closer and our tongues dance to their own beat. Little kids are playing all around us, so I'm not tempted to slip my hand inside her T-shirt. Anyway, after the *battleofthebra* I'm happy to just kiss and cuddle. We're having a good time, but we're sitting on top of Tasha's water-splash-ride and we're about to fall.

The newsman on Caroline says over 1000 Mods and Rockets are fighting in Brighton and Margate this afternoon and police are struggling to keep the gangs apart. I think of Shay and Gray who are down on the coast. Good to know they're in Portsmouth, miles from the trouble. But the bad news is a passion breaker: we stop kissing and Tasha starts talking. She says the Mods and Rockers are *disgusting* and *moronic* and *a disgrace.* If she stopped to ask she'd know I agree the riots make no sense, but it's nothing new is it? Some blokes love a good punch-up and that will never change. Fact.

I try to bring some warmth back into our afternoon, but our little friends smiley and happy are walking away across the grass. Tasha is on about the zoo now. She's glad we didn't go in coz she hates seeing animals being stared at by yobby families with screaming kids and booming voices. It all sounds a bit snobby to me, like she's got a mental picture of council estate oiks blowing raspberries at the llamas and laughing like hyenas. She's middle class, I'm working class, it shouldn't matter but I'm starting to feel maybe it does. I don't like the way she looks down on the world.

Caroline's playing great music but Tasha can't stand Tony Blackburn's jokes. I say I like them coz they're almost as corny as mine. Tash gives me a weird look then flicks the dial to *Pick of The Pops* on the BBC, but that's not right either. She says Alan Freeman is *pathetic...* I think he's fun. She says Doris Day's *Move Over Darling* is *insulting to women...* I think it's horny. She says *Juliet* by the Four Pennies is *banal...* I think it's cute.

Fluff finally plays this week's chart topper, *Don't Throw Your Love Away*, and we walk back to Baker Street. On the way I start chatting about how great it must be to have three number ones like the Searchers. Tash cuts me short with four sharp words, *does it really matter?* She makes me feel like an idiot and a twist of anger bites deep inside. I feel like going home when we get to the tube, but her sister is cooking us a meal. I'm hungry and I want to see what this *wild child* looks like, so we head west to Labroke Grove.

Monica's five star menu turns out to be beans on burnt toast.

'Sorry dah-ling,' she says, 'I just can't fucking cook!'

'Don't swear.'

'Piss off Tash, this is my *fucking* flat and if I want to *fucking* swear I *fucking* well will.'

'It's not a flat, it's a room.'

'Okay then, my *room...* she's so fucking pedantic Tony.'

Tasha gives a bored look that says she's above all this rubbish.

'Now she's an actress she thinks she has to act like James Dean.'

'Not really Tash, he's six feet under.'

I don't mind them bitching. It's not embarrassing coz it's easy to see they love each other really. They're just different, that's all. Tasha is dark and buxom, Monica is blonde and slim, a tiny bolt of lightning with electric blue eyes that sparkle with fun and secret promise. One thing they have in common: they're both very sexy. Monica is two years older but her mum was right, she's a real wild child. I don't know if she's a good actress but she sounds like one... loud and posh.

She wants to know all about the Infernos.

I tell her we rehearse in the loft... *My God, how romantic, very Greenwich Village.*

I tell her we play R&B... *Black music, love it, very sexy.*

I tell her I play the bass... *Met Paul at a party, Kings Road dah-ling, very chic. Had his guitar, played a lovely slushy song from their new film, can't remember what it was called, too busy swooning over those big brown eyes, very come-to-bed sexy, but no chance there sweetie, he's with Jane, very lovey dovey...*

I tell her we want to play the States... *My dream too dah-ling, Broadway here I come!*

I tell her we want to make a hit record, hear it on Caroline, sing it on *Ready Steady Go!*. *I met Cathy last week actually, real sweetie, just like she is on TV. I was at The Scene with Sophie who is an ab-so-lute hoot. Cathy saw us dancing and asked if we'd like tickets for RSG! How cool is that? Kingsway next Friday, fucking amazing...*

Being with Monica is fun. Right now she lives in a tiny room in west London, but the name of the street is Fifth Avenue, so she's on her way to New York, and I'm backing her to go all the way in a hurry. I've never met anyone like her before.

Tash and I walk back to the tube in silence. She's still moody and I'm getting sick of feeling I don't match up to who she wants me to be. Maybe she's pissed coz Monica and I hit it off, but I don't think so, truth is she doesn't give a damn. A quick kiss that means nothing then Tash says she's not sure when she'll see me again. We go our separate ways and it feels like a map to our future. She knows it, so do I.

And all I feel when she's gone is relief...

Bank Holiday Monday 18th

Welcome to London's St Tropez... Cricklewood, *North-West 2 mate!*

I'm stretched out on a towel beside the fish pond in our back garden. Sky: blue. Sun: hot. Waterfall: splashing. Fountain: sparkling. Radio station: Caroline. Music: superb. Yes indeed, it's a zipadeedoodah day. I laze in the sun writing a few lines about Cathy McGowan and *RSG!*. It's not a poem, not sure what it is really, see what you think...

> I see her every Friday on my TV screen
> She's so groovy and she really makes the scene
> She's the one who really blows my mind... 5-4-3-2-1
> *Ready Steady Go!*... I'm in the In-Crowd
> *Ready Steady Go!*... I'm gonna shout it now
> The weekend starts here... *Ready Steady Go!*

It's not finished: watch this space...

Mum and dad are at their caravan and the Piles are away too, so I've got the place all to myself and I'm soaking up the midday sun. Only trouble is, no sun cream. I looked in the place we keep all that stuff and all I could find was a messy old tube of gunk from the Planet Grot. No way I'm putting that on my bod, so I'll give it another half-hour then go inside and make a sarnie.

Okay, apart from yesterday's rollercoaster ride with Tasha, what else has been happening in *The Strange World of Gurney Norman*? (Cue cool jazz.) Life's still good for the Infernos: we've got ten songs now and they all sound fantastic... make that okay! Here's the list: *Twist & Shout; Hi-Heel Sneakers; Louie Louie; Road Runner; Route 66; My Babe; Walking The Dog; Poison Ivy; Money; I Wish You Would.* The Yardbirds played that last song at the Marquee and now they've put it out as a single. Colin bought a cheap harmonica at Blank's so he could do the Keith Relf riff and it sounds pretty good. Is there no end to Mr Nice Guy's talents?

Being in a group is like knitting a jumper: it's a lot easier with a pattern. We were in the dark when we started, but Steve's 12-bar blues *Open Sesame* advice turned on the lights. We've spent hours in the loft working thru songs. I know the Piles are sick of us making a noise - he came out on the landing the other night as we were climbing down the ladder and tried to tell us off - but I said we have every right to play music in my dad's house, as long as we stop by ten. That's the law and this time we're using it to *our advantage.* I know it can't be easy for them having a live R&B band playing right above their ceiling, but they don't have to be there do they? We all know they've got a place on the Thames, so if they don't like it they know what they can do. And I'll stop there before I start to sound all bitter and twisted...

So, deep breath, big smiley smiley, and back to the good news. The Infernos have got a gig. My mate Jonathan wants us to play at his birthday party in July. I've know him for years, he lives on my estate and he came up to the Inferno one night and liked what he heard. (He's got great taste in music!) He says he can't pay us but we'll get plenty of food and drink, plus the chance to play to a crowd. Well, not really a *crowd,* but he reckons there'll be about 15 people there so we'll see if we can whip up a bit of Beatlemania in his front room. Jonathan says it'll be mainly aunties and uncles, hope they like R&B.

Hang on, someone's ringing the doorbell, better let them in...

It was Jem. He's going to Ruislip Lido this afternoon with his mum and dad. Would I like to go with? Let's see... big lake, sandy beach, pretty girls, water skiing (watching not doing), plus one of Jem's mum's *outofthisworld* picnics. Do I want all that? Er... yes.

See ya!

Tuesday 19th

Remember me?

No it's not a talking tomato, it's TN. Too much sun yesterday? You got it in one. Jem and I were out in it all afternoon and we're both burning up today. It was great tho, swimming in the cool water, waving to the girls on the little train that runs thru the pine trees beside the white sand. The Lido's an amazing place, even more like St Tropez than my back garden. Anyway, forget Jem and me, I've got some hot news about Gray and Shay. You know I said they were miles from those Mods and Rockers riots in Brighton? Wrong. They were smack bang in the middle of the aggro. It happened like this...

Shay's got a mate who works at a glass factory near our school. They had a boys-only outing to Portsmouth last Sunday, which is another way of saying an all day piss-up. There were a couple of spare seats on the coach so Shay and Gray went too. As you know, it was hot and sunny and they had a great time. In the evening they met two Pompey girls at a funfair and ended up walking them home where goodnight kisses soared to upper LP levels on *The Infernos' Code d'Amour*.

By the time they got back their coach was long gone, so they headed for the station to see if they could get a late train home. It was gone midnight when they arrived and the place was deserted. Shay was thinking of kipping on a bench, then Gray found some empty carriages so they climbed onboard and fell asleep.

A few hours later they got woken up by a guard on the platform. They asked him how to get to Victoria and he pointed to a train that was just leaving. Five minutes out of Portsmouth they were fast asleep again. Next thing they knew someone was shouting *all change*. The sleepy guy on the barrier couldn't be bothered taking cash for tickets so they got a free ride.

'Excuse me, where's the tube?' Shay asked a taxi driver outside the station.

'No tube in Brighton mate.'

Brighton?

Yes, Brighton, as in *change here for Victoria*.

'What shall we do Gray?'

'Bit of brekkie?'

'I'm not hungry... he lied.'

Where to find a decent cafe? The front, where else? They started walking down a long hill towards the water. It looked great, sparkling in the sunlight. S&G were looking forward to eggs, bacon and a couple of hours on the beach, before a relaxing train ride back to dear old London town. They were near the sea now, they could hear the seagulls and smell the salt on the morning air. A lazy, sunny day stretched out ahead...

Then six Rockers burst round the corner running for their lives, chased by a gang of 50 Mods, followed by about 20 coppers, puffing, blowing and looking very pissed off. At first Gray and Shay just stared at the madness (they hadn't heard a thing about the riots) then they turned and sprinted back up the hill to the station where they hid in the toilets until things quietened down.

'It was like a Keystone Cops film,' Shay laughed. 'Cops chasing Mods chasing Rockers chasing us.'

'It was a bit hairy at the time,' said Gray, 'but we heard most of the Mods were down there for the crack. You know, pop a few pills, cause a bit of chaos and have a laugh.'

'We got talking to a couple of girls on the train back and they said a lot of that riot stuff was cranked up by the press. They saw a photographer offer some Mods a fiver to beat up a few Rockers.'

The TV said a few people were stabbed down there, so some nasty stuff did go on, but Gray and Shay came out of it with a funny story and the phone numbers of those two Mods on the train. Typical of my mates to be in a riot... by mistake!

Friday 22nd

Heard on the news 40 microphones have been found in the walls of the American Embassy in Moscow. Wonder if they're throwing them out... we could do with a few for our group.

Saturday 30th

Got a *Dear John* letter from Tasha today. She told me she'd met a student at a CND meeting in Oxford and *they really relate.* In other words, he probably talks about the bomb all the time and knows how to unhook her bra. I wasn't sad. I'm glad she's found someone she likes coz we were going nowhere. Remember when I was talking about hit records and she said *does it really matter?* That's when it ended for me. I'm crazy about music and that's not gonna change in a hurry. So mix Roy Orbison with the Stones and you'll find the way I feel... *it's over, you'd better move on.*

Hard Day's Night

June '64

Monday 1st

O-levels start in a couple of weeks... time to get serious.

No group, no girls, no nothing. Like I said, time to move on, do well in my exams, get to grammar school, keep my dreams of being a journalist alive. I've loved being at Whitefield, it's a great school with great teachers who gave hope to kids like me when we failed our exams and felt we were on the crapheap before we'd even started. I can still remember how frightened I felt the morning the 11-plus results came out. I feel sorry for the little kid I see nervously waiting for the rattle of the letterbox. When it came I froze in bed like a corpse, while out in the hall mum learnt my fate. After what seemed like hours she opened the door.

'Time to get up Tony.'

'Did I pass?'

'No, but don't worry, Whitefield's a good school, you'll like it there. Now come and get your breakfast.'

She was so gentle in the way she broke the bad news, couldn't have been any kinder, but my young heart was broken. When I think about it now I feel so angry: what a way to treat little kids, splitting them into winners and losers at that age with a few cold words on a scrap of paper. We all knew getting to grammar school was important. If I'd lived somewhere else my chances of being a writer could have been crushed there and then. That's no exaggeration. Some secondary mods are crap at getting kids thru O-levels, but my lucky star was shining the day I walked into Whitefield. Nearly two hundred kids started school that day, all part of the baby boom after the war, and I felt timid and small. But Gray was there beside me like a rock and when a teacher called Mr Lewis told us the school believed in us and we'd get our O-levels if we worked hard, I decided to do just that. Simple decision: a chance to prove that sad little boy who failed his 11-plus could bounce back and find his place in the sun.

Sorry to go on a bit, I'm as bad as Tasha, but that's how I felt five years ago. I've been working towards this moment ever since and now the exams are just days away. So I won't be writing for a few weeks, from now on it's revision-a-go-go for me and my mates.

Wish us luck, okay?

July '64

Thursday 9th

The magic moment finally came when the last exam was over. Gray and I walked out of Whitefield the way we'd walked in five years before. Together. Gray starts his first job in a few weeks, but Podge and I are hoping for a transfer to Hendon County Grammar School if we get the grades we need. I think I've done okay in everything except maths, which has always been a mystery to me. I've been eating, drinking and sleeping exams for the last six weeks, so I'm gonna try to forget it all now... until we get our results.

Okay, what's been happening while I've been on Planet O-level?

Well, the Rolling Stones did their first tour of the States and the word is their live shows didn't go too well. But they did record at Chess Records in Chicago, home of their R&B heroes like Chuck Berry, Bo Diddley, Muddy Waters and Howling Wolf, so some great new tracks are the pipeline. Meanwhile, the Beatles did their King Midas act in Denmark, Holland, Hong Kong and Australia, where everything they touched turned to gold. Ringo came down with tonsillitis the day before the tour, so a young drummer called Jimmy Nicol got the chance to join the Fab Three. He had a Beatles haircut and looked the part, but Ringo was soon back for a string of sell-out shows in Oz. Now all eyes are on Liverpool. The Beatles are going home tomorrow for the northern premier of *Hard Day's Night*. I can't wait to see it, can you?

*

It's no secret I love America. I like to keep up with what's going on over there and couple of things I've read recently have really made me think. The first was about a war America is fighting in a place called Vietnam. Some young guys in New York are in trouble for burning their draft cards and saying they don't want to go over there. They're probably not much older than me and my heart goes out to them. I can't begin to imagine how I'd feel in their shoes. There are so many exciting things happening in the world today, war just seems like it should belong in the history books.

There was some good news too. President Lyndon Johnson signed a new Civil Rights Act last week making racial segregation illegal in the States. It's less than a year since Martin Luther King gave his brilliant *I have a dream* speech and I'm not naive enough to think things will change overnight, but this new law has to be a step in the right direction. Lyndon Johnson became President when Kennedy was assassinated and I'm sure JFK would be happy to know civil rights are moving forward in the land he loved.

I've never seen any racial hatred here: nearly everyone in our part of London is white. You get different races and religions like Irish people in Cricklewood and Jewish people in Golders Green, but their kids get on okay at school. Gray and I had a mate from Pakistan called Tanvier. He was a good wicketkeeper/batsman and we played for the same team. We went to his house one night and he gave us *dhal curry,* which was lentils and vegetables with tangy spices. We'd never had curry before and he thought it might be too hot for us, but we did an Oliver Twist and asked for more.

Apart from Tanvier, we just know Londoners, but nearly all the songs we do in the group are by black American R&B stars. That's the great thing with music, it crosses all barriers. I was nine years old when I first heard *Rip It Up* by Little Richard and I didn't know or care what he looked like. I just knew his music thrilled me from the top of my little boy head to the tip of my fluorescent lime green socks. I still feel that way...

Sunday 12th

This day will go down in rock 'n roll history!

The Infernos' first ever gig was fab, we'll never forget it... and neither will the audience. I'm not sure how much Jonathan had said about our music. He comes from a quiet Jewish family and they weren't sure what to expect.

'What do they play?' asked an aunt, as we set up our gear.

'Folk songs I think,' said another.

'Not like that Bob Dylan.'

'No, these boys sing in tune,' laughed a jolly uncle.

'Jonathan says they're very good.'

'If they play *Hava Nagila* I'm dancing!'

Joe Brown had *Hava* as a B-side last year, but it's not big with the Infernos, so we kicked off with *Road Runner*. Gray started by strumming his electric 12-string at Slowhand speed as he ran his fingers up the strings, then I joined him on the punchy Bo Diddley riff. Colin belted out the words and Shay beat thunder out of his drums, while Jem and Mick sat on the side shaking maracas and a tambourine. It's hard to describe the sound we made, but you could hear us three streets away that's for sure.

We kept the volume way up high as we worked thru our ten songs to a roomful of shocked faces. We knew we weren't their cup of tea, but Jonathan was grinning and clapping after every number, and as he was the birthday boy the others joined in.

'Thanks for being such a great audience,' said Colin.

'Make that patient!' came a voice from the corner.

'Shut up Murray.'

'Listen, I love these boys, they have *chutzpah*.'

We didn't know what it meant but everyone was smiling.

'This is our last one this afternoon,' said Colin, sounding confident and cool. 'We got it from the Beatles... *Twist And Shout*.'

Murray was up like a shot. 'Come on you miseries... *dance*!'

And then an amazing thing happened: everybody started bopping and I mean *everybody*. Most of them knew the words coz they'd seen the Fabs on TV, heard them on the radio, and now they were happy happy as we gave the first song we ever learnt 600% zing. That's 100% zing per Inferno and the same again from Jem and Mick who were singing along with big smiles on their faces.

When we finished Uncle Murray was beaming at us like a proud dad. '*Mazel tov* boys,' he kept saying. '*Mazel tov*.' Jonathan's mum came over to say well done. Colin told her we could play some more, but she said we should have some food and drink. 'And give our ears a rest,' said the lady beside her, who was smiling but maybe not joking.

An hour later we were back in the Inferno all talking at once about the gig. It had been great to see everyone dancing like that but we're not idiots, we knew the sound was shit.

'If we sounded like that in a Mod club they'd slaughter us,' said Shay.

'I thought you *played* okay,' said Mick.

'Yeah,' Gray agreed, 'but our equipment's crap.'

'What do you think Jem?' I asked.

'It was a bit fuzzy.'

'We need more gear in a hurry,' said Shay and nobody was arguing.

One by one the lads drifted off, leaving me and Jem playing records and chatting like so many times before. But tonight was different, he moves to Newbury tomorrow. He's always been just a few doors up the road. Now his mum and dad have bought a pub out in Berkshire and I'll miss him when he's gone, but we'll keep in touch... that's forever.

Saturday 18th

I'm aching in places I've never felt before.

Podge, Gray and I spent last week putting up seating for the All England Sports at a new running track called Copthall Stadium. It was hard work, lugging heavy planks of wood around and fixing them to Meccano type frames. It took us twenty minutes to cycle there every morning and about two hours to ride home at night, at least that's how it felt. I've never worked so hard in my life, but after all those weeks of revision and exams it felt good to get out in the fresh air and do something different.

The money was good too, a pound a day, but the best thing was meeting Aidan and Conor, the well-known Irish double act, with their red hair, smiley faces, wiry bodies, and sandpaper hands. When they were around there was never a dull moment and they had their own way of swearing too.

'Fuck my hairy nob, how many more of these dese tings?'

'Kiss my hairy arse, I'll murder a pint tonight.'

It took two of us weedy schoolboys to lift those heavy planks and even then it was a struggle, but Aidan and Conor could lift one on their own and make it look easy. We couldn't keep up with them when it came to grafting or cracking jokes, but we must have done something right coz they asked if we'd like to go back to Ireland with them and work for the rest of the Summer.

'You'll get all the fucking you can stand at the county fairs.'

'Jaizus, they won't be standing after those country girls get hold of them.'

'They'll suck you off and blow you out in bubbles lads.'

Sounded good to us!

We were up for a trip to the Emerald Isle, but when we got home we all got the same reply... and it wasn't yes. There were questions, lots of questions. Where are you going in Ireland? How will you travel? Where will you stay? What will you eat? Of course, we didn't have any of the answers, so the door soon slammed shut. Shame really, it would've been good, but it's not gonna happen, no way. Still, there was a trip waiting for us when we got to work yesterday. Ciaran the foreman said he needed help to get some extra seats from his farm in Sussex, so Podge, Gray and I piled into his lorry and sped out of town feeling good. Ciaran's a nice guy, not as funny as Conor and Aidan, but he played Radio Caroline good and loud and bought us all a big fry-up too. 'You'll need the energy lads,' he smiled, as we tucked into our eggs and bacon. He wasn't wrong.

When we got to the farm Ciaran drove us to a barn full of wooden seats. 'Load the lorry and give me a shout at the house when you're ready to go,' he said before heading inside. The sun was beating down and we stripped down to our shorts but it didn't help. The sweat was pouring off us as we piled what felt like five thousand planks onto the lorry. It seemed to go on forever (now I know how the guys who built the pyramids must have felt) and when we finally pushed the last chunk of wood into place we sat down in a daze.

'Right lads, no time for slacking.' Ciaran was back and in hurry to get on the road. 'Come on up to the house and I'll get you a drink before we go.' And with that he jumped into the driver's seat and sped off across the dry rutted field like a bat out of hell. We stared in horror as the planks started to bounce, slip and slide off the back of the lorry. We were screaming at Ciaran, but he couldn't hear us. When he stopped and got out, his face was a picture as he stared at the trail of wood between us and him.

'Jaizus... what the fuck?'

Gray started to laugh, Podge was right there with him and I wasn't far behind. We were soon rolling round like a bunch of silly boy lemons. The shock of seeing all our hard work crashing down into the dust was just too much... we cracked up. Ciaran ran across the field. 'The rope, why didn't you tie the rope?' Answer: you didn't give us one mate. 'Jaizus, sorry lads, I'm a right fookin' eejit. Two quid extra each if we can get this sorted in a hurry.' We stopped laughing and started working. Two quid! Blimey, that was enough for an album *and* a single, or to put it another way the new *Hard Day's Night* LP, plus the Animals' mighty chart-topper, *House of The Rising Sun*.

I don't know if it was the thought of the extra cash, but we got things done in a hurry. Ciaran bought us a pint of Guinness (what else!) in his local up the country lane, then we raced back to London to slot the last few seats into place. It had been a long long day, but when Ciaran gave us seven quid each for five days work we felt rich.

I got those Beatles and Animals records this morning and I've been playing them non-stop. We'll earn a few more quid after the weekend taking the seating down again, then the lads will head back to Ireland. I still wish we were going with them to meet some of those red-haired girls at the county fairs. On the road with Aidan and Conor... now that would have been a good *craic!!*

Thursday 30th

I'm writing this on a coach back from Newbury. I've been down there for three days to see how Jem's settling in and I loved it coz it's *Beatlesfancity*. There's a brand new youth club right by the river and the only LP they ever play is the latest from the Fabs. Jem's made loads of mates already and when we went to an open-air pool near his mum and dad's pub a pretty young girl in a red bikini was definitely giving him the eye. So I don't have to worry, my kid brother's doing fine...

Went to see *Hard Day's Night* with Jem while I was down there. We hated it, really bad film... he lied. I'm sure you've seen it and think the same as us: absolutely stunningly brilliant! My cousin Chris in Walthamstow has seen it three times, all on the same day. She went with her friend in the afternoon, loaded up with sandwiches and a flask of tea, and didn't come out 'til God Save The Queen. I didn't think it was possible to be a bigger Beatles fan than yours truly, but Chris might just win that vote.

My fave bits were when Ringo was walking by the river with that little kid and when John was joking with an arty woman in glasses about whether he was *him* or not. I thought of mad Monica when Paul sang *And I Love Her*. I wasn't sure I believed her about meeting *Cathy* at a club, but there she was the following Friday on *RSG!* She told me Paul would sing *a lovely slushy song* in the film and she was right about that too. She could have guessed it coz a new McCartney love song was always on the cards, but then again maybe she did really meet a Beatle... *a-maz-ing dah-ling!*

I really like Monica, she's a lot more fun than her sister. I'd like to see her again, but that will have to wait.

Gray and I are going to Paris on Monday!

August '64

Paris

Monday 3rd

We're going to miss the ferry.

Trust us to travel on a sunny Bank Holiday: the roads are packed and the coach from Victoria seems to hit every jam going. I'm sweating on making the boat on time but Gray's chilling in the back seat, working out the chords to *House of The Rising Sun* on his acoustic. We're taking the guitar coz we figure it will help us meet girls on holiday and the plan's already working for Gray judging by that pretty French girl he's chatting up. You can't take him anywhere!

Dover. We blow some of our hard-earned cash on a taxi to the ferry and make it with seconds to spare. As we cruise out into the Channel, Gray takes his new friend Nicole for a drink and I'm happy to sit with with our bags and look at the sea. I'm at the back of the boat and a couple of seagulls follow us all the way to France. They're brilliant at catching the chunks of bread people throw and by the time we get to Calais they've had so much grub it's a wonder they can still fly.

It's early afternoon and we should be in Paris in a few hours. Nicole reckons it's a lot easier to get a lift in France if you're with a girl, but she's on the train Rouen so it looks like it's just Gray and me. We joke about dressing up in drag as we walk across town and find a good spot to hitch on the coast road to Boulogne. Five minutes later we're in the back of a little French car that looks like a tin can, with two lively ladies who are out for the day and up for a laugh. They ask us for a song, so Gray strums the chords he's just learnt and I sing about that house in New Orleans. It comes out sounding more like Bob Dylan than Eric Burdon, but they love it. *Encore! Encore!* So we give them a few more songs as we drive along with the top peeled back in the sun. They drop us on the road to Paris, then with waves, *aurevoirs,* and a lot of toot-toot-tooting, they're gone. Our first lift of the day and it was easy-peasy, we'll be with our supercool French teacher Michelle in no time at this rate.

Spin forward six hours and we're still waiting. We tried to buy some food and drink around tea-time but everywhere was shut. All we could find was a little café filled with kids and old ladies that sold us steak, chips, bread and a bottle of cheap wine for just over a quid, which wasn't too much of a rip-off, but still a drag when you've only got a tenner between you for the whole trip. The chips and bread were fine but the steak was definitely a bit dodgy. I'm not saying it was horse, but when we started talking about Roy Rogers it reared up on the plate like Trigger.

We took the wine with us to drink on the road. Looking back, I think that was a mistake. French families heading home from the beach saw two young guys strumming a guitar and swigging from a bottle. No wonder none of them picked us up. Nicole was right, what we really need is a girl. Nothing new there then! It's dark now, the guitar is back in its case and we've hidden the wine, but still no luck. We'll keep thumbing for an another hour or so then we'll have to sleep rough. We can't afford a hotel so nothing else for it. You know we were joking about dressing up in drag? If we had a long blonde wig now I'd put it on like a shot.

Still at least it's a clear night, look at all those stars...

Tuesday 4th

1.00am Here's the bad news.

Bright stars = no clouds = *une nuit très froide.*

It was my bright idea to sleep in this cornfield, I thought it would be warm, I'd read it somewhere. I guess it would make more sense if the corn was still here. This field's been cut and it's like trying to kip on the stubble of a giant's chin. It's as cozy as a bed of nails, but I can sleep anywhere so I'm soon dreaming of Paris. An hour later I hear a wild stallion pounding round the field, snorting angrily and stomping its hooves into the dirt. Maybe it's revenge for that dodgy steak... a ghost horse.

'Gray!'

'What?' says the horse. Turns out it's Lynchy running round in circles with his arms wrapped tight around his chest.

'Cold then?'

'Just third degree frostbite.'

As you will suss from our wildly hilarious banter, it takes a lot to get us down. But Gray can't do his crazed stallion act all night, so it's time to go...

1.30am When we got to this bridge we agreed the bricks each side were wide enough to sleep on. It's not great, but we're too tired to move. See you in the morning.

2.15am Okay, we're really getting pissed off now. A monster truck just hammered past and nearly knocked us into the river.

'This is fucking crazy!'

'Right.'

'Go?'

'Yeah.'

Banter... who needs it?

5.30am Now there's a witch in my dreams, a hideous old hag with mad staring eyes. What's that? I can't understand a word she's saying.

'Tone.'

Good, Gray's arrived, he won't take this shit that's for sure.

'Tony!'

I slowly open my eyes and see Gray looking up at an angry old bat who's leaning out of a window above us, making an early morning mountain out of a molehill. We're sitting on rock hard metal seats at a sticky table outside a dusty café in the village of the damned. The way this mad old woman is going on, you'd think we were trying to nick her precious chairs. If she doesn't shut up soon she'll do herself a mischief.

'Bread.'

Gray's eyes are bright with excitement but he must be joking if he thinks *Madame Looney* is about to serve up hot rolls and coffee.

'Bread,' says Gray again and he's off, almost running down the road with his guitar slung across his back. For a split-second the thought hits that this is all pretty cool, two friends together on the road, waking up in a little place they've never seen before and will never see again, the day stretching out ahead of them like an adventure waiting to happen. It's feels like we're living a page from Kerouac or a Bob Dylan song... and it all comes with the smell of fresh baked bread.

'Bread!'

Now I'm saying it and running to catch up with Gray who's standing by a magical sign that shouts it's message like merry Christmas bells.

Boulangerie!!!!!!!

Then reality hits. We push the door: it's shut. We push harder: it's still shut. Gray looks at his watch and to his surprise the face on his wrist says 5:35. It could be hours before we taste the crunchy bread that's teasing our taste buds. We can't wait that long, we're desperate men, we've been out in the wilds all night, battling ghost horses and monster trucks. Nothing else for it, we'll have to break in!

'Shall we walk round the back then?' says Gray, ice cool in the face of my madness.

'Just what I was gonna say,' I lie.

The baker turns out to be one of Noddy's friends from Toytown. As Bo Diddley so rightly says, you can't judge a book by looking at the cover. And you can't judge France by looking at a mad old lady with no teeth shouting out of a window. She was cold and fierce, but the baker is warm and friendly, with a thatch of white hair and a sunny smile. We use our O-level French to tell him where we've slept and who we're going to see. He says we'll love Paris, he and his wife went there for their honeymoon many years ago, and the lights on the Seine still shine in his eyes.

We get a loaf each and they're so fresh they burn our fingers. Can we buy anything to drink? He looks sad, he can't help us, then an idea... would we like water from the tap? *Oui s'il vous plaît.* He needs something to put it in so we give him the wine bottle from last night. He looks at the label and grins. *C'est de la merde!* We hold our heads and guts to let him know we agree. Time to pay. Gray offers him a handful of small coins and he carefully takes just the right amount and not a centime more. His name is Roland and he says to call in next time we're passing, which is about as likely as us getting a lift in Noddy's little yellow taxi, but it's nice of him to say it.

We come out with a warm fuzzy glow and even the angry stares of *Madame Looney* can't faze us as we head back past her café, munching on the best brekkie ever. We wave and smile, which is great coz it really winds her up, and she slams her window and disappears from our world forever. As if on cue, the sun starts to burn thru the early morning mist and we walk out thru the village until the buildings stop, then sit on a grassy bank and start hitching. It's good to know we'll soon be on our way.

Midday. We seem to have been away for ages. When I think about yesterday, last night and this morning, they all seem to melt into one. I think we're both a bit spaced out. We've been sitting here waving our thumbs in the air for hours. If we don't get a lift by tonight, we're going home. Michelle doesn't know we're coming anyway. She gave Podge, Steve, Gray and me her address at the end of term and said *anytime you're in Paris.* She probably didn't think any of us would turn up, but when we missed out on Ireland with the *fuck my hairy nob* boys, Gray said why don't we go to France instead? Having blocked one trip, our parents couldn't really say no, so here we are. It's quite a big deal coz, like most kids at school, we've never been abroad before. Podge couldn't make it, he's away with his mum and dad. Gray and I are starting to wish we were away with his mum and dad too.

Gray's gone back to the bakers to get some more bread. Meeting Roland has been one of the best things about this trip so far. He certainly did all he could to get our day off to a great start, only trouble is it's been sliding ever since. Hey... must stop writing. A big black Maigret car has just pulled up and guess who's inside? Gray!

12.15pm I'm a road runner baby. We're speeding down a country road, noshing bread and cheese, swigging from a bottle of wine that's not *merde*, trying our schoolboy français on Pascal the racing driver, and melting to the sugarsweet sounds of Françoise Hardy on the car radio.

C'est la vie my friends... next stop Paris!

Wednesday 5th

'I've just seen a naked woman.'

I'm still half-asleep but Gray's words wake me in a hurry.

'Where?'

'In the bathroom.'

'Not Michelle's mum.'

'No... her nan!'

Gray's in shock: if we had a bottle of brandy I'd pour him a slug. He's a tough guy, but right now it looks like he could pass out or throw up any second. Luckily, he just flakes out on his bed with his eyes shut tight.

'You alright mate?'

'My God, I hope I never see anything like that again.'

'What happened then?'

'I walked in and she was standing starkers in the bath.'

'Did she scream?'

'No,' says Gray, 'I did.'

I can't help laughing and Gray's right there with me, seeing the funny side of a sight he wishes he'd never seen... if you see what I mean.

'Do you think she's okay?'

'I'm not going back in there.'

'It's okay, I'll do it.'

It's not often I'm braver than Gray, but when it comes to old ladies I'm pretty fearless, so I'm happy to help. I walk down the silent corridor and try the bathroom door. It's locked but I can hear

Michelle's mum talking quietly inside and I guess she's bathing Lady Godiva, otherwise known as *grand-mère*. What a start to our stay with Michelle's family! We've only been here a night and we've already barged in on the dear old white-haired lady everyone loves and adores.

The bathroom door opens and Michelle's mum is standing there... naked. No, just joking, she's standing there smiling and saying good morning and the penny drops that she doesn't have a clue about the *grayseesoldladyinthenude* shock coz *grand-mère* is definitely away with *les fairies français* and wouldn't have had a clue the good looking guitarist from the Infernos was staring at her naked bod. In a word... phew!

Michelle's mum doesn't speak English but the French I've learnt from her daughter tells me she's saying we've slept well. She points at her watch and I see it's gone ten. She explains there's *petit dejeuner dans la cuisine* and after all the excitement that sounds *très bon,* so Gray and I are soon tucking into bread and jam with bowls of sweet milky coffee. A good bacon sarnie takes some beating in my book, but this comes close. While we're happily filling our faces, why don't I get you up to date on how we got here?

As you know, it was starting to look like we'd never get a lift, then Gray turned up in a big black Maigret car with Pascal behind the wheel, who turned out to be one of Roland's customers. He was heading into Paris and happy to give us a lift, which was great except he was a piss artist. Swigging wine with him seemed a laugh at first, but then it got scary. Pascal's first bottle of red went down in a hurry and he was soon hitting another. The more he drank the faster he drove, racing past any car that dared to get in his way. He was chatting, laughing, singing, having a one-man party, while we stared in silence at the road ahead.

I swear I don't know how we missed the lorry on that tight bend. I just closed my eyes and waited for the twist of jagged metal to strike as the scream of tyres filled our world, but somehow pisshead Pascal swerved to safety. And did he apologise for nearly killing us? Did he fuck! The madman laughed and I felt like punching his fat red boozy face, but he had our lives and the steering wheel in his hands, so I thought better of it.

'He's crazy!'

'Right,' said Gray from the back seat.

'What shall we do?'

'If we get out here we're stuck.'

'Stick it out 'til Paris?'

'Yeah, then first chance we get...'

So that's what we did, sat there scared shitless, while our psycho chauffeur did his crazy Toad of Toad Hall act. *Poop! Poop! the mad Pascal crid.* I'm sure Roland didn't know he'd got us a lift with a nutter. No way. Somehow the patron saint of drunken loonies kept us safe until we reached Paris and saw a sight sweeter than any oasis.

'Metro!' Gray's voice rang out like a victory bell.

'*Arrêté... Pascal... Arrêté ici...* STOP YOU PRAT!!'

I thumped the dashboard so hard it made him jump. He hit the brakes then had the nerve to look at me as if *I was crazy.* Bloody cheek! Gray and I were out of that car in a flash.

'The man's a cunt.'

Gray spat out the words and nobody on this earth could have put it better. When we bought our tickets for the Metro I still felt shaky, but riding the underground was fun and we soon found ourselves standing beside the *Arc de Triomphe,* at the top of a beautiful tree-lined avenue that's known the world over.

'Well, we made it Tone.'

'Just about mate... looks great.'

Five minutes later we were at Michelle's place, only trouble was she was in Spain at the time. Her mum looked a bit flustered as we explained who we were and where we'd come from, then she smiled and led us into her *appartement* on the first floor. It's really smart. Gray and I are in the spare room with twin beds and a view across the street towards the *Champs-Élysées.*

We had dinner with the family last night, that's Michelle's mum and dad plus Gray's sexy girlfriend *grand-mère.* (He'll kill me when he reads that bit!) We were both so tired we could hardly keep our eyes open, but we wanted to show what a good teacher Michelle is so we spoke non-stop O-level French for over an hour and managed to avoid saying we both fancied their daughter like crazy and if there was any chance of a little naughty romance while we were in town that would suit us just fine. Gray did tell them about me saying *je t'adore* to that other *mademoiselle* at school and they laughed and asked if we loved their daughter too and we said yes of course we did then we all laughed some more except for poor old *grand-mère* who just sat there with a faraway look in her eyes.

They were nice people, polite and kind, but we knew we were the last thing they'd been expecting. Michelle is due home on Friday, so before we went to sleep Gray and I agreed to keep things low key 'til she gets back. Of course we started today with the *oldladynakedinthebathroom* shock, but it looks like we got away with that, so now we're settling in for a couple of quiet days. No more dinners with the family, keeping the friendly chat going was hard work for us and them. We've still got a few francs so we'll eat out, but after that trip from hell with the mad Pascal we won't be doing much boozing. That maniac has put us off for life!

*

After breakfast with Michelle's mum, we went out to explore and soon discovered our seven quid in francs won't go far in this city. We looked at some of the menus on the *Champs-Expensive* and the prices were out of this world, across the universe, and into a galaxy where fat cats live on cream and caviar. Luckily we found a place that suited our budget right across the street from where we're staying. It's a corner shop that sells dee-lish French bread and big bottles of lemonade with metal caps like the Corona man used to bring. Throw in a hunk of cheese and a couple of tomatoes and you've got what we'll be eating for the next couple of days. Suits us fine, quite tasty in fact.

We walked round for a bit this afternoon, then it started to rain so we headed back and spent the rest of the day here in our room reading a couple of Sherlock Holmes books Gray brought with him. It's a bit weird reading about the foggy streets of old London town here in the heart of Paris, but it suits us just fine. I guess we're still getting over those two crazy days on the road. So an early night will be *superfabandsmashing...*

Cut to 221B Baker Street. Two familiar figures are deep in conversation.

'Now look here old fellow, this is a singular case of delayed shock.'

'I agree Holmes, you have clearly deduced that these two weary travellers need complete rest after their horrific encounter with the lunatic Pascal.'

'Elementary my dear Watson.'

'I have no doubt they will soon fully recover their strength and vigour.'

'Absolutely, old chap... *North-West 2 mate!*'

Thursday 6th

Sherlock was right.

When we woke up this morning we were keen to make up for lost time. We had breakfast in the kitchen with Michelle's mum (how *does* she make coffee taste so good?) then hit the streets. We went back to the Arc de Triomphe for a closer look, then strolled down the *Champs-Expensive* in the sunshine before crossing a bridge over the Seine and standing at the foot of the Eiffel Tower. A lot of tourist sights are disappointing when you see them for real, Stonehenge was half the size I thought it'd be, but the Eiffel's not awful. In fact, it was so amazing we just had to spend some of our precious francs and go all the way to the top. It's over a thousand feet high and the view was absolutely stunningly brilliant.

When we got down we blew some more cash on two cost-a-fortune Cokes, *'10 zillion francs, s'il vous plait monsieur'*, and loaded up with prezzies from a little souvenir stall. We got both our mums a mini Eiffel Tower in a snowstorm, our dads Eiffel Tower lighters, plus Eiffel Tower keyrings for everyone else.

'One thing worries me,' said Gray as we walked back.

'What's that?'

'D'you reckon they'll know where we've been?'

*

Taking the guitar this evening was Gray's idea.

'Michelle told me there's always buskers in Montmartre, maybe we can make a few bob.'

'Elementary my dear Lynchy.'

An hour later we're on a hill in the heart of the city beside a beautiful church called *Sacré Coeur*. The crowded streets are full of artists and musicians all trying to earn a few francs from the wide-eyed tourists. We start singing our latest greatest hit, *House of The Rising Sun*, on the corner of a narrow street and the echo comes back sounding good. Maybe too good coz three gypsy-looking guys with guitars and a double bass start mouthing off at us. We don't know what they're saying, make that growling, but I don't think it's *helloandwelcometopariswhereweareveryhappyforyoutobuskinour favouritespot*. It's more like *thisisourpitchsofuckoffnoworwewillslit yourthroatsandthrowyourmutilatedbodiesdanslaseine*.

My reaction is to do a Snagglepuss, exit stage left, but Gray doesn't like people trying to push him around. He keeps strumming his guitar like the gypsies aren't there. I want to chicken out but I can't let Gray down, so I start singing again and my voice comes out like a high-pitched squeak... funny that. There's a bit of macho pushing and shoving and my blood runs cold when I see one of the gypsies reach inside his jacket. I can already feel his rusty blade plunging into my chest, so I'm amazed when his hand jumps back into sight holding a harmonica. He says something to his friends, laughs out loud, then joins us in New Orleans with some great harp playing that's a mix between Dylan and Paul Jones of the Manfreds. He's a cool guy and when we finish the song he claps his hands and bows low like a Shakespeare actor. Gray is smiling now, he shakes our new best friend by the hand and we walk away with our pride and throats in one piece.

'There is a better place,' a pretty girl with long black hair and stunning blue eyes is talking to Gray like she wants to know him better.

'We show you,' says the girl at my side, with a voice like honey and a smile like a promise.

Two Dutch girls from Amsterdam, Reina and Sasze, warm and friendly and leading us to a bank of grass by a flight of stone steps where we can sing and play and talk and laugh. Reina's sitting close to Gray in white jeans and a Beatles T-shirt. Sasze's singing along with me on *Twist And Shout* and holding her hand to her mouth and giggling every time she gets a word wrong. Her summer dress is short and covered with flowers and she's so cute you want to wrap her up in ribbons and take her home for Christmas. (I have no idea what that means, but it's how I feel.) One song flows into another as the city lights start to shine below us and the golden tower reaches up into the night sky. Paris is a city for lovers and romance is in the air.

'What do you sing now?' asks Sasze.

'More Beatles please,' says Reina.

'What about *You Can't Do That,* Gray? That's a 12-bar, right?'

'Except the middle 8.'

'Skip that.'

'Right.'

'Sing it good Tony and I think you *can* do that.'

'Shut up Reina... she is terrible!'

But the giggle's there in Sasze's voice and her sexy little girl smile is sweeter than sweet. Gray kicks into John Lennon's song and I give it all I've got on vocals, trying to remember to keep my voice sounding billy goat gruff not Bob Dylan nasal. Gray skips the middle bit and covers with a chunky chord solo that reminds me what a great guitarist he is these days. We build to a big finale: Gray strums a big fat D Slowhand style and I chuck in a few *ooohhh-yeeaahs* just for the hell of it. The girls clap their hands, then get up to leave. Oh no... looks like our happy little balloon is about to burst.

'We go now' says Reina.

'Where?' asks Gray.

'Our hotel,' says Sasze, leaning down to take my hand.

I look at Gray and he reads my mind. *Is this really happening?* We try to play it cool, like we get this kind of thing all the time, but truth is we can't believe our luck. It's easy chatting to the girls as we walk arm-in-arm through the city streets. They tell us they saw the

Beatles in Amsterdam a few weeks ago when the Fabs took a boat ride thru the city.

'We saw you by the canal, didn't we John?' I say, sounding nothing like McCartney.

'Knew we'd seen them somewhere,' smiles Gray, sounding even less like Lennon.

When it comes to talking like the Fabs we're non-starters, but the girls love it and we're still laughing when we burst into their bedroom and settle in for a night *d'amour* and more and more. Gray's on one of the twin beds with Reina and I'm soon lost in Sasze's lips on the other. All the lights are off and murmurs of sweet pleasure start to wash over us, as our bodies move closer and kisses grow deeper.

'Reina.'

The voice is soft but different: sounds like Gray's caught an instant cold.

'Is that you John?'

'Thought it was you Paul.'

'Reina!'

It's not us it's *him*, the mad little bloke throwing the door open, turning on the lights, and screaming blue murder in Dutch. The girls jump up looking frightened, leaving us on their beds waving goodbye to our dreams.

'Just our fuckin' luck, Paul.'

'You said it John.'

'Get out! Get out!'

The angry man is dancing on the spot.

'You know how old my girls? I get police... you have big trouble.'

'Daddy, please,' says Sasze.

'We didn't do nothing,' says Reina.

Daddy gives them a verbal volley that's double Dutch to us, but we know it's time to go...

'Bye,' I say to Sasze.

'See you soon,' says Gray to Reina.

We walk out and daddy slams the door behind us. He sure has got a big voice for a little fella. He should be the singer in a rock 'n roll band.

'Shit, my guitar, left it in there,' says Gray.

'What ya gonna do?'

'Get it, of course.' The wild man of Amsterdam's gonna love this!

We walk back and knock on the door.

'Guitar,' says Gray in a wild west shoot-out type voice.

Dutch daddy turns into a purple people eater and screams something that sounds like: '*Youcangorighttohellifyouthinki'mgonna givebackyourguitarwhenyouandthatotherhooliganhavetriedtohave yourwickedwaywithmysweetandinnocentdaughtersandbythewayI'm yellingallthisinhystericalrantingtdutchbutanyfoolcanguesswhatIam ravingonaboutsowriteitinenglishorwe'llbehereallnightnowpissoff beforeIburstintoflamesandexploderighthereonthespot!!*'

He tries to shut the door but Gray's foot is in the way.

'Guitar.'

Gray's voice is ice cold and the message is clear. One way or the other, the guitar's coming with us. The stand-off is over in seconds, mad daddy grabs the acoustic and shoves it into Gray's hands, before slamming the door so hard the walls shake.

'Drink?' says Gray.

Good idea... we both need one!

*

Question: why do French bars charge so much for a glass of beer from the pump when half of it is froth? Bit of a rip-off, but the ice cold *bière pression* still tastes good after all the hassle. Blimey, I thought Tasha was a rollercoaster, but she's got nothing on tonight's bumpy ride.

'That's not the first time they've brought blokes back,' says Gray.

'Right, that's why he was checking up on them.'

'How old d'you reckon?'

'No idea... fifteen?'

'Your one was younger than that.'

'Yeah, probably, but she was cute.'

'I really thought we were in there.'

'So did I... fuck it.'

'We'll know better next time.'

'Next time?'

'Yeah, we're going back with a note.'

You've got to hand it to Gray, he's fearless under pressure. We borrow a pen and a scrap of paper from the barman and scribble

Michelle's number with a short note ... *Call us, John & Paul xx* ... then leave it at the hotel desk for room *soixante-quatre*. There's a chance mad daddy could grab the note and give it to the gendarmes who will then ring Michelle's mum to say she's got two English sex maniacs under her roof and the police van will be round in *cinq minutes* to take us away, but then again the girls might call us and that would be great, so we walk away hoping for the best.

We've lost track of time and when we get back to Naked Granny Towers the street is deserted. We get into the building with a late night neighbour, but what next? It's gone midnight and that means Michelle's parents have been in bed for a couple of hours. We can't ring the bell and wake them up, there's no way, so we spend the night out in the corridor and it feels like we're back on the road again. I grab a couple of hours kip but Gray's wide awake thinking about the warm bed he could be sharing with Reina. Jailbait or not, we know where we'd rather be. Michelle's mum finally comes out at about seven to buy bread *pour le petit dejeuner* and she's amazed to see us. We're too tired to explain, we just smile, shrug, and head for our room where we crash out in seconds.

Friday 7th

'Bonjour mes élèves, voulez vous quelque chose à manger?'

It's gone midday when Michelle sticks her head round the bedroom door and wakes us up with her laughing voice. She's back from Spain and it's great to see her. We're soon chatting away *dix-neuf* to the dozen over delicious cheese omelettes and bowls of caffeine-a-go-

197

go coffee. *Mademoiselle* keeps saying she's sorry she was away when we arrived and we keep saying it's not her fault coz she didn't know we were coming and neither did we until Gray hit on the idea last week. We tell her everything: the hassle of getting passports; the thrill of leaving England for the first time; our adventures on the road; the buzz of busking in Montmartre; but we leave out the bit about going to bed with naughty little girls!

Michelle is tanned from the Spanish sun. She looks great, happy and gorgeous, and our dreams of making it with her flood back, but that's never gonna happen so let's make the most of the one day we'll have together. One day? Yeah, last day today, has to be coz we're down to our last few francs. We tell Michelle we've got to get back for a gig coz it sounds cool, but the truth is we'll soon be like that well-known firm of solicitors, Skint, Broke & Brassic.

Michelle is sad we've got to go, but we're soon out on the streets for a whistle-stop tour of the city she calls home. She asks if we've been to the *Louvre* and we say yes thanks we had a wee-wee before we came out, which makes her laugh. Twenty minutes later we're face-to-face with the *Mona Lisa* and her eyes seem to follow us all around the room. Next we see an amazing statue of a young Greek woman called the *Venus de Milo*. She's over two thousand years old and her arms have fallen off but she's still beautiful. How anyone can carve curves like that out of marble is a mystery lost in the mists of time.

Next on Michelle's city tour is the beautiful *Notre Dame* cathedral. The hunchback's not home today, but weird gargoyle faces stare down at us. There's a warm feeling inside as afternoon sunlight filters through stained glass windows in shades of purple and blue. We're glad we came but we're in danger of culture burnout so Michelle takes us for one last treat, a boat trip on the Seine and the city looks even better from the river.

We get back to the *appartement* and Michelle's mum has cooked us a meal that seems to last forever... soup, salad, fish, pasta (Michelle knows we love it), cheese, fruit, chocolates and coffee. *C'est magnifique* and we're feeling good so we take Michelle for a goodbye drink. She wants to go to a little local bar she knows, but we're keen to go out in style so we grab a table *sur la terrasse* outside a café on the *Champs Expensive* and watch our last francs sail away on the waiter's silver tray. We're broke but who gives a damn? We sit back and enjoy the buzz that comes from sharing our last night in Paris with our beautiful French friend. It beats Golders Green Wimpy, that's for sure....

Saturday 8th

We're on the ferry back to Dover.

Michelle is not only gorgeous, she's a star. Gray was first up this morning and she asked him straight how many francs we'd got left. He didn't want to lie to her so he admitted we were *potlessfrancswise*. Next thing we know, Michelle's dad is driving us to the *Gare de Nord* and she is buying us tickets out to the coast. Then she gets us coffee and croissants and gives us both French kisses (on the cheek) before guiding us onto our train and waving goodbye.

'I said we'd pay her back for the tickets but she doesn't want it.' says Gray, as we sit on the ferry watching the white cliffs grow taller. 'She wanted to give us some English money too, but I said we'd be fine once we were on the boat.'

'How much have we got?'

'To the nearest hundred pounds?'

'Yeah.'

'A tanner.'

'You're joking.'

'No, that's it.'

Those croissants seem a long time ago and we're s-t-a-r-v-i-n-g.

We go down to the canteen where the guy behind the counter is about to close up. How much are bread rolls? Sixpence. We ask for one with extra butter.

'You two skint?'

'Yeah.'

'Just like my boy, soppy as a box of biscuits.'

He disappears and comes back with two bread rolls and a big plate of chips.

'Here you are boys, that's a tanner... special offer.'

He takes the money, winks and smiles, then slides the shutter down before we even have time to thank him. Gray and I do our famous magic trick where we make food disappear in seconds, then walk off the ferry feeling fine. We've only been away a few days, but we're happy to to be back in England, home of the Beatles, the Stones, the Animals, *RSG!,* Cathy McGowan and the totally fabtastic Infernos.

Yeah, it's good to be home!

Sunday 9th

You're not gonna believe this.

Gray came round today and we rang the operator and finally got thru to Michelle to say thanks for everything and guess what she said. *'Some girls telephoned for you today. They were sad when I said you had gone home.'*

We missed them by a day, how frustrating is that? Gray was sobbing on the carpet while I ran up the walls and across the ceiling. Oh well, only one thing for it, we'll have to add a new song to our set list.

All together now... *we were only twenty-four hours from Exeter!!*

September '64

Something

Good

Saturday 19th

Happy birthday to me
Happy birthday to me
Happy birthday dear To-neeee
Happy birthday to me

Seventeen today and a lot's happened since France. Ready for an update? Let's go...

Shay's got a job as a glass blower in a factory on the North Circular and Gray's working for an accountant in Golders Green. I can't see him lasting long in an office but he's making good money, eight quid a week, and he's got a new amp on HP. It's a Vox AC30, the same as the Beatles use. It makes his 12-string Danelectro sound absolutely stunningly brilliant.

I've got a new amp too, but mine's second-hand. My cousin Peter told me a mate of his in Arnos Grove was selling his Viking and was I interested? I asked if the viking came with a longboat and he said no, but it had a very horny sound. My how we laughed! It was a 30 watt amp, same as Gray's, and it came with two 18" speakers in a homemade cabinet. Sounded great, only one problem, I was skint, so how much did I need to beg, borrow or steal? Answer: 25 quid. The Infernos all said it was a mad-not-to-buy-it bargain, so I needed a job in a hurry.

I phoned Podge to talk about trying for a transfer to the grammar school (we both got the O-levels grades we needed) and he said he'd got a holiday job with a cleaning agency and he could get me in there too. They paid 30 bob a day, so I got stuck in for three crazy weeks. It was hard graft but I kept going coz I knew there was a bonus waiting at the end of the line of crummy carpets and greasy kitchen floors.

Getting the amp worked out fine, staying on at school was more of a sweat. Dad said he wanted me to go out to work and start paying my way and I dived straight back into the sulky mood I'd felt during the no-way-sign-HP-form thing. I didn't try to see things his way *at all.* All I knew was my dream of making it as a journalist was in danger. As usual mum was caught right in the middle and the whole thing got pretty shitty for all three of us.

I needed cheering up so I phoned the mad Monica and she invited me round for a drink. What happened next was...

the most amazing conversation I've ever had in my life!!

I'm gonna try to share it with you, just the way it happened...

TONY ARRIVES AT MONICA'S PLACE. FRENCH KISSES, THE KIND MICHELLE GAVE AT THE *GARE DU NORD*. MONICA TAKES TONY'S WINE AND PUTS IT IN THE FRIDGE. SHE'S ALREADY GOT A BOTTLE OF ICE-COLD WHITE ON THE GO AND POURS HIM A BIG GLASS...

Monica: So, how was Paris dah-ling?

Tony: Great, we went busking in Montmartre.

Monica: Fan-tastic! Did you screw anyone?

Tony: Er... no, nearly, but no.

Monica: What happened?

Tony: Long story...

Monica: Sounds like someone needs French lessons.

Tony: La plume de ma tante...

Monica: You know what I fucking mean!

Tony: You mean fucking...

Monica: Exactly dah-ling... by the way, ever sleep with Tash?

Tony: No.

Monica: Why?

Tony: Things didn't work out. I mean... she's quite moody.

Monica: I know, since daddy...

Tony: What happened?

Monica: Car crash... late night call... shattering news... no goodbyes... terrible shock... now mummy tries her best... made me even wilder... but Tasha's never... still his little girl you see... so close, then nothing... too sad for words.

Tony: She didn't say anything.

Monica: No, she never does... another drink? Come on, let's finish the bottle.

SHE FILLS BOTH GLASSES TO THE RIM.

Monica: So... she's moody, that's why you split?

Tony: No, it wasn't all her fault, I messed up too.

Monica: How?

Tony: It's a bit personal really.

Monica: That's why I'm asking dah-ling! I love a bit of scandal...

Tony: Well... truth is... sounds pathetic but I couldn't get her bra off, couldn't find the bloody clip, think she went off me a bit after that.

Monica: Did you try the front?

Tony: The *front* ?

Monica: She always wears front loaders.

Tony: Never heard of them.

Monica: My God dah-ling, you *have* got a lot to learn.

MONICA GOES TO THE FRIDGE FOR TONY'S WINE.

Monica: Not cold yet, but who gives a flying fuck?

SHE TOPS UP THEIR GLASSES.

Monica: I can't believe you're still a virgin.

Tony: I didn't say that.

206

Monica: You didn't have to, very sweet actually. I'd like to fuck you now, be your first, but it's all a bit weird with Tasha and...

Tony: That's over.

Monica: I know but it's still... and anyway, I'm trying to be a good girl for Ricky who is *depraved* in bed and such a sweetie out of it and if I start screwing round behind his back again he'll dump me and I'll be in *shreds* and it's just not worth the hassle for a quickie, even with you.

Tony: Shame.

Monica: Tragic dah-ling, but I'm happy to talk sex if you like, give you the benefit of my naughty past.

Tony: I don't know...

Monica: Oh well, if you're going to be all coy about it.

Tony: No, I mean I don't know what to ask.

Monica: Okay, let's start with where most men go wrong. No *finesse* dah-ling, no *special touch*. They come on way too strong, rushing, panting, big hairy hands grabbing and pinching at your...

Tony: Wangzangaroonies?

Monica: Is that what you called them when you were a little boy? How funny! Yes, grabbing your wang-zanga-wotsits... and your

207

legs... and your pussy. Too greedy you see, pigs at the trough, not the way to turn a girl on.

Tony: What is?

Monica: Perfect seduction? Sexy little steps dah-ling... gentle kisses getting warmer... his hand outside my blouse slowly undoing the buttons then feeling my breasts... moving down to my thighs and inside my panties... then we get naked and if we want to screw we screw, but only if he's wearing a plastic mac... I love that lost-in-the-madness rush of a wild fuck... then later do it again... slow and horny... and it feels so sweet you never want to stop.

Tony: Don't think I fancy that.

Monica: What?

Tony: You know... plastic... rubber... all that kinky stuff.

Monica: Sorry, not with you... oh, you mean *plastic macs*? You don't wear them silly, well you do but only when you roll one onto your prick. Durex dah-ling... got any on you now?

Tony: No.

Monica: Why not? You came here wanting to screw me, didn't you?

Tony: Well...

Monica: Of course you did, I'm gorgeous. But no Durex?

Tony: No.

Monica: Big mistake, buy some, keep them in your wallet, then you'll be ready if you get lucky. If she says no, golden rule, don't try to force her. A lot of men see sex as something they take from a woman. Truth is, if the sex is any good you don't *take* it, you make it together. Most girls know exactly how far they want to go before they slip into their best bra and panties for their big night out. Men waste hours trying to grab more than we want to give, shit for brains you see.

You don't have to fuck to have a good time. Kissing can be lovely all on its own, so can feeling her breasts and teasing her nipples with your tongue. If she wants you to slip your finger into her pussy, take it slowly, find her sweet spot and build an easy rhythm until you feel her pleasure rising, then give it to her harder and harder until she comes. Now it's your turn and I'm sure I don't have to spell out what she does to please you...

Tony: No, that's okay... it all sounds...

Monica: *Thrilling* dah-ling, I love it. There's so much more I could tell you, like the joys of the clit, but you'll have fun discovering it all for yourself. Enjoy it, don't be shy, that guilty sex-is-dirty crap has *gone*, ration books and grey dresses *gone,* it's all changing sweetie, can't you feel it? We've got the Beatles now for fuck's sake. The Kinks *You Really Got Me,* have you heard it? Raw, sexy, brilliant shit. Mary Quant, Biba, David Bailey, the Shrimp: it's all happening and dreams really do come true. Young and free in London, no better place to be. You want to know about sex and I'm happy to tell you, what's wrong with that? Nothing. But if we drink one more glass of wine I'll have to jump you and shag your balls off, so we'd better get out of here before I break every fucking boring promise I've made to Ricky.

I just stared at her and smiled. My senses were reeling: all I could see were the pictures she'd painted in my head. I liked the words she used when she talked about sex: pussy, breasts, prick, instead of cunt, tits, nob and *wangzangaroonies*. (Glad she thought I was joking about that last one!) I loved the things she said to me, even if I didn't understand them all, like what's a clit and how does it give you joy? Losing her dad has made Monica hungry for life. She loves the Sixties, the here and now, and she lives it all to the full. *Ab-so-lutely dah-ling!!*

We rolled out into the afternoon light and walked arm-in-arm down Portobello Road. The street market was closing but Monica saw a shop window dummy of a busty woman on a stall and said I must buy it. Then she disappeared into a second-hand clothes shop and came back waving a bra and straw hat. 'There you are dah-ling, you can practice on her 'til you've got it off... literally! Don't you just love the hat? Very BB in Saint Trop.' And that's how Brigitte came into my life. Monica walked us both back to the tube, then pulled my face down to hers and gave me a sizzling goodbye kiss.

'Now fuck off, you sexy bastard,' she laughed.

So I did.

*

I couldn't stop thinking about Monica for the next couple of days. I longed to call her, go round to her place, take her to bed and do all the things she'd told me about, but I knew she didn't want that. So I sat in my room and tried to decide whether BB was a fun mascot or the kind of pervy toy Anthony Perkins would have loved in *Psycho*. What? *My* room? Oh yeah, I forgot to tell you the new extension was up when I got back from Paris. Dad started in July and finished it in a hurry. It was great of him to do that, but there was still a big dark question mark over my future and that meant another clash between me and him.

I'd been feeling sorry for myself but spending time with Monica really made me think. She goes on about living life to the full, having fun and all that stuff, but it's easy to see she's still crying inside for the father she'll never see again. Tasha's moody, Monica's a little crazy, they're different but the same. How would I feel if my dad died? It's a horrible thought. We've never been close, but I love him, so why not try to see his side of things for a change? He's kept me all my life, paid for everything. Maybe it is time I got a job and stood on my own two feet. That's what Shay and Gray have done, why not me?

The dream, my journalist dream, that's the answer. Grammar school, A-levels, Fleet Street, that's been the plan for years and I'm so close to taking the next step it hurts. So what to do? I didn't want a big argument, just the right moment to talk to him. It came when he gave me a lift to pick up the amp I'd bought. He knew I'd worked hard to get the cash, so he was happy to help. I went for it on the way home.

'Can I stay on at school dad?'

'Well, you're nearly seventeen, don't you think you should get a job?'

'I need to be a grammar school boy to get the job I want.'

'Will they take you?'

'I don't know, no point asking if you don't want me to go.'

'Will you work hard?'

'Definitely. If I get some A-levels I might make it as a journalist.'

'That's a hard world to break into.'

'I know, but I'd like to try.'

There was long pause, maybe three years, while dad thought it all thru.

'Okay then, if the grammar school say yes you can go, but don't bugger around once you get there.'

'I won't. Thanks dad... thanks!'

Great moment.

Next day Podge and I went to see Mr Hailey, the totally brilliant headmaster at Whitefield. We weren't the first to ask for a transfer to the grammar. A few students had paved the way, like a really funny guy called Dave English, good footballer, great cricketer, and the kind of character who makes the sun shine on a rainy day. I'd heard Dave was doing well at Hendon County, so Podge and I knew we were in with a chance. Mr Hailey rang up for us and our new headmaster must be a good bloke too coz he gave us the thumbs-up there and then.

It was weird cycling into school on my first day. I felt the same way I did when I started Whitefield, kinda nervous and excited at the same time. I went with my mate Tommy, who's been at the grammar for five years, and he was great about making sure Podge and I got to know all his friends in a hurry. We bumped into Dave English too and he cracked a couple of jokes... just for a change! Good start.

*

Okay...

Get Ready...

Rumble of Drums...

Big Big Headline...

I've just seen a girl's naked breasts for the first time!

A beautiful moment... and I owe it all to the Infernos. It's what I dreamed of when I joined the group: I wasn't chasing fame and glory, I was chasing girls, we all were. Put a guitar round your neck and they'll come calling. That was the idea. Well, last Thursday we played that world-famous rock venue, the Claremont Youth Club. After the gig I got talking to a Suzy with the dancing eyes. Last night we went to bed together and I'm still buzzing.

It all started back in August when Colin got us the booking. He'd been pushing hard on the group since Gray and I got back from France. He said a string of gigs would sharpen us up and he was right. As you know, Col's the baby of the Infernos, but when it comes to stuff like blagging gigs on the phone he's got more front than the rest of us put together.

'We've got a gig at the youth club, so that's a start,' he told us a few days later. 'The bloke who runs it won't pay us, but if we do okay he'll give a proper gig and that's pays ten quid. A lot of other places are saying they want a photo and some blurb.'

So I wrote a biography ... *two of the group recently played in Paris ...* and we got some snaps done. We kept mucking about at first, then we got into it and they came out alright.

We practised four times a week thru August and early September in a church hall near Whitefield school. Gray's guitar rang out thru his AC30 and when I finally plugged my Star Bass into the Viking amp for the first time, the power was unbelievable. It gave Shay something to lock into. He's got his own drumming style now, keeping the beat duckarse tight as he drives the band along. Colin's voice still sounded a bit blurry thru the old Watkins Dominator, but that will get better when we can afford a proper PA.

We had a good chat about the music we want to play and it's gonna be a mix of R&B classics and new hit records. *House of The Rising Sun* sounded great on Gray's 12-string. Shay and I got a nice tight beat going and Colin sang it better than I did in Paris, but he didn't get chatted up by Sasze! Talking of girls, we were rehearsing in the church hall one evening and we saw some looking in thru the glass doors.

'Must be Girl Guides or something,' said Gray.

'Bet the vicar's double booked,' said Shay.

'Colin, go and see what they want,' we all crid. We *always* ask Colin to do *everything* coz we're lazy sods and he's Mr Nice Guy. We saw him chatting to the girls then he came back smiling.

'They've been listening and they want to know if they can come in.'

Blimey! Fans, sort of, we couldn't believe it, but it was good coz we pumped up the energy on our next song, *You Really Got Me*, the one Monica called *raw, sexy, brilliant shit.* It's a great number to play, sorta picks you up and carries you along.

You have to be smart about the songs you cover. I like that catchy Herman's Hermits hit, but it's way too poppy for us. *I Get Around* by the Beach Boys and *She's Not There* by the Zombies are brilliant records, but they're both way beyond what we can do right now. If we keep things simple we're fine and that means 12-bars or songs that stick to three or four chords, like *Do I Love You?* and *Best Part of Breaking Up* by the Ronettes. When we play them all I can see are the slits in their sexy silk dresses... steady on Carruthers!

Most of the new stuff we're doing would sound better with backing vocals. Gray and I are happy to give it a crack but we can't afford any more gear right now. It's case of softly, softly, catchy monkey... and as we're all nature lovers and believe in the freedom of wild animals across the globe, we'll forget the monkey bit and just wait to see what happens.

This is the official equation: Gigs = Money = More Equipment.

The girls at the hall liked our sound and that gave us a lift as we got ready for the bright lights of Claremont Youth Club. Okay, it wasn't exactly the Marquee, but when we got there we felt nervous coz we knew a few of the local faces were waiting to see what we were like and we didn't want to screw it up. When we started the place wasn't exactly buzzing, nobody listening and a bunch of little kids playing table tennis right by the stage, but at least there was no pressure. We played alright and later on a few cool Mods drifted in at the back and stayed 'til the end.

'Can you whistle?' asked one of the table tennis kids, as I slid my bass back into its case.

I knew the punchline so I ignored him, but it came anyway.

'Well, you can't sing!'

His cheeky laugh echoed out into the September night. A pretty girl from school had seen it all happen. She was a couple of years younger than me. Dark hair and blue eyes, warm and sexy, already a woman. I'd never spoken to Suzy... until then.

'Prat,' she said

'Don't you start,' I snapped.

'Not you... *him.* I like your group.'

She laughed and squeezed my arm. The thrill of her touch shot thru me like an electric shock. Spin forward to Friday night and there I was nervously pacing round my bedroom, trying to remember Monica's words of wisdom. (I'd bought a packet of Durex at Boots in Cricklewood, just in case. Embarrassing, or what? No wonder so many young guys end up buying a toothbrush!) Mum and dad were away at their caravan. *Hard Day's Night* was on the Dansette. Consulate cigarettes and Strongbow cider? Check. BB stored away in the attic? Check. Now for my Christmas party *piece de resistance...* one of the red bulbs from the Inferno in my bedside lamp. What girl could resist? Luckily for me, not Suzy.

She arrived with a smile and never stopped talking about our group and the songs we play. She's really into R&B but she loves the Beatles, Stones and Animals too. We laughed and smoked and sipped our cider, and when John Lennon's *You Can't Do That* filled the room we were up on our feet. Truth is I'm no dancer but it didn't matter, we both knew it was just a step along the way.

Paul and George joined John with *sweetasanut* harmonies on *I'll Be Back,* then we flipped the record back to side one. Suzy held me close and I kissed her. We lay down on my single bed and I felt her tongue exploring mine. I kept hearing Monica's voice, don't rush things, enjoy it, be tender, and her words flew me to a planet I'd never seen before. I slowly unbuttoned Suzy's blouse and kissed the deep valley between her breasts. Her bra was low-cut, black and silky and after all my trial runs with BB I was ready to unclip it with a *snap* of my fingers, but I lost my nerve and my fingers started to feel like I was back with Tasha.

'It's okay.'

Suzy's voice was soft and warm. She sat up and took off her blouse, then slowly slipped away the black satin and lace. I gazed at her beautiful breasts. She lay back with a smile and pulled my mouth down to her hard nipples. It was beautiful kissing her, holding her, floating in a *timestandsstillhaze*. Monica's little red book made sense now. Being in bed with Suzy wasn't scary, it was beautiful. It wasn't about making the right moves to get what I wanted, it was about sharing the moment, two of us together in one special place. (Sorry if that sounds mushy but it's how I felt.) In the heat of the moment I did try to go *all the way*, but Suzy slowed me down with a gentle whisper.

'No Tony.'

Two words, not sharp or angry, but they drew the line and I was happy not to spoil things. Happy, yes I was happy, she was happy, we were happy. When I walked her home we laughed all the way. I kissed her goodnight then ran down the street, my head buzzing with the thrill of it all.

And now it's my birthday: new girl in my life, new friends, new school, radio playing a happy song and I'm singing along, top of my voice, big smile on my face.

I'm into something good!

Enter The Vampire

October '64

Wednesday 14th

The vampire's eyes burned into me and my blood ran cold.

'Do you feel you're fitting in here?'

'Yes sir.'

'That's not my understanding.'

His voice was low and full of menace. The headmaster was out to get me and I wasn't ready for the attack. The day he took Podge and me into his school without any fuss, I thought he must be a good bloke. Turns out that was a bit like saying Henry VIII was a dream husband. I soon realised none of the students at Hendon County liked the head. Hang on, I don't know that for sure, but I never heard anyone say a good word for him, definitely not. He was a tall, thin man and had been a good runner in his time, but now his skin was deathly white and that gave me the idea he avoided the sun... like a vampire.

You know what I'm like, once I get an idea in my head it keeps on growing, and in my imagination I could see him flying through the school corridors at night, his long black gown stretching out like bat wings. With the rising of the moon his vampire teeth would snap into sight and he'd select his victim for the next day, while hanging from the ceiling of the school hall. All a load of rubbish, of course, but he *was* scary and now I was in his sights.

'You don't seem to have many friends Norman.'

'I do sir.'

'Really?'

He left the word hanging in the air like an axe above my neck. My mind was racing, trying to work out what this was all about. Then a snapshot clicked into focus, the headmaster staring down from a long window above the schoolyard, seeing me alone and jumping to all the wrong conclusions. *Norman is a loner, a misfit, he doesn't belong in my school.* If he'd looked out two minutes earlier he would have seen me chatting to Podge about the new Animals LP. Five minutes later I was talking with Tommy, Dale and Alex about playing football for the school on Saturday. But he didn't catch those scenes, he saw what he saw and he thought what he thought, and now I was falling apart under the pressure of his cold, cold gaze.

'I like to give secondary modern pupils every opportunity, but some find the transition to life here extremely difficult. Do you feel you can adapt?'

'I think so sir.'

'You *think* so, but you're not sure are you?'

He was like a bad guy Perry Mason, twisting every word I said.

'Why did you come here Norman?'

'I want to be a journalist.'

For a second a cynical smile seemed to flicker on his dry lips.

'Do you think that's likely?'

'A-levels will help.'

'Possibly, but I always find it best to be realistic when setting goals.'

I took that to mean *you've got no fucking chance* and at that moment I thought he was probably right. Like a vampire he had sucked the lifeblood from of me. The grammar school was different,

222

that was true. I had the brains to do okay, but a little encouragement would have been nice. Instead I was being dissected like a rat by a powerful man who was king of a world he ruled with ruthless efficiency. He sat behind his desk, quiet satisfaction written all over his face. He knew he'd shaken me, planted doubts, marked my card, and I felt my days were numbered.

'If you choose to stay here, I expect to see you make more of an effort. Do you understand?'

'Yes sir.'

'You may go.'

'Thank you sir.'

That last line still makes me sick. *Thank you sir.* Why the hell did I say that? He'd torn me to shreds and I'd just stood there. *Thank you sir* for kicking me in the balls. *Thank you sir* for treating me like a fool. *Thank you sir* for wanting me out of your precious school. In my heart I knew what he'd said wasn't fair, but I couldn't shake the feeling he knew something I didn't. Had he spoken to my teachers, maybe some of his favourite pupils, had they stuck the knife in my back? Paranoia: amazing how soon it gets a grip. If I walked away tomorrow, would anyone really care?

Good question.

Now it's late, I'm tired and I want to sleep, but the vampire is inside my head, all those clever questions, all those doubts and fears.

Monday 26th

I'm going to leave.

I've given it a lot of thought and I hate to say it but the vampire was right. I don't fit in at the grammar. The guys from the football team are friendly but I miss Graham, the good old days of *lynchandnorman,* in a school that felt like home. It's great having Podge at Hendon County, but we take different classes and most of the time I'm on my own. I scribble notes when the teacher is talking, then can't read them later. I liked the lesson notes we got at Whitefield, the support we got at Whitefield, the grades we got at Whitefield. I always felt ahead of the game there, now I'm the village idiot. I'd like to ask Dave English how he's fitted in here without skipping a beat, but I just heard he's been hurt in a horrible road accident. Everywhere I look, I see bad news.

So, the vampire will be smiling soon. I'll just be a name on a scrap of paper he can tear up and throw in the bin. I don't want to hang around where I'm not wanted. It's not fair on dad coz he's paying my bills and I'm struggling. A-levels? I've got more chance of riding on Santa's sleigh. Sleigh... slay the vampire! I'd love to but I'm afraid he's slayed me. It's half-term now and I'm going to see a careers advice guy at the town hall this afternoon. Mum's coming with me: probably sounds a bit pathetic, a big bloke like me taking his mum, but when I'm in trouble she's the one I turn to. Always has been.

I was happy happy on my birthday: funny how quickly things can change...

2.30pm He's a kind man. Small office, collar and tie, jacket over the back of his chair, photos of his wife and kids on the desk he sits at five days a week, 49 weeks a year, planning trips to schools where he tells students what they can and can't do for the rest of their lives. He means well, but I feel like I'm drowning in a sea of dreams that never came true. He's got all the brochures you'll ever need, Gas Board, Electricity Board, Post Office, Army, Navy, Air Force, banks, factories, offices, all tumbling over each other to get school leavers to sign up. There's more than enuff work for everyone. *Quit one job in the morning, start another in the afternoon.* That's what kids say, what they do, it's easy. Ever heard of an unemployed teenager? No, of course not, it never happens, so the kind man sits in his office with the windows shut tight and knows he can help me. But he can't.

I want to be a journalist and he tells me all the reasons why that's never going to happen. He's not snidey about it like the vampire, he's just being *realistic*. I sit there nodding, trying to look interested, but I'm not listening to a word he says. All I can hear are the voices in my head. *What are you doing here? You don't want any of these jobs. You know what you want to do. Why are you giving up now?* When I tune back in, the kind man is smiling and saying he could get me a job here at the town hall, good prospects, job security, generous pension when I retire. I see a full moon, my dead body on the cold ground, the vampire laughing, blood dripping from his fangs. I thank the careers man and say I'll let him know. Mum and I walk down to Hendon Central to wait for a bus.

'What are you going to do?'

225

'I don't know mum.'

I didn't know then and I don't know now. Truth is I'm really fucked up. So I sit here writing these words, knowing if I make the wrong move, I could regret it for the rest of my life.

Tuesday 27th

When I woke up this morning my bed was a mess. It looked like there'd been a bullfight in there, twisted sheets and mangled blankets. Restless or what? I decided there and then I had to talk to someone before I went crazy. But who? Mum's done all she can and dad's off the list. I don't want the Infernos to know coz the group's my last refuge and I want to keep it safe from the curse of the vampire. I can't tell Suzy coz that's over, she's a free spirit and I always knew she'd move on. I did call Monica but a stranger's voice said she didn't live there anymore and I heard a line from an old blues song... *if I didn't have bad luck, I'd have no luck at all.*

Podge was doing fine at school. I didn't want to get him mixed up in my troubles, but in the end I told him I was leaving.

'Do you still want to be a journalist?'

'Of course.'

'Don't go then, you haven't done anything wrong.'

'He makes me feel like I have.'

'He's just picking on you.'

'Why?'

'No idea.'

'He's like a vampire, after my blood.'

'Don't bleed then.'

'What?'

'Don't give him what he wants, not unless it's what you want too.'

Podge is a nice guy, gentle and funny, but at that moment he looked angry. Angry I was getting shoved around and... maybe... angry I was running away like... come on Tony say it... like *a coward*. Talking to him was great, really shone a light. I came out knowing what I had to do. Time to ride out the storm: hold onto the dream coz it's all I've got.

November '64

Monday 9th

'Mr Driver wants to see you.'

The little kid gives his message and runs off across the schoolyard. The grey, damp day matches my mood and now another teacher is after me. What have I done this time? You tell me coz I've got no idea.

'Sit down Tony.'

'No thanks sir.'

'You alright?'

'Yes sir.'

'You're not in trouble, you know,' he smiles and I feel the pinch of tension ease from my shoulders. Mr Driver, Jack Driver, the only teacher in this school who calls you by your first name. Small, dapper, grey hair, clipped moustache, tweed sports jacket, warm Yorkshire accent. I like him coz he took the time to explain why I'd been dropped as centre-forward of the first team in October. He said I lacked pace and he was right. How would I feel about playing right-half for the seconds? Fine. And then guess what? He *shook my hand*. Doesn't sound much, but when you're feeling like a stranger on the shore, little things like that mean a lot. So, I've given the seconds my best shot, if you'll excuse the pun, and I don't deserve to get dropped again. No way.

'How would you feel about skippering the team?'

I stare at him.

'I'm thinking of moving Anderson up to the firsts, so I'll be needing a new captain. Think you can do it?'

'Don't know sir.'

'Well I think you can Tony. I watched the second half on Saturday and I liked the way you encouraged the other lads. Were you a captain at Whitefield?'

'Yes sir.'

'Thought so, you're a good leader and the team needs that. Interested?'

'Yes sir, thanks.'

I come out walking on air and the next day I'm back for a meeting with Dale Best, the craggy first team skipper from Darlington, great player and nice bloke. How to describe Dale? One word: charismatic. The kind of guy young kids look up to and want to be like, a school hero. Suddenly I'm talking football with him and Jack and for the first time ever I feel like I belong in this place...

I was really up for the game on Saturday, winning tackles, hitting passes, encouraging the lads. It was 1-1 with five minutes to go, then like *Roy of The Rovers* I scored the winner and felt something I remembered from another lifetime. What do they call it now? Oh yeah... happiness!

This morning in assembly the vampire read out my name as one of the scorers in our win. He didn't look angry. It sounded like I was just another kid and that's all I want to be. Has he put his fangs away? Hope so.

Monday 16th

'I would like to see Tony Norman after assembly.'

The headmaster's words cut through me like a knife. All around me heads twist, eyes stare, *he's in trouble, what's he done?* We exit the hall in straight lines and I go to see the vampire. He sits behind his huge desk and stares at me with those cold cold eyes. He's ready to strike and wastes no time.

'First you appear to take no interest in school life, now it seems you spend all your time with girls.'

What's he on about?

'And your jacket is not suitable for school, this is not a building site.'

I see it now: walking out of school last Friday, donkey jacket over my blazer, laughing and joking with some really nice girls I've got to know, Vicki and Alison and her sister Kate, just friends, nothing more. The vampire drives past in a big black car like a hearse and stares at us, which is weird coz we're doing nothing wrong. Now it seems what he saw was some kind of crime, or is he looking for any excuse to pick on me? *Bully.* The word shoots into my brain. *Bully,* that's what he is, just a *fucking bully* and all that snot about building sites has come spewing down his snobby toffee nose. I feel a burst of anger and let it all out. I've got nothing to lose.

'First you say I've got no friends, then you say it's just girls, and none of it's true. If I'm such a problem how come Mr Driver's made me captain of the school seconds? He must see more in me than you do. I wasn't doing anything wrong with those girls, we were just laughing... or is that against the rules now?'

'Don't be impertinent.'

He looks furious, but the smug look has gone.

'What about that jacket?'

'My dad gave it to me. I wear it because it's warm, not to be a rebel.'

'You seem very sure of yourself all of a sudden.'

'I know I'm not as bad as you make out. '

'That's enough. Get back to your class!'

'Yes sir, but I'm not leaving school. If you want me out you'll have to expel me.'

I was shaking inside but at least I walked away with my head held high. I needed fresh air so I ran down the stone steps to the schoolyard. Podge would be glad I'd stood up for myself, but I knew I'd burned all my bridges and I'd be out by the end of the day. Every time the classroom door opened I expected to see the vampire standing there, but he never came. Final bell of the day, out into the street, no last minute summons as I walked to freedom.

And now I'm home but I'm not happy. I thought it all thru on the bus and I know what's going on. The bad news will arrive tomorrow in a letter, black and white, cold and clinical, that's his style, how he likes to do things. It's just a matter of time...

December '64

Tuesday 8th

I hardly slept that night and the next morning I was back to being that scared little kid waiting for a letter that would change my life. But it never came. It's over three weeks now since my clash with the vampire. He still scowls at me every time our paths cross, but he hasn't spoken to me. Not once. They say the best way to deal with a bully is to fight back. Is that what happened here? I don't know, but maybe.

Little by little my fear of the fang has faded and I've started to enjoy life at school. There's been a party every weekend. I missed a couple coz we had gigs with the Infernos but I was there last Saturday, dancing to *I'm Crying* by the Animals, *Baby Love* by the Supremes, *He's In Town* by the Rockin' Berries, *All Day And All Of The Night* by the Kinks, *Remember (Walking In The Sand)* by the Shangri-Las, *Little Red Rooster* by the Stones and *I Feel Fine* by The Beatles. Great music, good times.

Monday 14th

Tommy and I were invited to a party last Saturday by a pretty Jewish girl called Phoebe. She lives in Golders Green and likes to do things with style, which meant soft lights, Dylan and wine. At first we thought it was all a bit super trendy, but Phoebe was very friendly and before we left she led me into a quiet room upstairs for a snogging session that thrilled me to my toes. Then today another girl came up to me in the romantic setting of the school table tennis room and asked me to come outside.

'I hear you're a good kisser,' she said.

'Is that right?'

'Feel like proving it?'

'If you insist.'

The kiss that seemed to last forever.

'Did I pass?' I asked when we finally pulled apart.

'Maybe,' she teased, mischief dancing in her smile.

Wednesday 16th

I don't kid myself. I'm not suddenly Paul McCartney. I'm a novelty, the new kid in school, and the girls are checking me out, which is fine by me. I'm making some good friends here too. Couple of weeks ago a switched-on guy called Alex said I could copy his Geography and History notes, and I started to see how he picked out the main points from a lesson and got them down on paper. He didn't make a big thing of it, he was just happy to help and I appreciated that.

I like Alex a lot. He reminds me of a western hero, tall, slim, good looking, with a low voice and an easy smile. The kind of laid-back dude who'd ride into Tombstone, Arizona, and ask Burt Lancaster and Kirk Douglas if they could use an extra gun for the *Gunfight at the O.K. Corral.* He comes from a council flat in Mill Hill and has the mind of a university professor. Nothing fazes Alex, he cruises thru school and I can learn a lot from him. He's cool.

Then there's a zany guy called Jeremy, who's pretty much the opposite of Alex. He talks like a public schoolboy and bounces around with a wild kind of energy. He loves questioning teachers, asking them to justify what they're telling us. He's got a good mind and his words spin like quicksilver as he waves his arms around enjoying the thrill of the debate. Jeremy may seem crazy, but he's not. He's got a heart of gold and if he can can help you he will... any time at all. He reminds me of Dave English, with his posh voice and kind heart, and it was great to hear Dave is getting better after that nasty accident. Good news, very good. My first term at grammar school has been tough, but things are on the up.

Saturday 19th

It felt good breaking up for the holidays yesterday. *Good* coz all that vampire crap was over and *good* coz I didn't let him scare me away. *Don't give him what he wants*... excellent advice when I needed it most. Thanks Podge. Now Christmas is coming and the goose is getting... nervous! Fantastic end-of-term party last night, *BeatlesForSalespinningnewfriendslaughingjokingchattingdrinking smokingdancingsnogging* and it felt great to be there. It really did.

Thursday 24th

Christmas Eve and Tommy's on the phone.

'Doing anything tonight?'

'Nothing special.'

'Fancy coming on a blind date?'

Tom's all set to take out a girl he likes, but she doesn't want to leave her cousin at home, so we all get together and you know how last minute things sometimes take off? Well, this turns out to be one of those nights. Tommy says we're going to the pictures, but he won't tell us what's showing at the little fleapit near our school. We push him for clues on the way and he finally admits it's a holiday film. Guesses ring out in the frosty air. *It's A Wonderful Life? Scrooge? White Christmas?* Then we turn the corner and see Tommy's yuletide treat... *Summer Holiday.*

Brilliant!

We sit back sipping our orange drinks and eating our ice cream tubs as Cliff and his friends put on their dancing shoes, board their London double-decker, and set off for Greece singing their catchy summer holiday song. Cliff and the boys soon meet Una and the girls and it's *goodcleanfoottappingfun* all the way to Athens. Seeing it on the big screen on Christmas Eve feels cozy and when we get outside it's snowing. All together now... one, two three... aahhhhh!! We walk the girls home singing Cliff songs and when it comes to goodnight kisses my surprise date is sweeter than a solo on Hank B's red Stratocaster.

Happy, happy, jingle, jangle...

Thursday 31st

Christmas Day was a lot better than last year. Mavis and Dennis came over again and this time we had a great meal which was not followed by me chucking up in the bathroom 15 minutes later, which made a nice change. Then we all sat round while dad gave out the presents and I felt really choked when I opened one from my mum and saw it was a college style scarf for school. She knew I wanted one and it was her way of letting me know she was glad I'd held onto my dream. She didn't say it, she didn't need to, I saw it in her smile.

And now it's New Year's Eve and I'm looking forward to 1965. The Stones new album comes out in a couple of weeks, the Beatles are all set to make their second film, and a hot new station called Radio London has joined Caroline on the pirate airwaves. Okay, now get ready for the hottest news of all. The Infernos are finished, kaput. We haven't split up, but we are making big changes: new PA, new lead guitarist to boost our sound, plus a brand new name.

The Infernos are dead... long live The Rest!

January - May '65

The Rest

Welcome to the Magic Carpet Ride
back to last summer...

Friday 26 June 1964

'Scuse me mate,' said Shay.
'How much d'you pay for your drums?'

Keith Moon stared at him and gave a two word answer.

'A lot!'

Moony went back to breaking down his kit and Shay joined Gray
who was talking to the lead singer of the best group
they'd ever seen, as he sat rolling up mike leads
on the edge of the stage.

'We were the Detours, then the High Numbers, now it's
The Who,' said Roger Daltrey. 'If you want to see us again
that's the name to look for.

238

'We still like R&B but the geezer on guitar's started writing songs.
We're gonna try a few of them.'

Daltrey kept it polite, but looked pretty pissed off like the rest of the
group. They'd just played the Refectory, a small basement club
opposite Golders Green tube, and the manager had spent the whole
night telling them to turn down.

The Who didn't like that, so they played even louder.

Gray and Shay liked their style and loved their music.
Keith Moon flying round the drums like a trapeze artist,
taking crazy chances but never crashing and burning;
John Entwistle, brilliant bass player, rock solid;
Pete Townshend, great showman, outstanding guitarist, unique;
Roger Daltrey with a voice like a migrant worker
on a dusty road down in the delta.

Brilliant!

But the moody manager man didn't agree.

'You're banned!' he screamed as they packed up their gear.

Daltrey, Townshend and Entwistle cut him dead,
but Keith Moon leaned forward with a dangerous smile
and spoke for one and all.

'Suits us dear boy... now fuck off!'

Okay, that was then... this is now!

January '65

Sunday 3rd

Shay and Gray knew The Who were special when they saw that gig last summer and now they're the hottest Mod band in London. They've been playing the Marquee every Tuesday since November and they're so good it's frightening. We've all seen them, we'd love to be like them, *so we're coming alive in '65!* (© Cheesy Deejay Links Inc.) Shay found our new name when he went for a drink at The Rest Hotel in Kenton just before Christmas. We picked up our new PA a few days later and Colin's parents said we could keep it at their house which was nice of them coz it means great big speakers on the landing.

The church hall where those girls came to listen was great for rehearsals, but it's easier now to use a small hut on Colin's estate. Bare tiles on the floor, big draughty windows, one small electric fire on the wall. We can see our breath as we talk. This is not a good place to be a brass monkey, but we're on a mission. We need a new guitarist who can give us the power we need to take the next big step.

The kid who's trying out tonight is the same age as Colin. He doesn't say much when he arrives, just takes off his coat and tunes up. When he looks round he sees four Mods with short hair and smart clothes. His hair is kinda wild, his sweater baggy and his blue jeans torn. We run through some songs from our set and he tries to work with us but his guitar is in the wrong room. We like to keep things tight, play songs the same way time after time, but that's not his style.

"What kind of stuff do you like?" asks Gray.

"Blues, rock," he says softly.

"Green Onions?"

"Okay."

The transformation is stunning. Our freezing hut spins up through the sky and lands in Memphis. We thump out the Booker T. & the M.G.'s. riff as the shy kid turns into a demon, his guitar breathing fire. He's got every Steve Cropper lick down and adds a few tasty ideas of his own. We change the mood with a slow 12-bar blues and his playing leaves me breathless. Superb. But when we go back to the songs we play onstage, he's soon struggling again, like a cougar in a trap.

"See ya later," he says, when it's over.

"I'll give you a ring, okay?" says Colin.

The stranger nods and heads out into the frozen street.

We pack away our gear and sit round watching Shay putting his drums into their cases. There's plenty of time to talk – Shay always takes ages!

'*Green Onions* was amazing,' I say.

'Great blues guitarist,' nods Gray.

'But we're not a blues band, are we?' says Colin. 'I don't think he's right for us and anyway... he's a bit of a scruffy sod.' And that's that. No place for Paul Kossoff, the kid who loves to play the blues.

Sunday 17th

First gig as The Rest last night, Irish wedding in Maida Vale.
This is how it felt to be there...

We're a bit loud for some of the crowd, but it's a happy day and everyone's out to have fun. There are some beautiful girls here and I can't help wondering what might have been if we'd gone to Ireland with Aidan and Conor last summer. We missed out on those flame-haired colleens but people are enjoying themselves in the here and now and it feels good playing with our new gear. The PA is 50 watts of power with speakers either side of the stage, Gray and I have new Shure mikes too. Playing Jonathan's party with just one amp seems yonks ago.

The proud father of the Irish bride is all smiles. As the night goes on he brings Guinness for the band, but most of us can't stand the stuff. I'd prefer cider, but giving a list of the drinks we all want seems a bit cheeky, so Colin asks if we can have soft drinks instead and the daddy nearly passes out on the spot.

'Jaizus, a band that doesn't drink, never thought I'd see the day.'

A couple of songs into our final set, he appears with bottles of Coke.

'Hope it chokes you lads,' he laughs.

The party's really taking off. Couples who haven't danced for years are twisting and jiving, old moves jerking back to life. Grandads tap their toes, little kids run round in circles, good times everywhere. But something's wrong, we're slowing down, I look round at Shay and his eyes are glassy. He's been tucking into all that free Guinness and he's as pissed as a fart.

'Faster!' shouts Gray. 'Shay... faster you cunt!'

Shay hears Gray but it's no good, he can't keep his eyes open, he leans back and falls off his drum stool before anyone can catch him. It happens in slow motion and he ends up flat on his back with his feet in the air. We're halfway thru *Louie Louie* and I feel panic rising, but Colin stays ice cool.

'Don't stop,' he shouts to me and Gray. 'Keep playing!'

We spin back to our mikes and sing the chorus with him. Then something wonderful happens, the drums come crashing back in. Mick the roadie has pulled Shay into the wings, grabbed his sticks and jumped onto the kit. We finish the song and get a big hand like nothing's happened.

'*You Really Got Me,*' shouts Colin.

We hammer into the Kinks smash then finish with *Twist And Shout* to yells for more, so we do another 20 minutes and the father of the bride gives us a nice little bonus. A great night... and Mick can't stop smiling!

'Who's your mate?' asks the daddy looking at the flaked out body in the wings.

'Seamus,' says Gray.

'Thought he must be Irish, looks like he enjoyed the *craic.*'

That was last night... wonder how Shay's feeling this morning!

February '65

Wednesday 3rd

She gets out of bed and I watch her dress.

Her naked body is beautiful in the warm glow of her bedside light. Holly is tall, blonde and athletic. I noticed her the day I arrived at the grammar and little by little we got closer, laughing in the schoolyard, electric shock smiles in the corridors, until the day last week I brought in *Beatles For Sale* and we went back to her place to play it. Holly's different coz her mum and dad both work, so she has the house to herself 'til five-thirty. We're always here by four and the Fabs fill her bedroom as the passion we've been saving flows over us like a river.

No Reply rings out and I'm kissing her mouth, kissing her neck and feeling her firm breasts thru her white school shirt. By *Rock and Roll Music* I'm unhooking her bra (thanks BB!) and sucking her huge nipples. Peeling off her navy blue school knickers to *I'll Follow The Sun* is *funnysexy,* then *Mr Moonlight* spins like a starry sky as I play with her pussy and build the easy rhythm Monica knew she'd love. By *Kansas City* I'm driving her home, finger dancing harder and harder, then *Hey, Hey, Hey, Hey!* I feel her gasp as she pulls me deep into her lovely breasts. She's two years younger than me, I shouldn't be doing this, but we're both where we want to be and we love it.

Monica was right. You don't have to go the whole way to have a good time. I please Holly then she pleases me: how can something that feels so right be wrong? If we got caught one of these naughty winter evenings all hell would break loose. We both know the dangers and they add to the thrill. The minute I leave Holly, I can't wait to see her again, and every time I play *Beatles For Sale* I imagine her naked and smiling in the secret world we share.

Saturday 20th

Who's that staring in thru the window?

The usual Rest response: *go and see what he wants Colin.* Mr Nice Guy is back two minutes later with the kind of green mac you'd only wear for a bet. Inside it is a good looking guy with black hair carrying his Vox AC30 amp and a red Hofner Verithin guitar in a smart case. That uncool raincoat can't be his - it must have kidnapped him.

We're still searching for a lead guitarist and an ad in the *Melody Maker* has brought this guy our way. His name's Alfred Giulianotti and it will amaze you to hear he's Italian. He looks a bit nervous and asks if he can listen to what we're playing then join in when he gets some ideas. We go back to learning the Yardbirds' brand new record, *For Your Love,* and the opening chords sound great on Gray's 12-string. We stay with them for the verse... *Em, G, A, Am... Em, G, A, Am...* over and over as Shay locks into the beat, I find a bass line that works, and Colin sings the words from the sheet of paper in his hand.

Alfred's feet are soon tapping and he comes in on the third run-thru. He hits the chords with Gray then throws in a few lead lines that send a shiver up my spine. Music's weird, you know in minutes if someone's right for your band. Paul Kossoff wasn't, Alfred Giulianotti is, and the bonus is we'll probably be protected by the Mafia.

I'm already thinking the Italian stays... but the raincoat goes.

'Call me Fred,' he says and his smile shows he's starting to relax. He knows *You Really Got Me* and *All Day and All of the Night* and plays wild solos on both, same on *Louie Louie,* same on *House of the Rising Sun,* where Alan Price's keyboards come alive on Fred's guitar. He's amazing, but not at all flash. We say we like what he's doing and he looks pleased. He's a fine musician, but we don't know much about him. The four of us are pretty close: will he fit in?

The answer comes when Gray shows him the sheet music for a new song we want to learn. It's called *Heatwave* and The Who do a brilliant live version with maximum R&B. Fred starts playing the chords and singing about a girl who really can can-can and we stare at him like he's crazy.

'Who sings the *Heatwave* you want to do?' he smiles.

'The Who,' says Shay.

'The original's by Martha and the Vandellas,' adds Colin.

'Well, this is by Irving Berlin!'

What's that noise?

Must be the sound of our cool image crashing in flames. But Fred's not bothered, he's a good bloke and says he'll buy the record and learn it by the next time we meet, that is if we want him to come again. Of course we do, we like him and when his green mac takes him home we have a chat and agree we've found our new guitar man.

Saturday 27th

Fred turned up today with the chords for *Heatwave* and the words all written out for Colin. He showed us how it went and we worked hard, getting the power into the music first, then trying high harmonies as Colin punched out the lead vocals. A couple of hours later it sounded really good.

'Er... so am I in the group then?' asked Fred.

'Of course!' they all crid.

We sat round talking for a while when we finished and Fred was really chuffed to be joining us. He said he was hooked as soon as he heard our *raw and exciting sound*. 'You sure you were listening to us?' smiled Shay. Fred laughed, we all did, and it felt good, like we'd known him forever.

I'm even getting used to his mac!

March '65

Sunday 14th

It's great having Fred in the group. Give him any record and he can learn it in a few days. He's got a fast mind and a zany sense of humour: he's like a mix between Spike Milligan and Dave Davies of the Kinks. Gray's powerful 12-string is still at the heart of our sound, but Fred adds a new dimension with his flowing lead guitar lines and spot on backing vocals. Truth is, we've never sounded better, and it's great to feel part of the music scene coz it's jumping right now.

Radio London's a great station, they call it Big L and it's got these zappy jingles... *wonderful Radio London!* Since they came on air just before Christmas they've had a stream of new hits to play like: *Go Now* by the Moody Blues (Gray *loves* it!); *You've Lost That Loving Feeling* by the Righteous Brothers; *Ferry Across The Mersey* by Gerry & the Pacemakers; *Tired of Waiting For You* by the Kinks; *Come Tomorrow* by the Manfreds; *Game of Love* by Wayne Fontana & the Mindbenders; *Cast Your Fate To The Wind* by Sounds Orchestral (sheer class); *Funny How Love Can Be* by the Ivy League; *Don't Let Me Be Misunderstood* by the Animals; *Leader of the Pack* by those sugarsweet Shangri-Las; *Baby Please Don't Go* by Them (we do the flipside *Gloria*); *The Last Time* by the Rolling Stones.

I still listen to Caroline too. They gave *Yeh Yeh* by Georgie Fame and the Blue Flames loads of airplay and it went straight to number one. It's hard to believe there was no pirate radio a year ago. Music's exploded since then. Millions of kids got transistor radios for

Christmas and every time they turn them on there's a new song, a new group, a new something. I like that folk singer Donovan who's just been on *RSG!* three weeks running. He wears a Bob Dylan cap but writes his own songs, like *Catch The Wind*. There's so much great music around it's hard to know what to play next. The Who are moving on from R&B and we'd like to do the same, *Walking The Dog* and *My Babe* are starting to feel a bit tired, but we'll stick with the stuff we know for a while coz Colin's got us loads of gigs to play in the next few weeks and we're gonna be busy...

April '65

Tuesday 20th

Just back from a school field trip to the Lake District. We got hit by a blizzard high on a mountain called Helvellyn. The rock path was narrow and slippery and our hands felt like ice. Dale and I were really struggling up there. We decided to take a break and eat the chocolate in our packed lunches. Then Dale saw a plaque above his head, a tribute to a man who'd been swept away in a blizzard. Tragic for him and fucking scary for us, I was glad to get down in one piece.

Trudging round in the cold all day was a drag, but the evenings were great. Alex and I found a small bar that reminded me of the Witch's Cauldron, with wine bottle candles on the tables and good sounds. The guy who ran the placed loved Dylan and played his new album over and over. I think it's his best yet. Rocky tracks like *Maggie's Farm* and *Subterranean Homesick Blues* (killer title) are followed by four brilliant acoustic songs on side two, *Mr Tambourine Man, Gates of Eden, It's Alright Ma,* and *It's All Over Now Baby Blue.*

It felt good to forget about school for a while. Pam and Janet felt the same, they'd been sleepwalking thru a field trip from Esher and when we met at the bar one thing soon led to another. Hot kisses in a dark damp alley and then, on our last night, free wine from the tambourine barman sent us laughing into the spinning streets. This morning, back in London, first stop was a record shop for Dylan's LP *Bringing It All Back Home.* It's playing now and I can still taste that teenage gypsy queen's sweet lips as she tells me of her dreams.

Thursday 22

'If you play that record once more I'll have to break it.'

Dad's standing at the door and an hour of non-stop Dylan has left him shaken not stirred. I don't blame him, don't blame myself, the truth is we're still living on top of each other. I've got my own room, but my parents are just a few feet away thru the curtains I never open. We all need more space. Fridays can't come quick enuff...

Wednesday 28th

'Did you see it?'

Colin was on the line minutes after the *RSG! Sound of Motown* TV special tonight. An hour later he was sitting in the Inferno with Gray and Shay. We'd all seen the show and felt the same way... this was *lightning strikes.* We've always loved black American music and now Dusty Springfield had opened the door to our future and introduced us to her friends from the motor city.

Truth is, we've been listening to Motown for ages, but we didn't know it at first. *Money, You Really Got A Hold On Me, Please Mister Postman,* all great tracks on early Beatles LPs and we thought the Fabs wrote them, but they were Motown gold. We're not the only ones who've been slow to work out where all that great music was coming from. The Motown stars have just finished a UK tour and nobody came. After tonight's *RSG!,* that's sure to change in a hurry. This was our first chance to see and hear the might of Motown in one place at one time, singer after singer, group after group, song after song, looking great and sounding even better, absolutely stunningly brilliant. We wanted to taste it all, learn it all, play it all in our new *WeLoveMotown* group. Trouble was the show went past in a flash...

Luckily Colin was on the case and wrote down some of the songs. Here's a few that got our pulses racing: *Shop Around* and *Ooo Baby Baby* by Smokey Robinson and the Miracles; *Shake, Baby Love,* and *Stop! In The Name of Love* by the Supremes; *The Way You Do The Things You Do, My Girl* by the Temptations; *How Sweet It Is To Be Loved By You, Can I Get A Witness* by Marvin Gaye; *Kiss Me Baby* by Little Stevie Wonder who's only 13 (even younger than Colin); *Heatwave, Dancing In The Street, Nowhere To Run* by Martha Reeves & The Vandellas, plus the big finale, *Mickey's Monkey,* with Smokey on lead vocals backed by Dusty, Martha, Diana, Stevie, and all the other Motown stars. Dazzling.

We were still buzzing in the Inferno two hours later, excited voices all talking at once, jumping the queue to have our say. We'd found what we'd been searching for and we all knew Fred would feel the same way... Tamla Motown we love you.

May '65

Wednesday 26th

A flashy rehearsal studio in Marble Arch. A powerful light show makes us feel like real pop stars as we run thru some of our new Motown numbers onstage, *Stop! In The Name of Love, Dancing In The Street, Nowhere To Run, Shop Around, My Girl, It's Growing*. We know we can't get close to the originals, but the songs sound good just the same. Shay's nailed that solid Motown beat, I keep it tight on bass, Gray's 12-string rings thru the chord changes and Fred's fuzz box lead guitar covers the brass lines that bring the music alive. Colin's doing great on lead vocals and with three of us singing back-up, the sound is rich and strong.

We've played loads of gigs since Fred joined. Pubs, clubs, youth clubs, plus rehearsals, busy busy, living it all to the max. We did a gig in Wembley last week and two men in suits came up afterwards and said they were interested in managing us. That's why we're here tonight, third time this week, but it all feels a bit weird. We play, they listen, we pack up our gear, they ask if we can come again tomorrow or the next day. We ask them what they think and they say they want to see us again. If it's the same tonight Colin's gonna tell them bye bye. I think they're a bit creepy, watching us from the shadows, like they're the cats and we're the mice, but they won't catch us in their trap. Who needs it?

Monday 31st

Shay came round today for some *spaghetti special*. He brought a bottle of red wine called *Bulls Blood's* which sounded a bit revolting but tasted fine. Shay saw the manager of his football team over the weekend and told him about those weird blokes who wanted to manage us and he said we'd done the right thing to dump them and why hadn't we asked him to do it? Shay rang round and asked what we all thought and we said give him a try. We like Wilby, he's larger than life, more front than Selfridges, a real jack the lad, always ready for a laugh and joke. He drives a white van and if you see him coming run for cover.

'He asked what we want him to do,' said Shay.

'What d'you say?'

'Get us a gig in Soho '

'Could take a while.'

'Snowball's chance,' said Shay.

And we both knew he'd got that right.

June '65

Sunday 13th

The brunette walks into the garden in her bra and panties and sits beside the pond.

'Are you sure this is alright?' she asks.

'If anyone looks they'll think you're wearing a bikini, and anyway who cares?'

Not me. Mum and dad are in Leysdown and I've just spent the last two hours in their bed with the pretty girl who's enjoying the sun. The thing with Holly couldn't last forever, she's going out with a guy from the first team now, and I'm enjoying being with the brunette. We both feel the same way, it's fun being with new people, trying new things, nothing too heavy, don't try to pin us down.

Radio London plays *I Can't Explain* by The Who and the brunette smiles. It's out of the charts now but still sounds great, and she heard it by The Rest on Friday night. She likes our group and they like her, everyone does, with her slim figure, short skirts, and nervous giggle. She's a little shy but she wants to change, enjoy the treats she knows are out there waiting for her. Like most of the girls at school she doesn't want to *go the whole way*, but she's happy to dance pretty damn close to the edge. So we eat our sandwiches and drink our Cokes and know we'll soon be back in the double bed we'll share thru this long hot afternoon.

7.00pm The brunette's gone, but she's still on my mind. The phone rings and I think it's her.

'You won't believe this,' says Shay. 'Wilby's only got us that gig in Soho.'

June - August '65

Soho

Bank Holiday Monday, August 30th

I've loved playing the all-nighters in Soho,
loved everything about it. We've been running so fast
I haven't written any of it down. But this weekend's been
wet and windy, autumn knocking on the door,
a good time to look back.
Hope you enjoy the story of our summer in the city...

Soho... how did it happen?

Turns out Wilby delivers vegetables to a restaurant down there and the manager knew a guy who knew a guy who wanted a band to play Saturday nights at his club near the Marquee. That's where our dream of playing Soho began, now it was happening for real. Eight hours a night, starting at ten, 40 minutes onstage, 20 minutes off. Fee: £20 cash. Tough schedule, but with our new Motown set and plenty of gigs under our belt, we were up for it.

The Big Top was a basement bar off Wardour Street, not a top venue but we were shaking the first time we climbed onto the low stage and turned on our amps. Nobody said a word and as you know that wasn't like us. We were always talking, *always*... but not that night. A pool of cool faces stood by the bar, their eyes drilling into us. Like Martha says, *nowhere to run...*

We launched into *Heatwave* and steamed thru one of our best numbers. We were doing alright and the good word spread fast. Soon the basement was packed with Mods from the street, all wanting to see what this new group was all about. Then the manager of the Marquee walked in and said, 'The Who can't make it Tuesday, I want you guys instead.'

Nice scene in a 'B' movie, but this was reality so it didn't happen. No applause after *Heatwave,* we didn't expect it. We'd played enough Mod pubs and clubs around London to know they were a tough crowd, you had to work hard to win their respect. The trick was not to leave gaps between songs, punch them out, one after another, no small talk, no jokes, just music. But before we could start the next song, the manager rushed up to the stage. Small man in a crumpled suit, hair slicked back from his pale face, he didn't look happy.

Colin leant forward to talk to him and as they mumbled my heart sank. I knew what he was saying. The same thing we heard everywhere. *Turn it down.* Every time we went to see The Who, my ears rang for the next two days, but we were forced to play every gig like it was a vicar's tea party. It drove us crazy. The manager had his say, gave us all a quick nervous smile, and hurried back to the bar.

'Turn it down, Col?'

'No... up.'

'*Up*?'

'Yeah, he wants it louder, so people can hear us out in the street.'

This truly was a brave new world!

Cue feedback from amps and squeals from the PA, as we set our guitars and mikes to max. Then Fred and Gray hit the big meaty opening chords of *Anyway Anyhow Anywhere,* and magic filled the smoky room. Sheer volume lifted us to a whole new level. We'd never sounded this good... ever. I looked back at Shay and saw a mad glint in his eyes. He'd dreamed of hammering his drums like his hero Keith Moon and now his time had come. Two Mod girls walked out to the small wooden floor in front of the stage and started to dance. Quick nod from Colin. He knew, we all did. Good sign. We forgot our nerves and started to have fun as our music ran up the steep concrete steps and out into the neon night.

*

Soho was sexy, dangerous, exciting, shady characters in secret doorways and music, music everywhere. Jazz, blues, R&B, blaring from open windows, swirling in a heady mix above the rock 'n roll streets. Walking thru the late night carnival felt like gate-crashing a party on the wrong side of town and we loved it.

There were always hookers on the corner. Painted ladies living their lives on the edge. Mascara overload eyes, low-cut blouses, mini skirts so short they took your breath away. When they saw us staring at them between shows on that first night, the girls decided to have some fun.

'Looking for a good time, darlin'?'

The tall redhead was looking straight at me.

'Er... no ... no thank you.'

I swear my voice jumped an octave. I sounded like a nervous boy scout or something. The hookers laughed and I felt my face start to glow.

'How about you?'

A buxom brunette was smiling at Fred.

'Me?'

'Yeah, come here.'

Fred walked over.

'See anything you like?' asked the hooker, pushing out her huge breasts.

'Very nice,' said Fred, totally deadpan, staring down her busty cleavage.

The girls on the corner laughed louder. They were a million light years ahead of us in every way. They had their fun teasing us that first time, but from then on they took us under their wing. Always said hello when we met them on the street, asked how the gig was going. We started to feel at home in Soho, happy to join the faces of the night.

The manager at the Big Top was a good guy to work for. As long as we played loud he was happy. When it got late he'd say, in his thick Greek accent, 'Have some sweets boys, no charge, have some sweets.' I figured he was trying to keep our energy up. But sometimes when we asked for free chocolate bars to munch during our breaks, he'd give us a funny look. Weird. If it was a problem, why offer in the first place?

We'd been playing at the club for a month or so when drugs first appeared on the scene.

It was getting on for two in the morning as we walked into Wardour Street.

'I want some purple hearts,' said Shay. 'I'm knackered.'

'Know where can we get some?' asked Gray.

'See that black guy down there?'

'Where?'

'Big fat guy outside the Flamingo,' said Shay. 'I've heard he's a dealer.'

'Go and ask how much,' said Gray.

Shay took off to investigate.

It was late, but Soho was still buzzing. The friendly hookers were on their beat.

'Many in tonight?' asked the tall redhead.

'A few,' I said.

'I've had a few in as well, love!'

Her salty laughter sang like a midnight choir.

'Right, they're a quid each.'

Shay was back.

'I've only got a pound,' said Gray.

'Give us it, then.'

They both looked at me.

'No, it's okay,' I said, feeling puny. I didn't trust myself to start with drugs, didn't know where it would end. Shay and Gray were as good as gold, put no pressure on me.

'Right, back in a minute,' said Shay.

We watched him talking to the dealer outside the club where Georgie Fame made his name. Money changed hands, then Shay hurried back and walked a few yards down our sidestreet into a doorway.

'He told me not to open the stuff near him,' he explained, undoing the small twist of paper in his hand. There were two pills inside.

'I thought they were meant to be purple,' said Gray.

'Maybe it's just a name,' said Shay.

The white pills looked familiar to me. I'd seen them before.

'Can I have look?'

I picked up one of the tablets and turned it over. Written on the pill was one word. *ASPIRIN.*

'You bloody idiot, McKeown!' Gray shouted.

'Don't have a go at me, Lynchy!' snapped Shay. 'How was I meant to know?'

'Go and get our money back.'

Shay walked back out into Wardour Street and pointed at the man mountain.

'*You* get our money back!'

His timing was perfect. We rolled up. The girls on the corner asked what had happened. Graham told them and they cracked up too. Everyone was laughing but Shay, he still looked annoyed. The brunette with the beautiful breasts grabbed him and planted a big red lipstick kiss on his cheek.

'You live and learn love,' she smiled, 'you live and learn.'

Later that night, we told Pete Townshend the story. Not the real Townshend, his double was a regular at the club. Always came in late and danced 'til dawn.

'Forget street dealers,' he said. 'I get my sweets here.'

"Is that right?' said Shay dismissively.

'What do you think those *sweets* are?' snapped the Pete clone, his voice thick with sarcasm. 'Fucking Mars bars?'

We stared at him.

'The Greek's got anything you want, Purple Hearts, Black Bombers, French Blues...'

Of course, we made out we'd known all along. The stoned Mod swayed off.

'Hey man,' said Gray in a jokey druggy voice, 'must have a Kit Kat.'

'Yeah man, need some Smarties real bad,' I drawled.

'That manager must think we're a right bunch of clowns,' said Shay.

'Well, we are in the Big Top,' said Fred, quick as a flash.

'Come on you lot,' called Colin from the stage, keeping us in line as ever.

'Shall I go and ask for some pills?' asked Gray.

'No, sod it, let's just play...'

And that's what we did. Five teenage kids living out our *Beatles in Hamburg* fantasies thru June, July and August. Meanwhile, in a place called reality, I was still a grammar school boy, school desk waiting for my blazer and tie, one year from taking my A-levels. But in Soho I was bass guitarist with The Rest, onstage with my mates, playing the music we loved. My dreams of playing *RSG!* and touring the States seemed to move a little closer with every all-nighter. There were no scripts in Soho, every Saturday was a new adventure...

She walked into the club around one in the morning. Elfin face free of make-up. Short blonde hair, slim, stylish. Tight jeans and a loose black sweater. Some kind of art school angel.

The Rest were playing well that night. One more song before our break. Colin called it. *Midnight Hour.* Wilson Pickett's gutsy new single. We hit those big opening chords, D B A G, then kicked into the *Midnight* riff. The elfin blonde danced close to the stage. I couldn't take my eyes off her. Raw music, low lights and when her eyes met mine, I found myself inside my ultimate rock 'n roll fantasy. I was living every word of Pickett's song but when it ended I saw the blonde's friend tug at her sleeve and head towards the exit. She looked tired and edgy. The blonde started to follow, then looked back at me. If I wanted to meet her, I had to move. Now.

'Drink?' I asked.

There was promise in her smile.

'We're leaving.'

Her friend's voice was harsh. I ignored her, kept my eyes locked on the blonde's.

'Okay,' she smiled.

We slipped away from the ice maiden and sipped our drinks at the bar. We must have talked. What about? I have no idea. I was lost in her blue eyes. I led her to the deep shadows beside the stage. We lay down together and she was unlike any girl I'd even been with before. Her mouth was soft and sensual, her touch a gentle caress. She softly stroked my face then, showering me with gentle kisses, guided my hand inside her sweater. I felt her naked breasts. Her kisses grew deeper and hotter. Finally, we came up for air and she spoke, her voice most mysterious in the half-light.

'No man does this to me.'

A strange phrase. I didn't understand it and I didn't want to talk. I kissed her again and felt her soft tongue tracing slow circles around my lips. She really turned me on. I was in danger of bursting into flames, but she was about to reveal her secret.

'I don't go with men.'

I thought she meant she didn't go *all the way*.

'You're a virgin?'

'No,' she said. 'I'm a lesbian.'

I could have got angry, accused her of making a fool of me, but I knew better. I'd felt her pleasure, this was no one-way street.

'Are you sure you're...' my voice trailed away.

'I like you,' she said quickly, 'but I've got to go.'

She nodded back at the dance floor. The friend she'd come with was staring at us, fury in her eyes. If looks could kill, I was a dead man.

This was a strange game and I was way out of my depth. The beautiful stranger gave me one last lingering kiss.

'I'll be back,' she whispered.

I watched her walk across to her friend who smacked her once, hard across the face, then ran out in tears. The mystery blonde followed and this time she didn't look back.

I never saw her again... wish I had.

*

The all-nighters grew more surreal as they drifted towards dawn. The Big Top stayed open later than most clubs in Soho and a crazy parade of misfits found their way into our smoky basement, looking for one last hit from their weekend kicks. I always looked forward to seeing Nureyev and Fonteyn, my nickname for a freaky couple whose arrival told me our marathon was nearly over. Nureyev was short, tubby, bald and old. Fonteyn was years younger and much taller. They never spoke, just danced, lost in their stonedness.

He shook his body and punched the air like James Brown on speed. Sweat ran in monsoon rivers down his face, but he never took off his evening jacket and black tie. Her body was lean and she swirled with the elegance of a *prima ballerina*. I loved the way she moved. They always arrived for our last set and when we hit the final chord of the night Nureyev would stand to attention and nod his thanks to the band. A flashing smile from Fonteyn, and they were gone.

Now came the worst part of the gig, packing up our gear. At six in the morning it was a tedious chore, so we went for it with one last burst of mad energy. Twenty minutes later we were out on the pavement, shivery from lack of food and sleep. Time for Fred to take off to his part of town while we waited for Wilby to arrive with a screech of tyres and mad grin.

'Come on you little monkeys, get loaded up!'

We just had time to slam the heavy metal doors before the van roared off thru the deserted morning streets. No seats in the back, just the metal floor. Stray spuds and cabbages bouncing round our feet as we fought to keep the amps and speakers from crushing us.

'Take it easy!'

'You trying to kill us, or what?'

'SLOW DOWN YOU CRAZY BASTARD!!'

But Wilby was always out to beat his best time back to Cricklewood.

'Sixteen minutes,' he'd say proudly, as we finally skidded to a stop.

'You're fucking mad.'

'Who got you the booking in the first place?'

'You did.'

'Stop moaning then.'

No point arguing, Wilby *always* had the last word...

We tried to keep quiet as we carried the gear into Colin's house, but every time a speaker thumped into a wall or door frame, we'd run out and collapse in hysterics. The pressure to stay silent at the end of a long night was just too much.

We always blew it.

I'd finally get home floating on a happy high of tiredness and satisfaction, mum and dad away in Leysdown, house to myself. Breakfast with Shay and Gray: sausage, bacon, eggs, beans, toast and coffee never tasted better. And music of course but not too loud, side two of *Bringing It All Back Home*. Perfect. Then another coffee and the last Stuyvesant in the pack...

Talking, laughing,
running back the movie of the night,
The songs we'd sung and the people we'd met.
Freeze the moment, keep it safe,
Monica's words singing out like a mantra,
Young and free in London,
no better place to be...

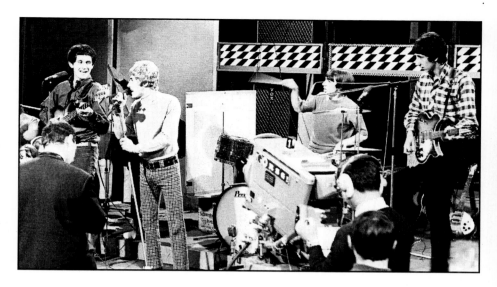

The Rest saw The Who play the Marquee and *RSG!* and wanted to be like them.
Following in their Soho footsteps gave Shay the chance to play as loud as Moony!

Wilson Pickett's *Midnight Hour* was a hot number
for us in the Soho summer of '65.

'The Kinks, *You Really Got Me,* have you heard it? Raw, sexy, brilliant shit.'

Donovan and Dylan led the way for the Mississippi Folk Trio.

With Podge, near Bal-ham!   With Tommy, waiting for Newport to call.

The Small Faces (above) and Walker Brothers (below) were in the chart Cathy and I wrote on the way to the Melody Beat Contest in Brighton.

Eric Burdon of the Animals, one of my all-time favourite singers. Gray and I took *House of The Rising Sun* to Montmartre, Paris.

She drives me crazy with her champagne eyes,
Queen of the Mods... ain't no surprise.

By the end of '66 The Rest were set to record my song *Ready Steady Go!*
as a tribute to Cathy McGowan and the TV show we all loved.

 My

Generation

September '65

Sunday 19th

Eighteen today and I've decided to have another go at being a folk singer. Spent my birthday fiver on my cousin Peter's acoustic guitar and Gray's shown me some simple folkie chords like D, G and A. I didn't do too well with that Bert Weedon book, but this time I'm gonna work until my guitar strings run red with minstrel blood. (Truth is I'll probably just do an hour a night then watch a bit of TV, but you have to sound a bit poetic if you want to be the new Bob Dylan.)

By the way, did you hear what happened at the Newport Folk Festival? I read about it in *NME*. Dylan played a couple of songs with a rock band and some of the crowd booed him. Bloody cheek! Stupid too coz both the tracks are already out on record with backing groups. *Maggie's Farm* was on *Bringing It All Back Home* and *Like A Rolling Stone* is on his new LP, *Highway 61 Revisited*. Meanwhile, the Byrds have had a worldwide smash with their brilliant electric version of *Mr Tambourine Man,* so how come the Newport crowd were so shocked? What do they want Bob to do, stand there strumming his acoustic and singing *The Times They Are a-Changin'* when he's 97 years old? The fools who booed him should take off the blinkers and open their hearts. Dylan is full of new ideas, new songs, new poetry, he has to be free to grow, free to move... like a rolling stone!

The Beatles had a better time in America this summer. They played to over 55,000 people at a place called Shea Stadium in New York. Brian Matthew brought it all to life on a show called *The Beatles Abroad.* There are so many pirate stations around these days I'd almost forgotten about BBC radio, but this documentary made me feel like I was really there. Pity the new Beatles film is such a drag. *Hard Day's Night* was sharp, witty and clever: *Help!* is like a reject from Saturday morning pictures and the Beatles lose the plot in a soppy storyline no one cares about. But... and it's a BIG BUT... the music is brilliant. I've got the LP and love all 14 tracks with *Yesterday, The Night Before, I've Just Seen A Face, You've Got To Hide Your Love Away, You're Going To Lose That Girl, It's Only Love* and *Help!* all shining bright at the top of the tree. How do the Fabs find time to write so many great songs? Search me, guv! The Stones are doing great too. *(I Can't Get No) Satisfaction* is their best record yet, love that dirty fuzzy riff.

October '65

Saturday 2nd

We've stopped doing the all-nighters in Soho. The manager at the Big Top wouldn't give us a pay rise and Wilby got tired of picking us up at six every Sunday morning so we've jacked it in. I've given up my paper round too. I do a cleaning job on Saturday mornings now for a family in Golders Green. I usually go round to see Alison afterwards coz we always have a laugh. We're not going out together but she comes to see The Rest a lot and if she's not there I miss her. I've had a few girlfriends, but it's nice to have a friend who is a girl I like for who she is, not what we do in bed.

Thursday 21st

Auditioning with The Rest at a big dance club in Greenford. Last time we tried out here we fell flat on our faces but that was BF... Before Fred ... and tonight we're flying. The Who used to play here and the local Mods really know their music, but we've got our new Motown numbers, plus both sides of a brand new single by our latest *must-be-like-them* group, the Action. *Land of a Thousand Dances* and *In My Lonely Room* sound clean and fresh and the crowd may not scream for more but we know we're doing fine. When the manager offers us a proper gig it feels good, like we've skipped another hurdle on the road to somewhere.

We're playing two or three nights a week now. Twelve quid a time, that's two quid each and two quid towards the HP for our PA and mikes. Wilby's still driving us around but he won't take any money.

He says he'll get his cut when we make it big, so he could be waiting a while. Colin's a diamond, he collects the gig money, gives us our share, goes to the music shop and pays another chunk off our loan. He's looking good onstage too in his hipster slacks and tartan shirts. Shay calls him our *bony Mod lead singer.* When it comes to organising the band Col's the boss, no doubt about that, and the good news is even tho I'm still at school I've always got money for cigarettes and cider... I waste the rest of it!

November '65

Friday 26th

Just started a new folk group with Tommy and Podge, I strum the guitar and we all sing. We come from London but we're called the Mississippi Folk Trio, so work that one out. Tommy's bought a big reel-to-reel tape recorder, it weighs a ton, but sounds really good. Have you ever heard your own voice? We all got a shock, I can tell you. Singing was tough at first coz those spinning reels don't miss a thing, but it's getting better and our best numbers so far are *Greenback Dollar, Stewball,* and *Michael Row The Boat Ashore.*

I'm still in The Rest, of course, but it's nice to play guitar for a change and I'm really getting into it, might even try to write a few songs. *I walked in the cold wind howling to the moon, chasing a dream I'll only find when vagabonds dance on diamond beaches in the crystal sunset dawn.* That's me trying to sound like Dylan, how am I doing? Yeah, you're right, back to the drawing board!

December '65

Friday 3rd

Guess what? Just won first prize in a talent show at school with eight other guys. It was like a Phil Spector band, singers, guitarists, drummers and keyboard players everywhere. We did *Hit The Road Jack* and if you want to hear the best version check out Ray Charles. We did it our way, which is to say not as well, but after just one quick rehearsal we did alright. Good jam, good fun, good to win, and I came away thinking about a girl with long blonde hair whose funny sketch in the show really made me laugh. How come I've never seen *her* before?

Friday 17th

The idea was to do a song from The Who's new LP to add a little extra zap to our Christmas shows and we went for a track called *The Kids Are Alright*. We've been doing *My Generation* since it came out as a single a few weeks ago and it's been going down a storm. We thought *Kids* would be great too, trouble was too many gigs, no time to rehearse, quick run-thru on Sunday afternoon and we thought it would be fine. Spin forward to tonight... it wasn't.

I forgot the chords halfway thru the first verse, Fred and Gray got in a tangle with their guitars and that threw Shay who lost the beat. By the time we hit the chorus a bloke from the RSPCA had turned up to ask if someone was throttling a cat. Colin was really angry and that never happens, ever.

'Sorry,' he told the audience, 'we don't know that one yet.'

'Why fuck it up then?' shouted a Who fan, full of Christmas cheer. Mind you, he had a point. In our hands the *Kids* sounded like a load of dead people, know what I mean?

Friday 24th

No booking Christmas Eve, so Shay, Gray, Colin and me head up to Soho for a night out. First it's egg and chips in a cafe with bright lights and canned carols, then out into Oxford Street where we meet a guy selling gonks from a suitcase on the pavement.

'Hi, I'm a gonk. In case you don't know, we're tubby little guys with floppy hair and cute faces and we're a big craze right now. You can take me home tonight, but please pay the man first!'

We stand round trying to decide how many we want and a tall slim guy joins us. 'How much are they?' he asks.

'Seven and six each or three for a quid,' says the face with the case.

I feel like I know the stranger and try to remember who he is as he picks a gonk.

'I wanted that one,' says Shay.

'Really?'

'No, it's alright mate, only joking.'

The stranger smiles, pays his money, and heads off thru the Christmas lights.

'Wasn't that Eric Clapton?' asks Gray.

'Thought I knew him.'

'Probably wanted to join The Rest,' says Colin.

'Too shy to ask,' laughs Shay.

'You lot gonna buy anything or what?' snaps Gonk Man and we get one each to remind us of meeting Slowhand. Was it really Clapton? You don't expect to see a star standing right beside you like that, but I think it probably was. That's the way London is right now, anything can happen anytime. You start out buying a cute little guy with floppy hair and end up talking to the best lead guitarist in the world.

So how do we top that?

Easy, stroll down to Wardour Street and see the Action at the Marquee. We love their single and it's great to find out they're even better live. Brilliant singer, beautiful guitar sound, excellent high harmonies, we come out on the kind of high Steve and I felt when we saw the Yardbirds.

'Fancy a drink in the Big Top?'

Great idea from Shay and nobody's arguing. The manager is happy to see us and it's drinks on the house. He must want something and sure enuff the band he booked for New Year's Eve has pulled out. We're all going to a party in Hendon, but when Colin comes back after a private chat and says it's 50 quid for the night, we all realise there's nowhere we'd rather be. Merry Crimble!

Friday 31st-ish

Great gig, love Soho, smiley faces, my generation, home now, so drunk, love The Rest, love my mates, love my gonk, love you, must sleep, happy route 66...

January - April '66

Keep On Running

January '66

Sunday 2nd

2pm I don't like 1966... so far it's been aspirin-a-go-go but New Year's Eve was great. A few people who follow The Rest heard about the Soho gig and turned up just after eleven. I wouldn't call them fans - that sounds too flash - but they like our music. There were only about twenty of them, but in club like the Big Top that makes a difference and the party started there and then. The mystery blonde didn't show, but Nureyev and Fonteyn arrived in the early hours and asked where we'd been. The manager gave us plenty of free drinks and I'm not saying a word about people eating special sweets, but we were still buzzing when our last song ran up those steep concrete steps and out into the street.

Don't ask about yesterday, you really *don't* want to know, but I'm feeling a bit more human today. I'm writing this in the Inferno coz my parents are home and I want to play *Rubber Soul* over and over and over and that drives dad crazy. It's okay up here, I can do what I want. I got the new Beatles LP for Christmas and this is the first chance I've had to really take it in. It's amazing how every record they make is their best yet and they've done it again. The songs are excellent and the ones standing out so far are: *Drive My Car; Norwegian Wood; Nowhere Man; Michelle; In My Life; If I Needed Someone; You Won't See Me.* It's nice sitting here on my own, gives me time to think. I need to stay focused this year, push on with the group, push on at school, busy busy busy...

8pm Back to the Marquee tonight, this time for the Graham Bond Organisation who play mean and moody R&B with a jazzy twist. Graham Bond on Hammond organ, Ginger Baker on drums and Dick Heckstall-Smith on tenor sax. They don't have a cool image, they don't try to put on a show, they just stand there and play some of the best sounds around like *Wade In The Water, Got My Mojo Working,* Hoochie Coochie Man and Traintime.

Has there ever been a better time for live music? Check out the posters in the Marquee. Coming soon... The Who, Manfred Mann, Jimmy James, Alan Price Set, Steampacket (Long John Baldry, Rod Stewart, Julie Driscoll and Brian Auger), David Bowie and the Lower Third, Georgie Fame, the Action, Little Stevie Wonder. And that's just one club... no wonder they call it Swinging London!

Friday 21st

George Harrison married Pattie Boyd today. She was one of the schoolgirls on the train in *Hard Day's Night*. Paul was best man, John, Ringo and Brian Epstein were there too. John and Cynthia tied the knot in '62 and Ringo married Maureen last year, so Paul is the only bachelor left now. George and Pattie are going to Barbados for their honeymoon, winter sun, happy happy, but a million Beatles fans will cry themselves to sleep tonight.

I feel like crying too, but it's got nothing to do with the Fabs. My A-level mocks are coming up and I'm struggling. Trouble is I'm not really interested in what I'm studying. I sit down to revise but my mind is soon off and running. Girls. Football. The Rest. All pulling me away from *The Snowy Mountains Hydro-Electric Scheme* and stuff like that. If I was doing A-level Motown I'd be okay, but I'm not. Must get my head down and do the best I can. Why do I feel like I'm about to take a shower at the Bates Motel?

February '66

Sunday 20th

Hi Tony, haven't seen you for a while. How did the mocks go?

Don't ask. Long faces from my teachers and promises from me to work harder. After all the bad news I was on the crest of a slump. Then dad got a week's work down in Margate and mum went with him, so I took the chance to bunk off school. At first I just sat around playing Simon & Garfunkel's *Sounds of Silence* LP feeling bluer than blue.

Then a weird thing happened: I started to write songs. Never done it before, but I got a couple of ideas. I don't have a tape recorder and I was sure the melodies would run away overnight, but they stayed with me and it was like the lyrics had been waiting in the wings. That is to say they came quickly and if I ever meet Paul Simon I'll buy him a drink, coz my songs are inspired by his. Definitely.

There's a track on *Sounds Of Silence* called *A Most Peculiar Man* about this guy who's so lonely he takes his own life. Loneliness must be terrible: my friends mean the world to me. So I wrote a song for a man who has nobody to turn to and it came out like this...

Lonely Man
All men fear when the bomb will fall
But for me life is worst of all
I am such a lonely man
Won't somebody please take my hand?

Sitting in my lonely room
I've got no light to ease the gloom
I've got no friend to call my own
And no one's calling on the telephone

All men fear when the bomb will fall
But for me life is worst of all
I am such a lonely man
Won't somebody please take my hand?

I got the idea for the second song from another *Sounds Of Silence* track called *Richard Cory*. The title came from the Fabs...

Follow The Sun

Man may live for many a day
Works so hard to earn his pay
But when his day's work is done
Got no time to follow the sun

We're all born to be free
Children with one destiny
9 to 5 can bring you down
Young dreams lost in the tears of a clown

Did you hear about poor Richard Cory?
Took his own life in the house up on the hill

Fight for what you think you need
Soon ambition turns to greed
Bigger house – bigger home
But in the night you're all alone

Did you hear about poor Richard Cory?
Took his own life in the house up on the hill

Man may live for many a day
Works so hard to earn his pay
But when his day's work is done
Got no time to follow the sun

It's mad how nervous I felt when I played the songs to Podge and Tommy for the first time, but they liked them. I wrote out the words so they could join in, then we recorded on the reel-to-reel. The tape came out okay: think I'll send it to the Newport Folk Festival. We don't play *nastynoisyelectricguitarslikethatcrazyrebelBobDylan* so maybe they'll give us a gig. In the meantime I need to get serious at school. Chasing my A-levels is tough, I might even write a song about it. And if you think the first two numbers I've done are a bit depressing, wait 'til you hear *Vampire School Blues!!*

March '66

Sunday 13th

Things are really taking off for the Action. They've got a fantastic new single out on Parlophone, same label as the Beatles, same producer too, genius George Martin. It's called *I'll Keep Holding On* and we've just spent two hours working on it. It's a Motown song, the original was by Marvelettes, and by the time we'd finished it was sounding pretty damn exciting. I get a real buzz off days like today, pity I don't feel the same about *The Snowy Mountains Hydro-Electric Scheme...*

Thursday 17th

Hold the front page, this could be our big break!

The Melody Maker Beat Contest is giving unknown groups a chance to hit the headlines. The final will be held at the London Palladium and the prize is a one-year recording contract with Decca. Imagine The Rest playing on the stage where John Lennon told the people in the cheap seats to clap their hands and the rich ones to rattle their jewellery. We'd love it, so we've done it, filled in the form that is, and sent it in with a new photo. Gray couldn't be there coz he was working (he's just started driving for Walls) so one of our best mates stepped in. We've all known Stewart since we were kids and he gets our *nicestmanintheworldaward*. Here he is with The Rest...

(l to r): Colin Green, lead singer; Stewart Hall (standing in for Graham Lynch) 12-string rhythm guitar and vocals; Shay McKeown, drums; Tony Norman, bass guitar and vocals; Fred Giulianotti, lead guitar and vocals.

Tuesday 29th

Remember the Refectory, the place where Shay and Gray first saw The Who? Well, we've just passed an audition and we start playing there in a couple of weeks. Amazing! The hardest thing was getting to the club with our new driver. (Wilby jacked it in a couple of weeks ago. No hard feelings coz we owe him a lot.) Mr Jones lives opposite Colin and he's got an old ambulance which takes all of us and our gear, but he's crap at finding places. Golders Green should take 10 minutes and I'm not saying he got lost but the Amazon's looking nice this time of year!

It went like this...

Colin: Next on the left Mr Jones... Mr Jones, it's next on the left... coming up... any minute... NOW!!... we just passed it Mr Jones.

Mr Jones: Sorry, I'll just turn round.

When we finally got there they asked us to play six songs. We finished with the new Yardbirds single, *Shapes of Things*. Shay nailed the beat, Gray's 12-string powered the chords, Colin sounded great on lead vocals, and Fred served up a *watchoutJeffBeck* guitar solo that knocked everyone out like they'd been hit by Cassius Clay.

Only one thing the manager could say after all that.

Yes!

April '66

Thursday 7th

Just back from another school trip, this time to Scarborough. No fairs to be seen, but plenty of snow and silly games walking by a river with Alex, Alison and her friend Vicki, soaked to the skin by the end of the day, good laugh, very good. Then yesterday a pretty girl snuggled close to me in the back of the minibus. I've known her for ages so I thought I must be reading the signs all wrong, but last night she slipped into my bed. She was wearing pyjamas which shouldn't have been sexy but it was. Alex was asleep in his bed right beside us, so no words were spoken or needed. I loved being with her but this morning it was like nothing had happened, except for the mystery in her smile.

Wednesday 13th

Six weeks to get ready for the biggest gig of our lives. *Melody Maker* want us to play one of their Beat Contest heats down in Brighton at the end of May which is...

veryscarythrilling

bigtime

Friday 15th

First gig at the Refectory tonight and we loved it.

All the faces who follow The Rest were there and we did our best numbers, *Shapes of Things, Keep On Running, Land of a Thousand Dances, In My Lonely Room, I'll Keep Holding On, Going To A Go-Go, Heatwave*, plus another brilliant Motown track we just learnt from Kim Weston, *Take Me In Your Arms (Rock Me A Little While)*.

Fred's always searching for new hit songs to cover, so we did The Who's *Substitute* and *Somebody Help Me* by the Spencer Davis Group, and they both went down a storm.

The Refectory's got a name for good music and we didn't let anyone down tonight. It's just the kind of gig we need to get ready for the *Melody Maker* competition.

We're hoping to take a busload of supporters to Brighton. We've got no idea how to do that, but we'll find out coz we'll need all the help we can get down there.

That's for sure.

Wednesday 20th

Great phone call last night.

'How are you dah-ling, still a virgin? Alright, don't tell me then you bastard. Must see you, long time no chat, how's the group, how's school? Can't believe you're still a little schoolboy. Now sweetie... *Dr Zhivago*... press preview... wangled two passes... don't ask how... premiere's not for days... they say Omar's *smouldering* and Julie's so fucking sexy I may have to turn lezzy... you'll love it.'

And I did. Took the day off school and met Monica in the West End this morning. Seeing a film at that time of day felt a bit weird, but we were soon swept away by *Zhivago*. Julie Christie stole every scene with her crystal blue eyes and kissable mouth and the cinema was so quiet it was easy to step into the film and imagine I was right there with her, sleighriding through the snow as hungry wolves howled the moon. It came as quite a shock to step out into a bright spring day in London.

Monica knew an Italian place where the lunchtime food was cheap and good and we were having fun until the dreaded Ricky turned up. He'd missed out on the film coz he had to work and I think he was a bit pissed off, or maybe he didn't like seeing me laughing and joking with his girlfriend which I could understand but one thing's for sure, he'll never own Monica, nobody will, she was born to fly free.

'I hear you bunked off school,' said Ricky with a thing called a smirk. I could play his game, clever duel of words, but who needs it? I stayed cool, finished my *spaghetti carbonara,* slowly drank my glass of house red, kissed my mad friend on the cheek and told Ricky I'd see him again sometime, which I sincerely hope I won't.

But Monica and me, our day will come... *ab-so-lutely dah-ling!!*

Friday 22nd

John Mayall's Blues Breakers are playing the Refectory and Eric 'Gonk' Clapton is standing on the exact same spot I played my bass a week ago. The room is packed, standing room only, and the band are cookin' on *I Got Love If You Want It.* I feel happy happy great night happy, then a guy who's trying to reach the bar pushes Colin and he bumps into Stewart who slops his pint over the sharp little Mod in front of him. Stew tries to say he's sorry, but the mean bastard in the suit nuts him in the face, and before I know what's happened I've grabbed the Mod by the lapels and thrown him back through the crowd. If I was a fighter I'd hit him while he's down, but I'm not so I hesitate. Big mistake. The suit is with a tough gang called the Finchley Boys and they're after my blood.

Someone hits me hard from the side and spins me round, then a pint glass smashes down on the back of my head and I fall to the floor. Everything goes into slow-motion, a gap opens up all around and I see the Mods moving in to give me a kicking. How long before the bouncers break it up? God knows, get ready, cover your face, cover your balls...

She steps out of the crowd in her long black leather coat.

'Fucking leave him alone!'

Her voice is tough and strong. I don't know her but nobody here would believe it. The gang aren't expecting a girl to stand up to them, they don't know how to deal with it, and she throws them long enough for the bouncers to drag me to my feet and pull me to the bar.

'You alright?'

'Think so.'

'Weren't you in that group last week.'

'Yeah.'

'Right, stay there, we'll get rid of them.'

The Bluesbreakers have played right thru the fight (first rule of any band) and suddenly I can hear them again as they build to a big finish and the bouncers shove the bad guys up into the street. Can't see Stewart, we've been torn apart by the crowd, but Colin's here looking as white as a sheet.

'Sorry Tone, it was all my fault.'

'Don't be daft.'

'They're just fucking cowards,' says a sexy voice still spiced with anger.

It's the girl who saved me. Dark hair, flashing brown eyes. That leather coat must have cost a fortune!

'How's your head?' she asks.

I run my fingers thru my hair and they get sticky with beer, but there's no blood.

'You were lucky.'

'Thanks to you... look, can I buy you a drink?'

'They're closed... see you next time you play down here... good group.'

She's seen The Rest, is that why she saved me, need to ask, get her number.

'Which way you going out?' the bouncer is back looking edgy.

'Just... out the front.'

'They're waiting for you. We can't help you out there, they'll kick your fucking head in.'

A surge of fear cuts thru my shock haze like a blade.

'Come on, quick.'

The bouncer drags me away, the girl stays put but Colin sticks close. I tell him I'll be alright, but he's not leaving me on my own, and there's no time to argue. The bouncer rushes us thru a side bar and up into the street, just yards from the Finchley Boys who are staring down into the club waiting for me to appear. What to do? Just one chance, an alley down the road to the left.

'Come on Col, don't look back.'

We walk away, hoping they won't see us.

'There they are... get the cunts!'

That's what we expect to hear any second. We duck into the alley and start to run, pitch black, can't see, then we hear it, the angry sound, running feet, loud like thunder, closer and closer to their prey, thru the gloom a cold wire fence, I tear at the gate like a madman, won't shift, we're trapped, Colin stays cool, grabs a bolt, slides it free and we're thru, but they're on our heels, must be, we spin round too see... nothing. The echo of our own feet bouncing off the high brick walls, that's all we've heard. Truth is we've lost them, relief hits us like a tidal wave, but we won't feel safe until we're home.

Keep on running...

Summer in The City

May '66

Saturday 21st

I'm with Cathy on my parents' double bed, I kiss her full lips, stroke her long blonde hair. We've only been together a couple of weeks but she holds me close and makes me smile. Truth is I'm starting to worry about the exams again. I tried to stay cool for a while, but the fear is back, so much riding on them. I don't want to be alone right now, too much time to think. We've played the Refectory twice since that beer glass night but the girl in the black leather coat didn't show. Maybe that's why I went and sat with Cathy on the school field, talked about the talent show, laughed as she ran her funny sketch back for me in the lunchtime sun.

I like being with her, she's warm and gentle, wacky and wise. We never stop joking, even when we're in bed, talking in silly voices, spinning crazy lines, weird and wonderful, a happy place to be. Cathy cares about me, I can see it in her eyes. She tells me The Rest will shine in Brighton and I hope she's right. I can't believe how many are coming, one coach full already and more bookings every day. I try to imagine what it will be like, standing onstage in front of a thousand people, but I can't see it, not yet.

Sunday 29th

9.30am On the way to Brighton with Cathy by my side. We've filled two coaches, a hundred supporters to cheer us on. Can't wait for tonight, don't want it to happen, we'll be amazing, hope we don't blow it. Too much in my head, too early in the day. Need to chill out. So we grab a pen and write down our Top 20 fave records of the year so far. Here they are in no particular order coz they're all stunningly brilliant...

1. Day Tripper / The Beatles
2. Paint It Black / Rolling Stones
3. Keep On Running / Spencer Davis Group
4. My Girl / Otis Redding
5. Shapes of Things / Yardbirds
6. Substitute / The Who
7. Pretty Flamingo / Manfred Mann
8. Daydream / Loving Spoonful
9. I'll Keep Holding On / The Action
10. Sorrow / Merseys

11. I Put A Spell On You / Alan Price Set
12. Homeward Bound / Simon & Garfunkel
13. The Sun Ain't Gonna Shine Anymore / Walker Brothers
14. Rainy Day Women Nos 12 & 13 / Bob Dylan
15. Monday Monday / Mamas & Papas
16. Barbara Ann / Beach Boys
17. Till The End Of The Day / Kinks
18. You Don't Have To Say You Love Me / Dusty Springfield
19. Sha La La La Lee / Small Faces
20. When A Man Loves A Woman / Percy Sledge

A-Level question: *1966 is an outstanding year for popular music. Discuss.*

Answers on a (Brighton) postcard please.

Midday. Okay, now it's getting scary. We're in the Regent Ballroom, Brighton, with all the other bands, listening as a man with a clipboard spells out how the day will run. He's focused, serious, doesn't want any fuck-ups. We're all amateurs but he's aiming for a professional show and that's fine coz that's the way we want it too. We try to take it all in, running order, rehearsal times, where to get onstage, how to get off. He's thought it all thru and it sounds good to us. Only weird thing is the voting system. Fans must vote for two groups not one. We don't understand how that'll work, but no time to worry about it now, we're on the move.

Up a million steps and suddenly we're out on the stage and the sheer size of the hall takes our breath away. It's massive and we feel the thrill, feel the fear, Colin, Gray, Shay, Fred, and me, we've all dreamed of today and now it's happening for real. Behind us there's a wall of gleaming Vox amps and soon we're plugging in and Shay's looking happy happy behind his sparkling set of Premier drums. We run thru a couple of songs and the guy on the mixing desk adjusts his dials to get the sound just right. Good to know he'll be there for us tonight.

3.00pm Walking with Cathy on Brighton pier, eating fish and chips out of paper bags, salty breeze from a mackerel sea, amusement arcades, young kids shouting, having fun. Sunday afternoon and the Melody Maker Beat Contest feels unreal, like it's never gonna happen. I'm meeting the boys back at the ballroom at seven, until then it makes sense to do our own thing, forget about the show for a while. Gray and Shay are off and running with two horny Mods from Cricklewood, Fred's with his family, Colin's with a girl from school, and I'm with Cathy, holding her tight, trying to ignore the butterflies flapping at the edge of my smile.

9.00pm 'And now, from London... THE REST!!' We dive straight into *Heatwave* and the sheer power of those exciting, rising chords lifts me. I think of The Who at the Marquee where we first heard the song: now we're playing it to a thousand faces and... hang on, something's wrong. Holly and her boyfriend are laughing, what's so funny? Cathy stares at me like she's got bad news and Alison is holding her hands to her ears and shouting... what?... we're too loud?... no, not that... she can't hear our voices... we look like clowns and it's not our fault. The cunt on the desk has forgotten to turn up our mikes, suddenly our vocals boom in, much too loud, and we're thru our first number before he finally pulls the sound into shape.

Irish wedding, why am I thinking of an Irish wedding? Got it, Shay falling off his drums, Colin holding us together, *don't stop, keep playing,* and that's what we do now, forget *Heatwave,* punch into *Going To A Go-Go.* I look back as Shay kicks into his thumping drum intro and he looks mean, like he's in a match, one nil down in the first minute, time to fight back, and that's just what we do, moving to the beat we found in Soho. Next it's the song Fred has written specially for tonight and *Eyes* shines in the bright lights like a Top Twenty smash.

We're really into it now, sweating, living every second, one last number and I swear *I'll Keep Holding On* never sounded better. The crowd are with us, dancing, swaying, a thousand faces watching as we build the excitement higher and higher until the final chord rings and Shay's symbols crash for the last time. Strangers clapping their hands, friends screaming for more, it's over, we loved it, now let's kill the sound man.

We're meant to jump off the front of the stage, but Shay forgets in all the excitement and comes face-to-face with the next group. They're not in the contest, they're here to plug their new single. 'Good group mate,' says a guy with long dark hair and a *Coates comes up from Somerset* accent. Shay says thanks and gets out of their way.

The Troggs walk out and play *Wild Thing.*

10.30pm They're counting the votes and we're in with a chance. The Eyes of Blue will win and that's the way it should be, great band from Wales, polished sound, two lead singers. All the other groups were okay except one, let's call them the *No Hopers,* and they were embarrassing. That two-votes-thing is still a puzzle and the idea's gone round our crowd to vote for The Rest and waste their second one on the band who've got no chance.

'And now the results you've all been waiting for... in first place, The Eyes of Blue! (Cheers) Runners up and also on their way to the semi-finals.... the *No Hopers!*'

No! This can't be happening! Cathy squeezes my hand as I stare at the stage in disbelief. The Eyes of Blue jump into the bright lights waving and smiling, happy happy, they deserve to be there, definitely, but the other tossers look shocked and I'm not surprised. It should be us up there... what the hell went wrong?

Monday 30th

We've been talking about nothing else.

'We tried to be too clever,' says Shay.

'Whose idea was it?' asks Fred.

'Fuck knows.'

Gray and I say it together and Colin still looks sick at the way we've screwed things up. If our supporters had voted for us and the Eyes of Blue, we would have got thru. But we all got caught up in a crazy scam and the *No Hopers* picked up a hundred votes they didn't deserve which was enough to dump us in a box marked 'Losers'. The worst thing is we know it was all our own fault. So stupid.

I'm selfish. I don't want to go into my exams with nothing to look forward on the other side, so I show the lads a small ad in the *Melody Maker*. 'Make Your Own Record'. Three hours in a London studio for 25 quid. How many numbers can we do in three hours? Fred reckons four and that sounds good to us. We'll make our own EP, bounce back from Brighton in a hurry.

June '66

Thursday 23rd

I've been living a nightmare: exams, revision, exams, exams, my head splitting with facts like a dam set to burst, big silent rooms, lines of desks, busy pens on endless sheets of paper, as I sit staring at the typed questions wondering whether I should run with the devil or drown in the deep blue sea. It's a horrible time, text books 'til midnight, crawling into school the next morning, taking three A-levels, knowing I could fail every one.

I live for Saturday nights when Cathy comes round. We go to bed and for a while the world makes sense again, but laughter is harder to find now. I try to explain why I'm so *edgytwitchymoody* but she's still a year away from all the shit I'm going thru and anyway when her time comes she'll cream it, no problem. She's bright, very bright, but she can't find a way to lift my gloom. This has been the worst month of my life. At least it will soon be over... for better or worse.

July '66

Friday 8th

On the beach in Sussex, high tide, starry sky, last night of a trip to unwind with friends from school, riding our bikes down from London, sleeping in tents, lazing on sunny afternoons, dodging summer showers, good times, good timing, just what we needed after the A-level horror show. The pyjama girl from Scarborough is here. I've wanted to be close to her but she does what she wants when she wants, and she's kept me dangling on a string. But now the driftwood fire is fading to glowing embers and I kiss her teasing, laughing lips as secrets ride the moon.

Saturday 9th

No tears tonight. None needed. Back in London and at a party. I'm dancing with Cathy, but the girl from the beach is across the room. I'd love to be with her, but I'm feeling guilty. Cathy stayed with me thru the hard times and I know that wasn't easy. When we first got together we laughed so much and I don't want to hurt her now. The room feels hot and stuffy, so we walk into the garden.

'I've been seeing someone else, I'm sorry.'

Soft words, sadly spoken, but the voice isn't mine, it's Cathy's.

It's over.

Tuesday 12th

The girl with the secret smile is still a mystery, which is another way of saying she doesn't want to go out with me. She told me straight. Her eyes are on college and I don't fit her plans. Like Cathy, she's moving on: time for me to do the same. We're in the studio next week to record four songs for our first-ever EP and after all the *examsandgirlsandtwotimingbastardguiltystressagogo* it'll be good to be back with the boys.

Saturday 16th

I'm really getting into the World Cup. All the games are on TV which is a major bonus and after a grotty goalless draw against Uruguay, the team really clicked tonight and beat Mexico 2-0 with goals from Roger Hunt and Bobby Charlton, who hammered the ball into the net from at least 30 yards.

Come on England!

Colin's voice cracks as he tries to hit a high note,
Gray and I sound like choir boys on speed, the key is so high we're
getting nosebleeds, and it's all our fault. Yes folks, The Rest have
done it again! Here's how we screwed things up this time...

We meet Fred at the recording studio in Tin Pan Alley and he's worried coz he's realised we've been tuning our guitars too low. There's a thing called *concert pitch* and all the top bands tune to that when they're making records. Fred reckons we should do the same. Gray and I agree it makes sense, so we tune our guitars to his then sit back and wait for Shay to set up his drums. We have a 5-course meal, watch *Dr. Zhivago* six times, read *War And Peace*... then Shay's ready! It's a three hour session and we're halfway thru it by the time we start playing.

We've been rehearsing our four songs for a week, *Heatwave, Going To A Go-Go, Land Of A Thousand Dances,* and *Baby You've Got It.* Bit risky that last one coz it's the Action's brand new single, but Fred worked out the chords in a flash and it's been sounding good so we're going for it. The engineer looks like he's done a lot of these cheap *Melody Maker* deals and he's not exactly a ball of fun, but he knows what he's doing and he tells us to record the music first.

We've never been in a studio, so we just play the backing tracks like we're doing a gig, one take per song, and we're thru in no time. Now for the vocals and Colin's struggling from line one, trying to sing the songs higher than ever before. He's got no chance. We've done him up like a kipper. It's just as bad for Gray and me, tearing our throats out trying for high harmonies. It's a relief when the engineer says we're out of time.

'What d'you want to do about mixing?' he asks.

'Don't know anything about it mate,' says Shay. 'Can you do it?'

'Okay, pick the stuff up next week.'

Another useless group, that's what he's thinking, and we troop out into Denmark Street with our tails between our legs. Only nine o'clock? Feels like we've been in there years. Another fuck up for The Rest. What is it with our group? Votes that turn *no hopers* into winners, concert keys that open the door to hell.

If it ain't broke don't fix it, that's what they say, but you know our trouble, we think too much, and when we need to get it right, we blow it, yes indeed, every single time. Recording an EP was meant to be a buzz, but we've come out of it with the moody blues. Fred heads home and the rest of us drive into Soho for a drink.

'Stevie Winwood,' says Colin, as we sit drowning our sorrows in The Ship in Wardour Street. We all spin round and see the Spencer Davis Group at the bar. We've got nothing to lose so we go and ask them where they're playing tonight. The Marquee, should have guessed, quick drink before their last set. Stevie seems a bit shy, but Spencer's a nice bloke and we tell him we do *Somebody Help Me* and *Keep On Running.*

'Hope you're paying the royalties,' he laughs.

We don't want to be a drag so we wish them all the best and head out into the street.

'Who's coming then?' asks Shay.

Answer: all of us.

Mr Jones drives our gear back to Cricklewood and we walk into our favourite club. *SDG* are good but Winwood stands out a mile and his take on the Ray Charles classic *Georgia* is just amazing. We talk about the gig all the way home on the tube and it's like the the studio thing never happened. That's the best thing about The Rest, we're never down for long.

Wednesday 20th

Sports day at Hendon County Grammar. The vampire headmaster sits high on a grassy bank looking down on hundreds of pupils who line the running track on the school field. He is in his element, talking and laughing with his VIP guests. He was a good runner at university and as this year's senior mile draws near, his sense of anticipation grows.

Where did the idea come from? Screw up the race. Ruin his day. I'm not the only one with a score to settle and a mind far sharper than mine has thought up this fiendish plan. We walk out of the changing rooms into the afternoon sun and there's a buzz in the air as we gather on the start line. I look at the vampire and his eyes are bright, this is his moment.

'On your marks... get set... GO!'

The flag falls and we set off at a snail's pace, Tommy, Podge, Jeremy, Dale, Alex, me, a few others, all in a line, keeping perfect stride, the slowest we can run without walking. At first the kids around the track don't know what to make of it, then the penny starts to drop and an excited whisper builds as eyes zip from the vampire to us and back again. *They're taking the piss... look at the head's face!* The excitement of the mob sets in, the whisper becomes a cheer, the cheer becomes a roar. We round the bend at the end of our first lap and kids are on their feet shouting, while we stay deadpan, like this race means a lot and we're doing the very best we can.

Back at the start line: will the vampire storm down the hill and stop us in our tracks? The whole school is watching him, but he seems stunned by the contempt we're showing in front of his VIP guests. Then someone bursts onto the track. Small, dapper, grey hair, clipped moustache, tweed sports jacket. If it was anyone else we'd ignore them, but this is Jack Driver and we hear the tension in his voice.

'Okay lads, you've had your fun, now let's have a race.'

We answer as one.

'Okay Jack.'

The pace picks up and the race is run, but the kids stand and cheer us all the way home...

Thursday 21st

Why did we do it? I guess we all had our own reasons. For me, the vampire is a snob. I've grown up working class, but who gives a shit any more? There's a million things I love about the Beatles, but ripping apart the class system is high on the mountain. Can you imagine anyone from our generation looking down on John Lennon for the way he talks? Did you see that brilliant comedy sketch on *The Frost Report* with three guys playing upper class, middle class and working class types, ripping the whole crazy system apart with razor sharp lines? All that crap doesn't matter, it's what we do, think, believe in that counts, that's who we are, but the vampire can't see it. He clings to his crumbling past, as the kids in his school turn their eyes to the future, and I walk away without a backward glance.

Saturday 23rd

I won't find out if I've scraped any A-levels for a few weeks, but I've got to start looking for jobs right now. No easy way to get into journalism, so I'll write to newspapers, magazines, anyone I can think of who might help me get a start. I've made a Top 10 list: *Melody Maker, New Musical Express, Disc, Record Mirror, Daily Sketch, Daily Mirror, Daily Express, Daily Telegraph, Evening News, Evening Standard.* All nail biting stuff so it's good to turn on the TV and watch England in the World Cup. We beat Argentina 1-0 today so we're thru to the semis. It was all a bit mean and moody and Alf Ramsey stopped his players swapping shirts at the end. Hurst from

307

West Ham got the winner, but we need Greavsie back. One game from the final... exciting!

Monday 25th

Van Morrison sings up a storm on *RSG!, Here Comes The Night, Baby Please Don't Go,* but he didn't say much tonight. We were both in a tiny room at the recording studio in Tin Pan Alley waiting for the records we'd made. It's not often I sit with someone like him, so I started chatting.

Tony: I'm in a group called The Rest.

Van: Right.

Tony: We do *Gloria.*

Van: Right.

Tony: Good song, did you write it?

Van: Yeah.

Tony: Saw you do it on *Ready Steady Go!*

Van: Right.

Tony: Have you been recording with Them?

Van: No, we've split up.

Tony: What you doing now?

Van: My own stuff, thinking of trying America.

Tony: Great, we'd love to go there too.

Van: Right.

BORED RECORDING ENGINEER WHO THINKS WE'RE USELESS WALKS IN.

Bored man: The Rest?

Tony: Yeah.

Bored man: Wanna come thru and pay?

Tony: Okay. (To Van) Good luck in the States!

VAN: Thanks.

He didn't want to talk, I knew that, but we shared a goodbye smile. Van was great with Them, but making it on his own in the USA, that's gonna be tough. Meanwhile we've got our own problems. I've just played our our new tracks and they're embarrassing. Acetates are demo discs that wear out after a few plays and the way we sound on these things that's just as well.

Tuesday 26th

England are in the World Cup Final. We beat Portugal 2-1 and Bobby Charlton got two more goals, so World Cup Willy's smiling tonight.

Friday 29th

Fugg me, fugg me, she crid. It all came true in St Albans!

People think The Rest meet loads of girls at gigs, but we don't. By the time we've packed the gear away, everyone's gone home. But tonight was different. Two girls stood right by the stage all night. A bit older than us, short skirts, big hair and loads of make-up, not exactly pretty but horny.

Definitely.

They were staring straight at Shay and me...

They started talking to us in the break, asking about the group, where we played. They were impressed we'd just made an EP, lucky they've never heard it! They were still there at the end of the show and when they asked if we wanted to go for a walk we said fine. Five minutes later we were down by some very dark tennis courts and Wimbledon's never seen the kind of action they were about to serve up...

Shay disappeared with Ginny and Shaz pulled me into a luscious French kiss as she ran her fingers inside my shirt and started to squeeze my nipples, gently at first then harder and harder. She took my hand and guided it up her skirt, no panties, no hang ups. Shaz knew every step of the game she was playing, gently running her nails down my stomach and over my prick, then unzipping my fly and slowly sliding my jockeys over my thighs. She pulled me closer and I gasped with pleasure as I slipped inside her. It felt warm and wonderful and I knew in a heartbeat why people love sex, love screwing, love fucking so much. It was beautiful and new and I wanted it to last forever, but soon I was longing to come.

I tried to relax, think about something else, and that's when I felt the wire fence twanging. Shay was shagging Ginny, I was shagging Shaz, and the noise was like the beat of a factory line in the heart of Motown city. Bang, bang bang, fugg, fugg, fugg. I started laughing but Shaz thought I was shaking with the thrill.

'Yeah, come on, fuck me you bastard.'

I shook even more, but my laughter turned to raw passion as she started to bump and grind her pussy, pulling me deeper into the crazy dance as I pumped into her again and again and again and when I came I thought my head would explode. We held each other tight as Shay and Ginny built to their own hungry climax in the black velvet night. A couple of minutes later we were all walking back, laughing and joking. The girls waved goodbye and went home to add another notch to their bedposts, while Shay and I thanked the lucky star that sent those sweet groupie girls our way...lucky we had some *plastic macs*. (Thanks Monica!)

Saturday 30th

11.45am World Cup Final day, Shay and I walking down Empire Way feeling good on the morning after the *fugg me fugg me* night before. We've cycled over to buy a couple of programmes and taste the Wembley buzz before the big match. It's already crowded here, Union Jacks everywhere, scarves, rattles, hats, red, white and blue, smiling faces, anxious faces, all waiting, hoping, dreaming of Bobby Moore lifting the golden trophy as England are crowned champions of the world this afternoon.

'Now look here old chap,' I say in a Sherlock Homes voice, 'do you recall the tennis courts of St Albans?'

'Absolutely, the thrashing of the high wire fence...'

'The lusty cries of the dusky maidens...'

'Fugg me, fugg me, she crid.'

'Happy days Watson, happy days!'

Yes, happy days, happy happy, the long wait to lose your cherry then you do it on the same night, and up against the same fence, as one of your best mates. Groupies, we love them, but today's all about football. Better get back soon, make the cheese and Branston sarnies, put out the crisps and peanuts, the lads are coming round to see the game. Here we go!

2.55pm Brilliant to watch the teams walking out of the tunnel, lining up on the Wembley turf, national anthems blaring, love all that stuff. There they are, the England stars, Gordon Banks, George Cohen, Ray Wilson, Nobby Stiles, Jack Charlton, Bobby Moore, Alan Ball, Roger Hunt, Martin Peters, Bobby Charlton and Geoff Hurst. Jimmy Greaves is fit, but Alf hasn't picked him, so Hurst better play well coz he's taken the place of one of the best goal scorers in the game.

4.45pm How did that happen? Seconds to go then Germany nicked a goal, 2-2, and now we face extra time. Can't take much more of this...

5.30pm They think it's all over... it is now! Final score 4-2 and Geoff Hurst got a hat-trick. Always said he was a good player! The Germans were moaning the third goal wasn't over the line but the Russian linesman did us a favour. Then Hurst hammered the fourth to end to any arguments. Now 90,000 fans are going wild as Bobby Moore leads his team up the famous steps to receive the Jules Rimet trophy from the Queen.

What a day and it's not over yet... we've got a gig tonight!

10.00pm The Refectory is packed. No Finchley Boys, they don't turn up for small bands like us, but the girl in the long black leather coat is here. I put my hands over her eyes and whisper *surprise,* but when she turns round I see a stranger. Disappointing, I'd love to see her again, but I soon forget it coz I'm here with all my mates and England have just won the World Cup. Alex, Podge, Tommy, Stewart, Gray, Shay, Colin, all talking, laughing and drinking in our break, then Fred says he wants to start the last set on his own. He walks up to the mike holding his guitar and a briefcase. What's he up to? He takes out a Napoleon XIV hat he's made from old newspapers, pulls it down over his eyes and launches into a zany version of *They're Coming To Take Me Away Ha-Haaa!* The crowd love it, clapping along with the beat, as Fred surfs a goodtime wave that rolls and grows. England fans are dancing in the fountains in Trafalgar Square tonight and we've got our own party going on, playing the songs we love in the group we love, nowhere in this good old world we would rather be...

August '66

Tomorrow
Never Knows

Saturday 6th

'Colin's in hospital.'

I've known Gray for ten years and I've never seen him like this.

'Shay rang... they think he might die.'

Why say something like that? It can't be true, makes no sense, Colin's only 15, lead singer of The Rest, nothing can happen to him, we're invincible.

The phone cuts thru the shock, it's Shay, says he's coming round. Fifteen minutes later he's telling us what happened last night.

'He got run over outside his house when he got back from the gig,' says Shay. 'Mr Jones was over the road trying to sort out his ambulance so he could pick us up. Colin told him we'd all gone home and Jonesy asked him to check the back lights before he went in. Then there was a big bang, Colin flew through the air and crashed down on his head. The cunt who hit him was on the wrong side of the street, probably pissed. Must have been one hell of a smack, they found one of Col's shoes in a garden. Jonesy woke his parents and when Colin's mum saw his body in the road she had an epileptic fit. He was still unconscious when they took him away. He's in a bad way... may not make it.'

We feel so useless. Our friend is fighting for his life and we can't believe he's not out there somewhere buying a new shirt for tonight. Must do something, help in some way. We ring Colin's house, his mum answers but she's too choked up to speak. Mr Green comes on the line, Colin's in a coma, fractured skull, no other news, just pray for the best. He starts to talk about the accident, but his voice trails away.

'We thought we'd lost him...'

I feel so sorry for him, so sorry for Colin, still feels like this can't be happening but it is.

'Must tell Fred,' says Shay. I go and make more coffee while they ring. We all want to speak to him, saying the same things over and over, but it's good to hear Fred's voice, quiet and strong, trying to take in the terrible news that's shaken our world.

Sunday 7th

Rang Mr Green. No change. He asked me not to call again, it upsets Col's mum, he'll let us know...

Tuesday 9th

'They think he's gonna make it,' says Shay.

'Thank God.'

'He's semi-conscious, but they're still worried.'

'If he'll ever...'

'Yeah.'

'Can we see him?'

'He wouldn't know us mate.'

Shay's voice is flat, he hangs up.

Wednesday 10th

Nearly a week now, still semi-conscious. You may think I see Shay and Gray every day, ring Fred, stay close, but it's not like that. It's easier to be with people who don't know Colin, don't know what's going on. Went to the pictures on my own tonight, fleapit still showing *Alfie,* liked the way he talked to the camera, laughed at his jokes, knew the game I was playing, trying to push the truth away, finding it waiting for me outside in the street.

Thursday 11th

I'm getting nowhere finding a job. Some of the papers have written back, *no vacancies at the present time, we will keep your details on file*, all that crap, the rest haven't even bothered. Journalism: must have been mad to think I could break in, closed shop, no chance, need a job, something else, but what? Dad asked how I was getting on last night and I shouted at him, said I'd still got a few quid saved from the group, he could have that if he was so worried about money. Mum stared at me like I was crazy.

Friday 12th

The only person I can talk to is Alison, I see her every day, she's a good friend, but when I leave her the dark clouds always roll back. Bob Dylan is in hospital, motor bike smash, nobody knows when he'll get better, if he'll get better, just like Colin. Fans burning Beatles LPs in the States, Lennon looking worried, saying he's not anti-God, not greater than Jesus, Paul, George, Ringo, right there beside him, their friend, a friend in trouble, just like Colin. But we can't see him, can't talk to him, so we sit in the dark, wait and worry, hope for the best, and fear the worst.

Saturday 13th

The phone rang this morning, sharp as a dentist's drill, too much cider last night, too many cigarettes, but I knew the second I heard Mr Green's voice, good news, brilliant news, we've got Colin back, fully conscious, talking, listening, trying to understand his lost week, must feel like a nightmare.

'We saw him last night,' said Mr Green 'He knew us, remembers everything until he was hit, then it's all a blank, maybe just as well. Can you ring Fred? I've been round to see Seamus and he's telling Graham. Can you go down the hospital today? Colin said he'd like to see you.'

An hour later we're there, taking it in turns to go in, sit by his bed, one at a time. Gray and I wait in the corridor and a nurse starts chatting, asks if we're in Colin's group, what he does, lead singer, she's not surprised, he's got plenty to say, now he's on the mend, we must have been worried, but he's going to be fine, may take a while, but he's going to be fine, our friend Fred rang, he's coming in this afternoon, and calls from girls, lots of girls, Colin's fan club, that's what she calls them.

Outside, waiting for the bus, talking about Colin. He still looks terrible, bruises, bandages, big black eyes, hate to think what he was like that night, the night he nearly... don't think about it, he's gonna be okay, that nurse, kind smile, he's gonna be okay, definitely. We get on the bus, go upstairs, Gray and me in the front seat, Shay just behind, good to be together, lost in our own thoughts. I see a dark alley, Colin beside me, he didn't have to be there, wouldn't leave me, wouldn't leave his friend, and I can't help it, I start to cry.

'It's alright mate,' Gray's voice is gentle, his eyes full of tears.

Shay puts his hand on my shoulder and I cover it with mine. Saturday lunchtime, people, cars, shops, life goes on, same as always, watch it roll by, no words needed, share the moment, this special moment, drink it in, start to believe.

Cricklewood: we run down the stairs, out into the fresh air.

'Right,' says Shay. 'Pub... and we're not coming out 'til we're drunk!'

Good Day

Sunshine

Monday 19th

Good morning!

Nineteen today and it is a *good* morning, the future starts here. Tube from Golders Green, change at Embankment, get off at Blackfriars, special journey, good time to write, so much happening, loads to tell you. Colin came out of hospital yesterday. He was in there for six weeks and he needs to rest at home for a couple of months, then he should be fine, bit of a problem with his memory but they say that will clear. He's already talking about gigs in December: can't wait for The Rest to get back together again. We've got something special planned for Christmas: tell you more later...

All those midnight hours and early mornings worrying about my A-levels, and when the results finally came it was no big deal. Colin was going to be okay, that's all I could think about, but passes in English and History were still good news. Alex has got a university place in London and Tommy's going to study in Bradford. They'll both get grants to cover their fees, plus some cash to live on. I'm happy for them but I'm thru with studying and Podge feels the same way. He took his A-levels to our local paper, the Hendon & Finchley Times, and landed himself a job as a sports reporter. He was really excited about it, but he still found time to think of me. 'Don't give up Tony. If I can do it, you can too.' That's what I call a friend.

*

Dad knew I was worried about Colin when I went mad at him that time. It was stupid and I felt even worse when I realised he'd been trying to help me all along. One of my cousins is a printer and dad asked if he knew where I could look for jobs. 'Try the *Printing & Allied Trades* ads in the *Daily Mail*, might be something there.' It was a longshot but the *Mail* is the newspaper in *Paperback Writer,* so I took that as a good sign and one morning there it was... *trainee journalist required.* Spent all day on my letter, kissed it for luck when I put it in the box, and maybe that worked coz a week later I got an interview.

Robin Needham was a big chap, well spoken, kind smile, bit like Billy Bunter, but much smarter, top man at the London offices of D.C. Thomson, the Scottish newspaper group. I felt so nervous when I was shown in to see him I thought I might clam up, but I didn't, far from it. He asked me one question and ten minutes later I finished my answer. It all came flooding out, how I'd wanted to be a journalist since I was a little boy, ignored all the cynics who'd told me it was impossible, and how if he gave me my chance I'd work night and day to be the very best I could be. When I finished I felt emotional and he looked worn out. 'Well, nobody could doubt your enthusiasm,' he smiled. 'I'd like you to do a current affairs test now and send in a piece of creative writing within seven days, maximum one thousand words, sound okay?'

Yes, yes, yes, okay to me, very, very, absolutely, thank you very muchly.

I rushed home and wrote... a song. Came to me on the tube, no idea why, for Cathy McGowan, based on those words I wrote yonks ago. I could hear the tune in my head, hardly spoke to mum when I got in, yes, interview was fine, thanks, thanks, grabbed my guitar, pad and pen, started to find some chords, E, G, D, A, *Ready Steady Go!*, dusty lines jumping back to life as the melody sang. An hour later I'd got it, rang Gray, told Shay, please come and hear it, hope you like it, and they did.

Next day I knew it needed... *something*. No need to force it, plenty of time, and I had a story to write, about a pop group who nearly die on the road to a talent show then - unlike The Rest - walk away as winners, smiley smiley, happy ending. I asked my sister Mavis if she would type it up for me. She took one look at my scrawly writing and said I'd have to read it to her, which helped me iron out the bumps and make the story flow. We had a good laugh doing it and the typed sheets looked superb, totally professional. Thanks Mavis.

The letter went in the post the next morning and I treated myself to the new Beatles LP *Revolver*. I'm sorry if I sound like a cracked record, but the Fabs have done it again and again and again and again and again and again and again and again and again and again and again and again and again and again... that's one for every track on their best LP ever. I can't pick out any of the songs coz they're all so good... *Taxman, Eleanor Rigby, I'm Only Sleeping, Love You To, Here There and Everywhere, Yellow Submarine, She Said She Said, Good Day Sunshine, And Your Bird Can Sing, For No One, Doctor Robert, I Want To Tell You, Got To Get You Into My Life, Tomorrow Never Knows.*

The Beatles looked shaken when their records were going up in flames in the States, but fanatics lit those bonfires. Millions of true American fans still love John, Paul, George and Ringo, coast to coast, heart and soul. They played the last concert of their USA tour in Candlestick Park, San Francisco, at the end of August. Wonder where they'll play next? Hope it's London, I'll queue all night for a ticket, got to be there to see the Fabs.

Have you noticed how good things start to happen once you're on a roll? More headline news: The Piles have moved out. I've got a new bedroom, upstairs, right by the bathroom, the whole deal. Alison helped me paint it and I wanted to thank her so we went to the final of the Melody Maker Beat Contest at the London Palladium. Guess what? The Eyes of Blue won, best group by far, and no sign of the *No Hopers*. We had a great time together and when we got back to Ali's we kissed goodnight and it felt like our lips were on fire. We didn't see it coming, we've been friends so long, but now we're much more and we're happy that way.

When the letter from D.C. Thomson arrived I went for a walk and opened it in the park, couldn't bear the thought of mum seeing my face if it was bad news. But it wasn't, I stared at the words, read them over and over, *we are pleased to inform you...* I got up and started walking, found myself at Pennine Drive shops, bought a bunch of flowers, ran all the way home, told mum I'd got the job, hugged her for being there, always. Then I called the newspaper office, fixed an appointment for the next day. That night we had steak for dinner and I bought a bottle of wine, thanked dad for telling me about those ads in the *Daily Mail*, told him they'd changed my life. He looked pleased. 'Glad it worked out,' he said. Just four words, but they meant a lot to me.

Then I went upstairs, sat on my bed, played *Revolver*, George Harrison, *Love You To,* listened to the sitars, found a magic carpet ride for my song. Played it to Gray and Shay and they said it worked, it's ready... *Ready Steady Go!* This is our plan: when Colin's better we'll teach him the words and ask Fred to add some genius guitar, then we'll go back to Tin Pan Alley, make the record and send it to Cathy McGowan for Christmas. Maybe she'll put us on the show, give us a break, just like Donovan, then we'll have a hit, hear our song on Caroline, take it all the way to the USA...

Ready Steady Go

I see her every Friday on my TV screen
She's so groovy and she really makes the scene
She's the one who really blows my mind
5 .. 4 .. 3 .. 2 .. 1

Ready Steady Go!
I'm in the In-Crowd
Ready Steady Go!
I'm gonna shout it now
The weekend starts here
Ready Steady Go!

Drives me crazy with her champagne eyes
The Queen of the Mods - ain't no surprise
She's the one who really blows my mind
5 .. 4 .. 3 .. 2 .. 1

Chorus

I hear her voice on a Summer breeze
Magic Carpet Ride high above the trees

Ready Steady Go!
Come on children
Ready Steady Go!

*

Back at the newspaper office, feeling jumpy as a cat.

'Congratulations, but I must say your current affairs paper was probably the worst I've ever seen from a successful applicant. I want you to promise you'll read the papers every day from now on.'

'Yes Mr Needham.'

I must have looked scared coz his gentle face softened and he smiled.

'However, your short story was one of the *best* I've read and since we're looking for a writer...'

'Thank you very much, I won't let you down.'

'I know you won't, now about salary...'

'I don't care about the money.'

His Billy Bunter smile broadened.

'Not the best way to negotiate Tony, but actually it makes no difference in this case. The rate for the job is nine pounds ten shillings a week, does that suit?'

*

As soon as I got out I started shaking like a leaf, sat on a wall, took a few deep breaths. I'd been so frightened you see, frightened something would go wrong at the last minute, *unfortunatelywe'vedecided,* but the final twist never came. I'd done it, I was a journalist, living my own movie, and the bells of London rang out as I walked down Fleet Street into the sunset, Beatles music playing good and loud, a song for me, a song for you, a song for the Sixties, final credits written in the golden light of this brilliant time and just like Monica said, dreams really do come true...

North-West 2 mate!!

What happened next...?

From the day I started work as a journalist, my lucky star was shining. Just one year later I was London pop correspondent of *Jackie*, the UK's top teen magazine, with over a million readers. Suddenly, I was meeting pop stars, going to press parties, getting free records and concert tickets. I couldn't believe it, but I loved it.

Then in '68 I got a job as a features writer on *Top Pops* and that took me all the way to the end of a wonderful decade. I interviewed brilliant musicians like Jimi Hendrix, Jimmy Page, Peter Green, Marc Bolan, James Taylor and The Who. I reviewed Jefferson Airplane and The Doors at the Roundhouse and Bob Dylan on the Isle of Wight. And yes, I finally got that dream interview with John Lennon.

Back in Cricklewood, my good times with The Rest kept on running. We didn't record *Ready Steady Go!* in '66. By the time Colin was ready to come back after that nightmare accident, the bad news had broken that TV bosses were taking Cathy McGowan and her cool show off our screens. Another ace decision from the men in suits.

But the spirit of the Sixties lives on!

Fast forward to now and *Ready Steady Go!* by The Rest is up on *YouTube* and *iTunes*. Great making music with them again. Loved it.

And finally, what happened to Monica? Did we ever get together? Well, that's a funny story... maybe I'll tell you about it sometime.

Tony interviews Jimi Hendrix, London 1969

With a little help

So many people to thank for the help they've given me while writing this book, but you know who I'm going to start with... Colin Green, Fred Giulianotti, Graham Lynch and Shay McKeown of The Rest. We had great times together in the Sixties and we're still mates today. *North-West 2 mate!*

I was working on this book for two years before I finally found someone to back me and make it happen. Michael Baldry loves Sixties music as much as I do. His cousin Long John Baldry was a great blues singer and we've named our publishing company after the band he shared with Rod Stewart, Julie Driscoll and Brian Auger. Thanks Michael for all your help, advice and support.

I've been lucky enough to work with some outstanding editors during my career and David Wilson is up there with the very best. His expert advice ensured I trimmed the excess baggage and kept this story moving forward. Thanks David, your professional guidance helped in so many ways. Here's to the next book we do together...

It's over 40 years since I worked with Chris Walter, the excellent freelance photographer at *Top Pops*. I managed to contact him at his home in Los Angles and it has been really good to talk again. Thanks for your photographs Chris, memories of a golden time.

from my friends...

Barry Norman is another good friend from the Sixties who has been brilliant with the help he has given me. He told me he had some never-before-seen photographs he'd taken at *Ready Steady Go!* After a nail biting (for me) search he finally found them in a dusty box at home and it is a thrill to publish these exclusive 'lost classics' here for the first time. Thanks for everything Barry.

One of the great joys of working on my**cool**sixties has been speaking to friends I knew back then. Thanks to Jennie Halsall for her memories of the day we shared at the Stones in the Park concert. Good to be in contact via the internet with Steve York in Mexico, and to reminisce with Karen de Groot and Kate Simpson about happy days at *Top Pops*. Thanks also to my friends Tony Pollins and Tommy Wright of the Mississippi Folk Trio. Great to rerun the good times we shared recording on the old Grundig reel-to-reel.

And finally love and thanks to my wife Melanie for her endless patience, particularly over the past six months while I've been writing this book. It can't be easy living with a man who is happily lost in a time warp linking him to the golden light of the brilliant time known as the Sixties.

Thanks for being there Mel... and for believing.

Photo Credits

Front & Back Covers

Tony Norman ... The Rest Collection
John & Yoko ... Chris Walter
Mick Jagger & TN ... Chris Walter
The Rest ... The Rest Collection

Photo Section # 1

John & Yoko ... Chris Walter
Mick Jagger & TN ... Chris Walter
Brian Jones ... Barry Norman
The Beatles ... Rex Features
The Rest ... The Rest Collection
President Kennedy ... Robert Knudsen, White House photo.
(John F. Kennedy Presidential Library and Museum, Boston.)
Cathy McGowan & Paul Jones ... Barry Norman
Tony Blackburn on Radio Caroline ... Dave Kindred

Websites

Chris Walter ... www.chriswalterphotography.com
Barry Norman & The Rest Collection ... www.mycoolsixties.co.uk
Dave Kindred ... www.kindred-spirit.co.uk
Rex Features ... www.rexfeatures.com
Framus Museum ... www.framus-vintage.de
John F. Kennedy Presidential Library and Museum, Boston, USA.
www.jfklibrary.org

Photo Credits

Photo Section # 2

The Who ... Barry Norman
Wilson Pickett ... Barry Norman
The Kinks ... Barry Norman
Donovan ... Barry Norman
Tony Pollins & TN ... The Rest Collection
Tommy Wright & TN ... The Rest Collection
The Small Faces ... Barry Norman
Walker Brothers ... Barry Norman
Eric Burdon ... Barry Norman
Cathy McGowan ... Rex Features

Photos in Text

The Rest ... The Rest Collection
Mick Jagger ... Barry Norman
Mick Jagger & TN ... Chris Walter
Brian Jones ... Barry Norman
Ursula Andress in Dr. No ... Rex Features
President Kennedy ... Ted Spiegel, White House photo.
(John F. Kennedy Presidential Library and Museum, Boston.)
Framus Guitars ... Framus Museum, Markneukirchen, Germany.
Radio Caroline ... Dave Kindred
The Rest ... The Rest Collection
Shay McKeown & TN ... The Rest Collection
Tony Norman ... The Rest Collection
Jimi Hendrix & TN ... Chris Walter

Classic Rock and Roll Photography

www.chriswalterphotography.com